Sex in the Parish

Sex
in the
Parish

Karen Lebacqz

Ronald G. Barton

Westminster/John Knox Press
Louisville, Kentucky

Book design by Ken Taylor

First edition

Published by Westminster/John Knox Press
Louisville, Kentucky

PRINTED IN THE UNITED STATES OF AMERICA
9   8   7   6   5   4   3   2   1

Library of Congress Cataloging-in-Publication Data

Lebacqz, Karen, 1945–
     Sex in the parish / Karen Lebacqz and Ronald G. Barton.
          p.   cm.
     Includes bibliographical references.
     ISBN 0-664-25087-4

     1. Clergy—United States—Sexual behavior.   2. Clergy—Professional ethics.   I. Barton, Ronald G., 1937–   II. Title.
BV4011.5.L44   1991
253'.2—dc20   91-4520

This volume is dedicated to all those pastors and laypeople who shared with us their stories of pain and struggle, joy and hope.

Sex in the Parish grows out of the work of the Professional Ethics Group of the Center for Ethics and Social Policy at the Graduate Theological Union in Berkeley, California. This phase of our work was supported by a grant from the Lilly Endowment, Inc. For reviewing materials and sustaining our spirits during the process, we thank John Landgraf, Fumitaka Matsuoka, Lynn N. Rhodes, Harlan Stelmach, Barbara Brown Zikmund, and especially Maura Tucker, whose indefatigable humor and constant wisdom were a godsend.

84/29

Contents

Contents

Sex in the Parish

Introduction:
The Sexual Puzzle

This is a book about sex. Specifically, it is about sex in the parish—about pastors and parishioners, about how pastors handle their sexuality in general, and about what they do in particular when they find themselves sexually attracted to a parishioner. Above all, it is about whether sexual intimacy between pastor and parishioner is wrong, and if so, what makes it wrong.

Sex is one of the most joyful, powerful, celebrated, and yet confusing aspects of human life. It is mysterious and humbling. It is also common and ordinary and everyday. Precisely because we experience sexuality in complex ways, we are often confused and uncertain about its meaning, its place in our lives, and what to do about our sexual feelings and desires.

CONFUSION

This confusion affects pastors as well as others. One pastor admitted:

> I am often confused and fearful as to how to express my sexuality in a healthy manner inside or outside the parish. This is probably the number one theological/practical issue I'm faced with as a parish minister.

This statement demonstrates what we have found to be altogether too common: clergy are struggling with various aspects of their sexuality and what it means to be a sexual person in a public role such as ministry.

For some, the regulation of sexual conduct may be plain and simple. Sexual ethics seem straightforward and clear-cut: "Be monogamous." "Celibacy in singleness, fidelity in marriage." We have heard these maxims from many. But for others, ethical issues involving sexuality are complex and answers are uncertain. The pastor quoted above expresses this sense of complexity and uncertainty. She speaks of being confused and fearful.

She is not alone. In our surveys of pastors, male and female, young and old, rural and urban, southern, northern, eastern, and western, we have found that many pastors struggle with their sexuality and with their theology of sexuality. While sexuality and its role and meaning may be clear for some, for others it is not.

In our view, the fact that sexuality is confusing for many is not in itself a bad sign. Simple aphorisms such as "be monogamous" or "celibacy in singleness, fidelity in marriage" may have their place, but they also do not cover all the realities and complexities of human life, including life in the parish. In spite of—or perhaps because of—the so-called sexual revolution of the 1960s, church people and leaders are not clear about roles, rules, possibilities, and limits in the sexual arena.

The confusion is partly about what behavior is acceptable. Is it permissible for the pastor who is single to date a parishioner? What about dating other staff in the church? As long as both parties are "consenting adults," is anything wrong? If something is wrong, what is it? Is it only adultery that makes sexual contact wrong? Is sexual attraction itself wrong, or is it wrong only if acted upon? There has been precious little attention to such issues in the literature on professional ethics.

Some years ago, Charles Rassieur published a book about clergy sexual ethics under the title, *The Problem Clergymen Don't Talk About*.[1] He was right: sexual ethics has not been much discussed in the literature on clergy. In recent years, several books have plunged boldly into the topic. *Ministry and Sexuality*, by G. Lloyd Rediger, is a compendium of cases drawn from his counseling experience with clergy.[2] Rediger offers examples of pastors involved in pedophilia, rape, transvestism, sexual harassment, and a range of other problems. *Is Nothing Sacred?* by Marie Fortune details a case in which five parishioners and a clergy colleague made allegations of sexual misconduct on the part of "Rev. Peter Donovan."[3] These are the only full-length treatments specifically devoted to the question of clergy sexual ethics, although Peter Rutter's *Sex in the Forbidden Zone* is intended to apply to clergy as well as to other professionals.[4]

Some of the literature dealing with sexual ethics for clergy assumes flatly that sex between pastor and parishioner is always wrong. Peter Rutter declares that any professional-client relationship of trust constitutes a "forbidden zone" in which sexual contact is unethical. Charles Rassieur is only slightly less guarded, assuming that "the professional dimension generally implies that there are certain limits to the degree of intimacy the professional relationship will allow."[5] Marie Fortune argues forcefully that Rev. Peter Donovan's actions were wrong, but, as we shall see in chapter 5, it is not clear whether her argument would constitute a blanket prohibition in other situations.

Most of us know pastors who have married a former parishioner and whose marriages are as "graced" as any we know. This would seem to undermine any assumption that ministry simply constitutes a forbidden zone in which all romantic or sexual interest is wrong. We concur with Rutter that 90 percent of relationships that begin in the forbidden zone will die in a short time because they are based not on genuine love but on projections growing out of the context in which the partners met. Nonetheless, some of these relationships do not die. How do we explain the possibility of a genuinely loving relationship? Are marriages wrong if they began with a relationship in a forbidden zone? Is there some way to understand both the dangers of sexual interest between professionals and their clients, and also the possibilities for ethical sexual contact? These are the questions to be addressed in this book.

The confusion about sexual ethics is not merely a confusion about behavior. Part of the confusion that pastors and others feel today arises from the fact that we define sexuality more broadly today than we once did. "Sex" used to mean a rather narrow range of behavior—specifically, genital behavior or behavior that was presumed to lead toward the genital. Today, when people talk about sex or sexuality, they often mean something larger: our entire way of being as male or female in the world.

THEOLOGY AND SEXUALITY

This broader perspective reflects a deeper issue at stake: what *theology* informs sexual ethics? How do pastors understand who God is and how God operates in the world? How does this understanding affect the decisions they make on a daily basis? Some years ago, Rassieur cautioned that "every task performed by a pastor is a theological task" and that pastors ignore the theological dimensions at their own peril.[6] For the pastor quoted above, sexuality is not just a practical issue but a theological issue. She sees correctly that confusions about sexual feelings and behavior often reflect confusions about how to understand God and what God is doing in human life. What we think is acceptable sexual conduct depends in part on how we define sexuality, and this in turn depends on how we understand God and God's creation.

Although clergy are trained theologically and spend much of their lives reflecting on the theological meaning of human life in all its dimensions, this does not guarantee that they will have a clear theological perspective on sexuality. One pastor lamented, "My theology of sexuality is in little pieces, like pieces of a puzzle that I haven't yet put together." This pastor may in fact behave very ethically. But she nonetheless reflects many pastors' struggle to articulate the *grounds* for that behavior, to find an adequate theology of sexuality.

For both these women pastors, and for other male and female pastors as well, sexuality is not just a practical issue; it is a theological issue. And it is a theological issue that is not yet resolved. It is like "pieces of a puzzle" that are not yet put together.

THE STUDY

This book is an exploration of that puzzle. It is the outgrowth of a four-year study of intimacy in the parish by the Professional Ethics Group of the Center for Ethics and Social Policy at the Graduate Theological Union. Part of that study focused on issues of sexual ethics. We began our study before the public revelations of the Jim Bakker and Jimmy Swaggert cases. Our concern was not just for sexual abuse in the parish, but also for healthy sexuality—how to create it, nourish it, express it.

In order to explore a range of experiences and expressions of sexuality in the parish, we conducted several informal surveys of pastors and lay people across the country. In one survey, we created six "vignettes" dealing with hypothetical ethical dilemmas about sexual behavior. These vignettes were shared with over two hundred pastors from around the country and have been incorporated into a videotape on clergy sexual ethics.[7] We asked pastors and lay people to respond to the vignettes, telling us what they thought ought to be done and why. These vignettes gave us some sense of how pastors would respond to a variety of possible situations of pastoral attraction to parishioners and co-workers in the parish.

A second survey instrument was a questionnaire sent to pastors around the country, asking them to respond to ten questions about their experience of sex in the parish. The survey was small and not intended to be scientifically controlled. It is therefore only suggestive of the range of problems and issues that pastors face as well as of the resources that they bring to those issues. We make no claims to speak for or represent all pastors. Moreover, our sampling was largely Protestant, mainline, and Caucasian and therefore does not tell us much about ministry among other groups.

Nonetheless, our respondents included men and women; gay, lesbian, and bisexual pastors; older and younger pastors, some with many years of experience and some newer to the parish; and pastors from Maine to New Mexico, from Georgia to Oregon. In short, while our sample was small, it does give us a preliminary picture of "sex in the parish" as it is experienced by a sampling of ministers from around the United States. In addition, we tested our preliminary findings with groups of pastors around the country and found that the experiences and insights we describe here "ring true" to a range of practicing pastors.

Finally, we conducted in-depth interviews with more than twenty pastors who agreed to share their histories and stories with us. We asked them to tell us something of their sexual history and to explore the questions they have. We heard stories of pain and promise, of joy and heartbreak, of problems resolved and of potential problems ahead. These stories form the third source for the reflections we offer in this volume. While none of the stories will be told in its entirety here, the value of stories is that they put particular dilemmas or issues into a larger context that is often revealing of an underlying ethical framework.

When we put together the data from these sources, what we find overall is not unlike the pastor's claim that she is dealing with pieces of a puzzle. The data look like pieces of a jigsaw puzzle, with bulges here and notches there. Sometimes they look as though they should fit together and then elude our efforts to make them do so. Few have straight edges or sharp corners. Our task in this volume will be to piece them together into a coherent picture, to make them "fit" in some way. The effort to do so will also illumine some missing pieces on which more research is needed.

As we go, we will reflect on the difficulties in finding the contiguous pieces, and on the shape of the puzzle that finally emerges. Some pastors are still struggling to find the edge pieces and boundaries, so that they may know even the broadest configuration of what the puzzle looks like. They remain confused and seeking. For others, the pieces are fitting together and the puzzle is taking shape. Their theology of sexuality is being formed. Both the joy and the struggle that pastors experience in dealing with sexuality must be comprehended if the puzzle is to be pieced together.

Our goal is ethical analysis. We want to suggest what is right and wrong for pastors in their sexual behavior. But we want that analysis to be adequate to the task. Sexuality is a complicated arena of human life. Ministry is a complicated context. No ethical analysis of an issue is adequate if it fails to take seriously the real-life struggles and dilemmas of those who encounter the issue in their everyday lives and the learning that results. We therefore take seriously what our pastors have said about and done with their sexuality. In order to deal with this complicated arena in a complicated context, there is no substitute for firsthand experience.

At the same time, no ethical analysis is adequate if it fails to provide perspective on what people say and do. Experience may give raw data, but it does not provide final answers. Two pastors facing similar situations might choose differently. Which choice is correct? Is it possible that both could be right? In order to answer these questions, we have to go beyond the actual choices and the feelings and hunches on which they may have been based, and offer some grounds for arguing that one choice is better than the other.

THE PLAN

In order to do that, we will be adding pieces to our puzzle as we go. We will begin in chapter 1 by looking at the good gift of sexuality and at some of its special vulnerabilities and joys as those are experienced in the parish. Here, we largely let pastors speak for themselves, though we also take note of how their insights are corroborated in some of the theological literature on sexuality.

In chapter 2, we examine the dynamics of sexual desire and temptation, with a particular nod to male sexuality, since the majority of pastors are male. Here, our framework is largely psychological. We are interested in how male clergy in particular experience the temptation to step over sexual boundaries, and what they do about it. We will ask how clergy establish a "radar" or early warning system to let them know when they might be approaching acceptable limits. As we do this, we take special note of the emphasis given to trusting one's own feelings, and explore where this might originate.

In chapter 3, we explore the story of one pastor who did not set limits, and for whom warning systems failed. His story helps to illumine why limits do not always work and how a complicated mix of psychological and social factors are at work when limits fail. It points us to the significance of some structural issues in ministry.

In chapter 4, we turn to an analysis of power and role in order to explain what makes sexual contact between pastor and parishioner suspect. Here, the power of the professional person in general and of the pastor in particular becomes the key ingredient to an ethical appraisal of pastor-parishioner sexual contact. Utilizing this central feature of professional power, in chapter 5 we suggest a framework for ethical analysis that takes seriously the dynamics of desire, but also takes seriously the role of the pastor and the vulnerability of the parishioner.

In chapters 6 through 9, we test the adequacy of the framework and expand it by examining particular questions for women in ministry, for single pastors, and for those pastors who identify as gay, lesbian, or bisexual. In each of these cases, we find that the power dynamics described for clergy in general need to be nuanced. This influences the ethical framework.

We therefore look to see whether the cautions we raise about professional power might be modified for the pastor who is female, single, or gay. Here, we find it important to attend to structural issues in ministry and to nuance our ethical framework accordingly.

In chapter 10, we turn to those who carry particular responsibility for the structures of ministerial practice—"bishops" and their ilk. We consider briefly some of the ethical dilemmas faced by denominational officials: how to protect parishioners without assuming that all pastors are unethical and guilty of misconduct, how to balance concern for the well-being of the pastor with concern for the well-being of the church, and so on.

When all is said and done, we know that we will not have solved all the problems associated with sex in the parish. We have become convinced that most ethical frameworks offered for sexual conduct within that setting are inadequate. To be adequate, an ethical framework must account for pastoral power, for sexism and its effects on both pastors and parishioners, for heterosexism and its implications, and for other social and psychological factors that set the stage for sexual behavior. An ethical framework must be adequate to deal not only with sexual abuse but with those who enter sexual relations with honorable intentions.

An ethical framework alone will not be sufficient even if it succeeds at doing all of this. Structures are needed to support pastors in their efforts to be ethical and to provide mechanisms for dealing with unethical behavior when it occurs.

One of our pastors put the matter this way:

> We're very muddled about sex. We're so inundated with sexual innuendos. Lots is on television but there is little understanding about the meaning of relationship. We need to reclaim the meaning that sex is given by God

to draw us into deep relationships. We often violate people.

She concludes: "This is important."

We concur. Whatever our success at providing an ethical framework for sex in the parish, of one thing we are convinced: the effort to do so is needed, and it is important. In the midst of the sexual puzzle where pieces do not always look as if they go together, in the midst of the muddle left by popular culture and failed traditions in the church, we need to reclaim a Christian approach to sexuality. We need to take seriously the dynamics of male and female sexuality, of power dimensions in society, of forms of oppression and their impact on our spiritual and sexual lives. This book is one effort toward that end.

1
The Joy of Sex
—In the Parish?

In March 1987, Jim Bakker resigned his powerful TV ministry after disclosing that he had had an affair some seven years previously. One of those who had initiated the investigation of Bakker was Jimmy Swaggert. Less than a year later, in February 1988, Swaggert also admitted to sexual misconduct and resigned his ministry. The stories gained national attention and notoriety.[1]

The Professional Ethics Group began our work before these stories hit the news. Yet we were very concerned about sexual abuse in the parish. One of our members had consulted in several cases involving egregious instances of manipulation and abuse of parishioners. Another member had counseled numerous clergy during times of career transition or stress, and was well aware of sexual acting-out on the part of pastors under stress. Like others, therefore, we began our work with a particular concern for prevention of abuse. Indeed, the very first public presentation by a member of the group about our work carried the title "Why Sexual Contact Between Pastor and Parishioner Is Wrong."

We were so concerned about what was *wrong* with sexual contact between pastor and parishioner that we neglected to ask whether anything might be *right* with sex in the parish. One critic finally said, "What about the positive role of sex in the parish? You make it sound as though there is no positive role for sexual energy or awareness." We suddenly realized that in our concern for prevention of abuse, we had not focused on whether sexuality has a positive contribution to the parish. Unwittingly, we were adopting the old attitude that sex is always to be seen as something surrounded with taboos and negativity. Because of our concern for the abuse of sexual energy or attraction, we had failed to make room for its contribution.

In *Office Romance: Love, Power, and Sex in the Workplace,* Lisa Mainiero offers an intriguing perspective on the possibilities for sexual relating among co-workers. She argues that, so long as co-workers are not in hierarchical relationship, "office romance, despite the complications, is more than worthwhile."[2] Among the benefits she lists from romantic and sexual interest among co-workers are: increased productivity, heightened motivation, softened interpersonal conflicts, increased teamwork, and enriched personal relations. Since the church is also a workplace, it is to be expected that some of these benefits might also occur in the church when pastors and parishioners experience sexual interest.

We began to wonder how pastors experienced sexual energy and attraction. Was it always something to be refused? Did it have any positive role to play? Therefore, when we designed our questionnaire for pastors, the first questions we asked were these: Is there a positive role for sexual awareness or energy within a congregation (e.g., does it make people feel more "alive" and enthusiastic)? Is this a resource that you consciously use, or a potential problem that you consciously avoid?

While our respondents could not know the history that led to the posing of this question, we hoped that they might reflect for us on their own experiences of how sexual energy or awareness can contribute to the dynamics of church experience.

And so they did. But their responses covered the waterfront! In this chapter, we share those responses, letting pastors speak for themselves for the most part, with little attempt on our part to interpret or analyze. Their responses will in fact look like pieces of a puzzle that have not yet been tied together. We will, however, indicate where the current literature supports the insights of our respondents.

SEXUALITY: AN AMBIVALENT GOOD

Most pastors are aware of sexual energy as a force that influences dynamics in the church. But they experience this energy differently.

Some specifically avoid sexual energy or find it primarily negative or problematic. One woman pastor wrote:

> There seems to be very little positive role for sexual awareness or energy. In fact, sexuality seems almost not to exist, except perhaps in a negative sense or at an "intellectual" level. I probably unconsciously avoid sexual energy as a resource, because introducing a "taboo" results in fairly sharp criticism by the congregation and instant claims that this is just my personal "opinion" and will not be taken seriously.

This woman pastor experiences sexuality as a "taboo" topic that she dares not broach for fear of criticism and reprisal.

Among men as well as women pastors, there were those who said they did not find sexual energy to be a positive force in the church. One pastor simply said, "there is not a sexual energy here." Several responded to our question with a flat "no." Thus, for some pastors, the positive role of sexuality is missing or hidden. They are more aware of the dangers than of the joys of sex in the parish.

One woman elaborated on what she sees as the dangers of claiming a positive role for sexual awareness in the church: "No. I mean there is energy that can be expressed in creativity, in humor, or in connecting with other people. But it isn't helpful when it becomes sexually expressed. . . . I have heard male ministers talk about using sexual energy, but I think that's destructive. I think they aren't very self-aware." This woman's negative response comes partly from what she has seen among her male colleagues. She is reluctant to allow space for a positive role for sexual energy, lest that space be misused and abused.

But she also distinguishes between good uses of energy and the sexual expression of that energy. While approving certain uses of energy—for bonding, for creativity, for humor—she rejects any direct sexual contact between pastor and parishioner. Interestingly, she makes room for sexual relations among parishioners: "Romance does develop between members, and that's good." Thus, she clearly distinguishes the pastoral role from other places where sexual awareness or energy might enter the church.

One male pastor acknowledged the constant presence of sexual awareness, but said, "I often choose to avoid this element, especially in my work with young people, for whom these elements are the most volatile." For this pastor, the problem was not with his own comfort level about sexuality, but with what he perceived his congregation—especially the youth—to be able to handle. Like the woman pastor who feared the taboos in her congregation, a number of pastors thought they were ready to deal with sexuality openly themselves but did not think their congregations could handle it well. One man wrote, "I don't believe it can be presented in the church in a way to make people more alive. That would require more candid responses about intimacy than a church as a whole is prepared for."

However, several pastors found sexual energy problematic not just because of their congregation's level of awareness or ability to deal with it, but because of their own histories or proclivities. One said, "Being a bit afraid of my own sexual energy and enthusiasm, I'm guarded." Another shared this interesting bit of his story:"I have been treated for sexual addiction and am regularly involved (weekly) in a '12 step group' for sexual addicts. I have always been extremely careful that there be no acting out with parishioners—so I have seen it as a problem to be avoided." Sexual addiction might seem to be the extreme end of a spectrum. However, it is not unknown in the church. In *Ministry and Sexuality: Cases, Counseling, and Care,* Lloyd Rediger also describes a case of sexual addiction among the clergy with whom he has counseled.[3]

Nor was this pastor the only one in our survey who spoke of sexual addiction as a problem in the church. Another called himself a "sexaholic":

> I would classify myself as a sexaholic, when it comes right down to it. My drug of choice, my drug of addiction, if I'm feeling bad about myself, and I want to fix myself, is that I go, not necessarily to get laid, but to find a woman and have her tell me, "Oh, you're good and you're good looking and you have a good mind, etc."

Both of these pastors are careful not to "act out" sexually in the church, but both raise questions about the addictive nature of sexual patterns. Later we will deal with some of the dynamics of sexuality and addiction that help to explain such patterns. What is important here is to note that some pastors avoid explicit use of sexual energy because of their perceptions of what the *church* can handle, but others avoid it because of their perceptions of what *they* can handle.

What all these pastors reflect is a sense of the ambiguities of sexual energy in the church—its potential for abuse as well as for good. As one pastor puts it, "I believe there is sexual energy—whether it is 'positive' or not, I'm not sure." Like the self-described "sexaholic" quoted above, this pastor noted that "flirting" and a kind of "courting" behavior is common in church—people dress their best, try to look their best, and tend to be on their best behavior. Thus, he was aware of sexual dynamics in the church, but was unsure how to classify them.

Sexual dynamics are always present in human interaction. Recognizing this fact, some pastors are keenly aware of the ambiguities involved in any kind of sexual expression, and they find sexuality both potentially a great gift and potentially dangerous in ministry. One said, "By openly, creatively, and honestly exploring the dynamics in the congregation, its effect can be positive. When hidden and repressed, it becomes dangerous." This pastor recognizes the constant presence of sexual awareness and energy, and appears to suggest that failure to deal openly and honestly with that energy is dangerous.

A woman pastor echoed the sentiments of this male pastor when she wrote:

> Absolutely yes, there is a positive role, and I both consciously use it and consciously avoid it. I consciously use it because sexual energy is part of our common story and a very basic bonding. It is a great gift and a way of recognizing God's creativity in us. It draws us to one another. However, it is also problematic—I believe more problematic than helpful in the ministry.

Both of these pastors, and others besides, saw sexual energy as ambiguous—a power that could work for good and express important parts of who we are as children of God, but also a power that could easily run amok or create problems.

Thus, even those who affirm the positive contributions of sexual energy or attraction find it an ambiguous gift. One pastor, who said that people "come alive" when their sexuality is nonjudgmentally affirmed, went on to say: "My own response is to make use of this resource somewhat timidly, however. It's so hard to find settings for growth that are not so threatening that people misunderstand or back away." Some would like to think sexual awareness good in theory but have a hard time in practice finding an appropriate expression for sexual energy.

For some, sexuality is neither positive nor negative but simply a fact of life. Many pastors spoke of understanding sexual awareness or energy as a "given" in human life. "Sexual awareness and energy are natural aspects of all human interaction and community," said one. Another concurs: "since sexuality and sexual identity is our most basic form of being, our most obvious and distinctive component of who we are, it is everywhere present." For some of our pastors, sexual awareness just *is*, and must therefore be dealt with, like it or not.

THE JOY OF SEX

And yet, for all the ambiguity involved in sexuality, most pastors saw at least some positive role for sexual awareness and energy in the church. One male pastor said it succinctly: "Our sexuality is a life-enhancing gift from God which needs regular affirmation in worship and in the religious community's other activities."

For many, sexual energy is a positive and good part of their work, a resource to use and nourish: "Sexuality is our capacity for intimacy. It is expressed in different forms—for example, the kiss of peace is sexual. Any worship that is true worship is sexual. It's all the same energy. . . . I use sexual energy as a resource." This woman pastor has been serving in ministry for more than fifteen years. She says, "I'm clearly a woman and happy to be a woman," and she declares that she can "talk about that in sermons." She is not afraid to see God as "lover" or to push her congregation on the importance of understanding the "erotic" in human life. Where one of the pastors quoted earlier found sexuality a dangerous and even a "taboo" area, this woman finds the opposite.

Here, we see a positive role for sexuality as a resource to generate energy within the parish. This woman pastor was quite clear that she relates "intimately" but not "genitally" with parishioners. So in affirming a positive role for sexual energy, she is not proposing to blur the lines between her personal sexual ethics and her role as minister. She simply understands sexuality in broad terms and sees sexual energy as a valuable aid to ministry. Moreover, she deals with a congregation that appears comfortable with that.

This positive experience was mirrored in the responses from some men pastors. One wrote, "Yes, there is a positive role for sexual awareness as an enlivening agent and to maintain sensitivity to gender issues." He says that he doesn't know how conscious he is about using this resource, yet he does use it. The apparent side effect, he claims, is that younger adults seem to be attending church more frequently. Another also finds sexual energy a positive and good resource. Noting that people "come alive" in settings where their sexuality is nonjudgmentally affirmed, he

thinks this represents a positive role for sexual awareness in the church.

Both these male pastors, and many others, affirmed
a positive role for sexuality. Indeed, about two-thirds
of our respondents overall affirmed sexual energy or
awareness as a positive resource in one way or
another.

DEFINING SEXUALITY

Part of the problem faced by our pastors is that this
"life-enhancing gift from God" can be understood in
several ways. Whether our pastors affirmed sexual
awareness in the church depended in part on how
they understood our question and how they defined
sexuality. The picture may look fractured because
pastors' responses to sex in the parish depend on
some underlying assumptions about how sexuality is
to be defined and what it means. Part of the ambivalence about the joy of sex can be explained by sorting
out the definitions of sexuality that appear to be
operating.

One option is to define sexuality as something that
is integral to our being. One young woman pastor
wrote, "It is hard to separate sexual energy from an
energetic sense of aliveness in general." Similarly, a
male pastor responded, "it seems artificial to separate
sexual energy from spiritual or psychic energy."
When sexuality is understood as part of the self,
something unavoidably built into the very way we *are*
in the world as human beings, then pastors are
concerned to encourage a healthy acceptance of it, so
that people feel whole. "Sexuality is very much a part
of being human. We affirm both femininity and
masculinity." As an integral part of what it means to
be human in the world, sexuality is to be celebrated as

"one of God's best gifts." As a sense of self, sexual energy or awareness is positive, good, something to be affirmed and celebrated.

However, sexuality can also be seen as something that happens "between" people, outside of the self, between self and others. Sexual energy is not just personal energy, then, but interpersonal energy. In this context, pastors found it more ambiguous. While most recognized that such interpersonal sexual energy is always present, many were concerned to channel it: "The positive role energy can play in a congregation will be directly proportional to each person being able to exercise what the Bible calls 'self control.' " (See Gal. 5:23.) "That energy is going to be there. It's important to reinforce it into acceptable contexts." When sexuality is viewed as something outside the self, happening between people, then pastors' responses were more uneasy. The energy is seen as "normal" and yet as needing to be controlled.

In sum, whether or not sexuality was affirmed as a positive resource for the church depended in part on whether the pastor responding was focusing more on sexuality as an integral part of who we are as human beings, or on sexuality as a dynamic between people. The latter was most troubling to our respondents:

> Because sexual needs and distinctions are facts of our humanity, I believe they should be openly acknowl-edged and decision-making carried out in light of them. . . . But seeking to use sexual "energy" as an ally must be done with eyes wide open to the dangers of clergy and parishioners falling victim to temptation of illicit *expression* of sexual intimacies.

For many pastors, there was a difference between accepting and affirming the *fact* of sexuality in all human life and accepting and affirming specific decisions about what to *do* with sexual energy or attraction.

There is also a certain ambivalence about what it means to have sexual energy available *in the church*. Context makes a difference. The combination of sexual energy and church made some respondents uneasy. As noted above, a number felt that their congregations were not ready to deal with sexuality, or that it was a topic that needed to be handled very carefully in this context. One pastor complained about the adage that there are three sexes—male, female, and clergy. Besides not being funny, he argued, it was not true: "I believe that most of us as clergy are . . . sensitive, aware, and in touch with our own self-awareness and perceptions so that sexuality, both in us and in our parish, is invariably quite out front."

And yet, a male pastor reported that "when I preach on sexual matters, people who are otherwise open-minded close up." At the same time, one woman reported that she had recently preached a sermon series on "the seven deadly sins." On "Lust Sunday," as it became dubbed, the church was packed. "This tells me," she reports, "that people need to hear more about sexuality from the church. Up until recently I have avoided it because I am afraid of the response. Now I am questioning what more I can do and how I can do it."

If our respondents are reflecting correctly the mood of mainline churches in the United States, there is both a hesitation and a hunger to talk about sex in the parish. There is both an ambivalence about and an affirmation of sexual energy. There is both acceptance and avoidance of sexual attraction as a normal part of human life. There is a joy about sex, but also a concern about sex in the parish.

Can there be a joy of sex in the parish? What are the positive meanings and possibilities for sexual awareness and energy? Are they compatible with the purposes of the church? Can they be a resource for growth and spirituality? These are the kinds of questions the ambivalence about sexual energy evokes. And so we turn to see what *theology of sexuality* might inform a positive understanding of sexuality in the church.

TOWARD A THEOLOGY OF SEXUALITY—OR A SEXUAL THEOLOGY

We did not ask our pastors to spell out their theological perspective on sexuality, though we did ask what tools helped to inform their perspective. Yet in answering the question about a positive role for sexuality, many pastors pointed to theological issues. Their insights are paralleled in contemporary literature that seeks to find new theological meanings for a Christian approach to sexuality and sexual ethics.

In an article titled "Making Love as a Means of Grace: Women's Reflections,"[4] Rebecca Parker argues that sexual intimacy can be a means of grace, a resource for healing and transformation in our lives. Sexuality, she argues, serves at least three functions that connect it with spirituality and grace. First, it gives us a profound sense of our communion with all of life. Boundaries fall away. Sexual intimacy is therefore sometimes described in terms reminiscent of mystical ecstasy or communion. Second, it also heightens our sense of personal presence and power. It can initiate us "into a clearer sense of strong selfhood." In the giving and receiving of sexual joy is found relational power. Third, there is a strong connection between sexual pleasure and creativity. Sexuality is connected, perhaps especially for women, with being ripe, fertile, full of energy, and alive. "Our fundamental bodily experience is that sexuality is bonded to the power of life. Sexual energy is life-giving energy." Sexual energy, then, has to do with bonding and communion, with integrity and self-hood, and with creativity and life-giving power.

All three of these aspects of the joys of sex are found in the responses we received from pastors. Our respondents spoke of energy, creativity, communion, and integrity as gifts of sexuality in the parish.

One wrote, "Sex and religion seem to be quite closely bound together in much of history. To separate them may well be going against a fullness God intended." This pastor expresses a judgment voiced in different ways by many of our respondents: that sexuality participates in some way in the *fullness* of human life.

This link between sexuality and the fullness of life appeared in several forms. First, sexuality was linked with *energy*. As one woman put it, "It is hard for me to separate sexual energy from an energetic sense of aliveness in general." A male pastor concurs: "It seems artificial to separate sexual energy from spiritual or psychic energy." One simply said, "There is energy—i.e., charisma—in being Christian." And yet another proclaimed, "The 'New Birth' can make us feel far more 'alive' and enthusiastic."

For all these pastors, male and female alike, sexuality is a gift of God that connects us to the kind of energy that is available for Christian witness and life. "As people are conscious and aware of sexual energy it gives them an ability to enter into all aspects of life with commitment, energy, and passion."

Closely related to this general sense of energy or aliveness or fullness was a link drawn between sexuality and creativity or creative power. "Power comes from God," declared one pastor. "Sexual power comes from God. And sexual power is creative, not just in babies, but in God's whole world." This pastor links sex with power and with creativity.

Because power and creativity are gifts of God, sexual energy is therefore a positive thing, a joy. It comes from God and is connected to God's purposes of creativity and power for human beings. A woman said, "It is a great gift and a way of recognizing God's creativity in us." For these men and women in the parish, sexuality is spiritual at root and has a positive function, because it makes us aware, responsive, and creative.

Several women pastors among our respondents specifically linked sexual energy with *bonding* or *intimacy*: "Sexuality is our capacity for intimacy." "Sexual energy is . . . a very basic bonding . . . . It draws us to one another." When the fullness of life is understood as including intimacy or bonding between humans, sexuality is seen as part of such bonding.

Sexuality as a gift of intimacy includes not only intimacy with other humans, but also *intimacy with God*. One woman linked sexuality with prayer and with the desire for union with God: "My own experience of prayer is often sexual: intense, longing for union. And the experience of union." Here, she recognizes that the longing for union is both spiritual and sexual—that "eros" in its deepest sense of desire for union has both dimensions.

Indeed, her statement is strikingly akin to one made by James Nelson in *Between Two Gardens*. Nelson begins this volume with a reflection on his own prayer experience in which he writes of prayer as a sexual and spiritual experience: "I was feeling unmistakable sexual arousal. My entire body-self was longing for the divine."[5] Like most of our respondents, Nelson defines sexuality broadly: "Sexuality is our way of being in the world as female or male persons."[6] And like most of our respondents, Nelson argues that there is a positive dimension to sexuality as an expression of our spiritual selves: "The Christian spiritual life," he posits, "is meant to involve the totality of the self—yes, the sexual self."[7] Sexuality expresses our wholeness as people, it relates us to others, it is a place for the expression of love, and it is an embodiment of the desire for union with God. Thus, sexuality and spirituality are linked.

In a similar vein, many women respondents linked sexual energy specifically with spirituality. One put it this way:

> Yes, there is a positive role for sexual awareness or energy in the church. When we talk about spirituality, we need to talk about the whole person. We've left sexuality at the door. Part of what is positive is being aware. It has to do with a certain spiritual energy and can be channeled positively.

In this statement, sexuality is necessary for spirituality—for human wholeness. Sexuality is creative energy. If spirituality has to do with being whole persons, then sexuality is an integral part of spirituality.

Indeed, some would say that if sexuality is part of *what it means to be human,* then it is so closely linked to our spirituality that it becomes impossible to separate the two:

> I wouldn't say that sexual energy is a resource to be used as much as I would say that it is a part of who I am. When I try to subdue that energy, I am less dynamic as a person and a pastor. When I am at peace with that part of myself and others, there is a light, free sense about ministry generally.

For this woman pastor, sexuality is not something that she "has" outside of herself, but something that she "is." In a similar vein, one man said, "That's who we are." Hence, proper integration of sexual energy is necessary for healthy living—and, significantly, for one's ability to serve as pastor. The "light, free sense about ministry" that is brought about by acceptance of the dynamic energy of sexuality is crucial to some pastors' understanding of what ministry is and should be. Sexuality thus links them to the fullness of life by enabling and enhancing vocation.

All these pastors—male and female alike—point toward a "theology of sexuality." That is, they point to a link between our relationship with God and our human sexuality. Indeed, we might say that they point toward a "sexual theology," in which God is understood and appropriated for human life and ministry *through* God's gift of sexuality. It is through the energy, the creativity, the bonding, the intimacy, and the integrity of sexuality that God is present and revealed in human life. Because sexuality is linked to the fullness of life in these ways, sexuality is one of the ways in which God is mediated to humans.

In concluding her argument for making love as a means of grace, Parker writes, "wherever passion, energy, joy, personal power, and creativity emerge and converge, the experience can be felt as erotic." Like many feminists, Parker uses the term *erotic* in its broad sense of pushing toward union, and therefore sees it as an appropriate term for describing the human-divine encounter as well. In Christian tradition, God is imaged in terms of passion, energy and creativity, joy, personal integrity and power: God suffers because God loves—passion; God is the creator, the whirlwind, the constant force entering human life—energy and creativity; God rejoices over the lost sheep who is found, over the sinner who repents—joy; and God through Jesus offers us the quintessential embodiment of personal power and integrity. If these are the characteristics of God, and if they are also experienced in sexual relating, then when sexual relating exhibits these characteristics, God is happening.

Or, to put it the other way around, sexual intimacy can be the place where God's nature and grace are revealed. In such a view, it is perhaps not stretching the point too much to say that sexuality takes on a sacramental quality, a quality of bringing God into human life. Hence, as Parker puts it, making love can be a means of grace. One pastor expressed exactly this perspective when he wrote, "For me, sex with my wife is an act of worship, an opportunity for both of us to lose ourselves in a higher reality of love and connectedness."

This pastor's reference to a "higher reality" may suggest a body/spirit dualism that is precisely what most of the pastors quoted here want to avoid. But we do not think he intends such a duality. We think he intends to suggest that the physical act of lovemaking is itself a way of worshiping God. Sexual intercourse can bring God into our lives and connect us to God. This is precisely what Parker is arguing.

This does not mean that one should have sexual intercourse with everyone! The pastor quoted here also said that to be formed in God's image means for him that "each person is a sacral vessel of the divine, thus, a sacral presence." Recognizing the other as created in God's image sets limits on sexual behavior, since "that person is not to be used as an object for the fulfillment of my desires." Rather, we "celebrate and worship God in the other." Most of the time, this means doing so in noncoital ways. But the point here is that coitus itself can be a way of embodying God's presence in the world.

Sexual intimacy is not the "be all and end all" of human life, as Parker rightly notes. But it has potential for "undergirding all that is good, and joyful in our lives." It is this link between sexuality and grace that allowed one woman pastor to say, "I would hope that being a better lover has made me a better theologian, and vice versa." And it is the sense of this link that makes some of our pastors—women especially—want to affirm the positive role of sexual energy and awareness in the parish.

In short, by lifting up the gifts that sexuality brings to human life, these pastors find sexuality connected on the deepest levels to our spirituality and to what it means to be human in God's world. There is a link between our ability to be humanly sexual and our ability to articulate a sense of God's presence in our lives. It is this link that our pastors are exploring.

Pastors who see God mediated through sexual intimacy are not only developing a theology of sexuality, but are actually talking about a "sexual theology"—a way of talking about God that is at root physical, sensual, and mediated through common forms of physical intimacy such as sexual touching and intercourse.

Several church studies of sexuality in the past several decades have also tried to avoid the narrow definitions so often given to sexuality and to affirm a positive place for sexuality in Christian spirituality. "Sexuality expresses God's intention that we find our authentic humanness in relatedness to others" argues the United Church of Christ (UCC).[8] Like many of our respondents, the study committee from the UCC defined sexuality broadly, distinguishing "sex" in the genital sense from "sexuality" as an "integrated, individualized, unique expression of self."[9] Thus, sexuality is an integral part of individual integrity and interpersonal relation.

Echoing the emphasis on the importance of sexuality for bonding, the Catholic Theological Society of America (CTSA) declares that "sexuality is the Creator's ingenious way of calling people constantly out of themselves into relationship with others."[10] Here, we see echoes of the emphasis on sexuality as providing bonding or communion and hence contributing to the fullness of life. As the CTSA recognized, possibilities of union and intimacy pervade our transactions with others, "adding interest and delight, promising mystery and disclosure and delivery from loneliness."[11] Sexuality, then, is not simply something physical. It is personal, social, and spiritual as well.

These theological reflections, both formal and informal, might be summed up in the understanding that sexuality is a gift from God intended to foster *creative growth toward integration.*[12] At its best, sexuality fosters creativity, enables growth, and moves toward integration, wholeness, and integrity in human life. At its best, it helps us to overcome our alienation from one another, it builds trust, it moves us toward "an eagerness for the freeing growth of the other,"[13] and it supports work and vocation. When it exhibits these characteristics, then it can be said to participate in God and to bring God into human life. Hence, we can talk about a "theology of sexuality" that affirms the goodness of this gift, but we can also talk about a "sexual theology" that understands God as God is known in and through the physical dimensions of human living. As Nelson puts it, "Bodily experience must be the starting point for any theological reflection at all."[14]

JOURNEY TOWARD INCARNATION

To understand God in and through the physical dimensions of human living is to speak of an incarnated God—a God made flesh and known in and through the flesh.[15] Thus it is that one of our respondents said, "I do use sexual energy—as it is released in the arts, in explicit affirmations of the incarnational dimensions of faith."

This "incarnational" theology was echoed by others. "I have a deeply incarnational theology, formed by an intensive study of the mystics, creation-centered theological readings, resonant with the Word made flesh of John's gospel," said one. "My faith is incarnational—and therefore 'bodied forth,' " claimed another. Not all of our respondents spoke of an incarnational theology. But many did. And others expressed the concepts even if they did not use the explicit words.

For most, the move to an incarnational theology— or to new depths of understanding within such a theology—had meant significant change in their own theological perspective and personal experience. As one woman pastor put it, "My personal Christian upbringing was repressive and guilt-producing, so where I am now—sexually and in every other way— required me to overcome the harmful early effects and develop a whole new theology."

This pastor was not alone in expressing a significant shift from an early, repressive understanding of Christian sexuality toward an incarnational theology that could affirm the goodness of all creation, including sexuality. A male pastor described his journey thus: "The Christian tradition has been against any other sexual relationship than heterosexual marriage. This, and its basis in given Scripture, formed my early limited concepts of sexuality. More recent exposure to understanding Scripture has changed my mind." And another one simply said, "my Baptist pietistical tradition has been pretty much left behind—now I have developed my own theology which is what is now being called creation spirituality."

For a number of pastors, then, there has been a shift from an early perspective oriented primarily toward keeping strict rules regarding sexuality toward a more open understanding and acceptance of sexuality as a good and creative part of human life in its various forms.

A number of factors contribute to this change. The pastor just quoted identifies new learnings about scripture as important for his journey. Many pastors rooted their understanding of a theology of sexuality in scripture, and their choices of significant scriptural texts covered the gamut from the Song of Songs to Jesus' encounter with the woman at the well.

But while scripture or new appropriations of scripture may be instrumental in pastors' views of sexuality, they are not the most important for many pastors. The pastor quoted above who said that his early "limited" concepts of sexuality had been changed attributed that change not only to scripture but to another, more central, source—his experience of gay and lesbian people:

> But probably most important was associating with homosexual persons on a professional basis; that helped me to reinvestigate the whole area of sexuality. . . . Now there are persons with different life styles and sexual preferences that have helped me to understand that they are fully persons under God. What God ordains, I'm not sure I have the power to put aside.

This pastor was not the only one to speak of the difference brought about in his theology by encounter with gay and lesbian Christians and non-Christians. Another pastor wrote:

> There was a time, a particular time, when as a pastor I was confronted by the issue of sexual orientation, particularly homosexual. . . . It was in that experience that I came to a fuller understanding of faith. . . . What was different about that experience was coming to know gay men and lesbians personally. The inclusive spirit of Jesus was a decisive force influencing where I came out on the issue.

Indeed, quite a number of pastors spoke of their encounters with gay and lesbian men and women as having a significant effect on their understanding of sexuality and on their theology.

Other experiences were also determinative. Primary among them were experiences of good sex, good marriage, and the grace of forgiveness and love: "A theology rooted in God's acceptance of me and the goodness of sexuality as a part of God's creation has developed in me out of experiences of grace and forgiveness, primarily in my marriage relationship. Intimate acceptance and love here have allowed me to see the affirmation of sexuality throughout the Scriptures." For this pastor, his own experience of being loved and accepted in marriage and in sexual intimacy led to a reappraisal of scripture. Another pastor wrote that his experience in the sexual arena "has further convinced me of the incarnation being a physical expression of God's love." Many pastors mentioned the centrality of their marriages to their own understanding and acceptance of the goodness of sexual love as an "embodied" expression of God's love.

Ironically, perhaps, divorce was also a tool through which some pastors came to new understandings of sexuality. "Because of a divorce, I've grown more sensitive to those divorced," wrote one, who concludes that he experiences a "sigh of relief that many hidden pains are now more freely discussed." He also sees such openness as demanding exploration of boundary issues and hence of pastors' expressions of their sexuality. Another pastor, who "came out" as gay in seminary but later married and tried to live as a straight man, says that it was during the twelve years that it took to break off the marriage that he finally began to put his theology and his sexuality together.

Painful experiences such as divorce, or trying to live a life that is antithetical to who we really are, can

themselves be a way of coming closer to God and
hence growing theologically. The "joy of sex" in the
parish sometimes means the "pain of sex" that results
in a deeper relationship with God.

Other experiences were also formative for pastors.
Quite a few mentioned family or upbringing, sexuality workshops, and former pastors or mentors. Others
spoke of "experience" generally, without specifying
particular experiences, for example, "my theology
comes from life experience and the values which have
been softened by experience." "My own experience
as a sexual being and work as a pastor has changed
my theology." One pastor, however, said that his
experience had not shaped his theology and that he
thought his theology was more liberal than his practice!

As scripture and experience are two roots of theology, tradition is yet a third. While many pastors see
their traditions as giving a "narrow" view of sexuality
and sexual ethics that must be overcome, tradition has
played a positive role for some in forming their
current theology of sexuality. One spoke particularly
of using the patristic writings, especially Irenaeus.
Another spoke of how church values of the 1950s still
informed his view, though he thought the stress on
virginity from that period had been "softened" today.
A number of male pastors said that tradition shaped
their views but did not specify how. Significantly, *no*
women mentioned tradition as an important source of
their theological views. This is perhaps because of the
painful legacy that the traditions of the church have
left for most women (see chapter 6).

Finally, to scripture, experience, and tradition can
be added "reason." Several pastors spoke of the
importance of the sciences for shaping their views of
sexuality. Others mentioned contemporary arguments about sexuality—especially the works of James

Nelson, Karen Lebacqz, and others. A number of sources on homosexuality were mentioned—Boswell, Mollenkott, and various gay novels and other expressions of gay spirituality.[16] The writings of Matthew Fox on creation spirituality were important for some pastors.

Men as well as women mentioned feminist thought and analysis as significant for changing their views on sexuality. One male pastor wrote:

> Reading of feminist materials which I got from my wife and some lesbian students in the congregation has been important. Part of what that did was to validate part of myself I always had known was there but didn't know what to do with—the intuitive, gentle side of me. I knew it was there as early as high school when I was an athlete. I tried to be more macho than I wanted to be. There was no model or affirmation for the gentle side of me. Gay and lesbian and feminist perspectives made it OK.

Finally, some mentioned liberation theology as a helpful source.

These sources—scripture, experience, tradition, and reason—are reminiscent of the traditional "Methodist quadrilateral" or four-fold source for ethical reflection.[17] The quadrilateral may have been used deliberately by some pastors; others may have used it inadvertently. Some used only a portion of it, but the collective wisdom of the pastors suggests that all four elements are present, either positively or negatively, for most pastors.

Put together, these sources are leading some pastors toward an affirmation of the "joy of sex" in the parish. If God is love, if God is incarnated, then bodily love *is* an expression of God's presence. To be a better lover is to be a better theologian, and vice versa. There is room for the joy of sex—even in the parish.

2
Dynamics of Desire

In the previous chapter we looked at the positive role of sex in the parish. Because human sexuality is an integral part of who we are, it makes us alive and energetic, it connects us to others, it deepens our spirituality. Many pastors surveyed affirm an "incarnational" theology in which the physical dimensions of human life are understood as vehicles for God's presence.

If sexual energy and awareness are good gifts in ministry, then why is there a problem? Is there something special about the church or about being in ministry that makes this gift problematic?

We think so. Precisely because sexuality is such a good gift, and because it brings gifts of energy and enthusiasm to the church, then it is to be expected that sexual attraction will also arise between pastor and parishioner. As one commentator put it, if pastors were not at all "turned on" by their congregations, what would that do to the liveliness of their ministries? Where energy runs high and enthusiasm abounds, it is to be expected that sexual attraction will also occur.

And so it does. As Robert Carlson puts it in "Battling Sexual Indiscretion," the effort to find God opens "that same well of yearning that exists in all of us and sometimes encourages us to sexual desire."[1] In

Sex in the Forbidden Zone, Peter Rutter explains that when two people work closely in a context where familiarity and trust develop, closeness, comfort, and a sense of completeness may be experienced. "Under these conditions," he suggests, "images of sexual union flood us."[2] Because sexual intercourse is a symbol for our deepest intimacy, any relationship that moves us can stimulate desire for that deepest union and therefore can be sexualized.[3]

What happens when pastors feel sexual desire? Sexual affairs and indiscretions by well-known religious leaders such as Jim Bakker and Jimmy Swaggert make newspaper headlines. But what about the average pastor? Are all pastors sexually attracted to members of their congregations? If they are, how do they respond?

Perhaps equally important, how do pastors know when they are responding out of sexual attraction? Do they have a "radar" or early warning system to keep out of trouble, and if so, what is it? What standards do clergy set for themselves, and how do they adhere to those standards? How do they know when they are reaching the boundaries of acceptable behavior?

In order to answer these questions, the Professional Ethics Group asked the pastors in our survey two questions. First we asked, Have you ever been sexually attracted to a member of your congregation or had sexual fantasies about a member? If so, what happened? Then we asked, How do you decide when you are reaching the limits of acceptable intimacy with a parishioner? What alerts you to the possibility that an inappropriate boundary might be crossed? These questions were intended to elicit information about how pastors handle sexual attraction to parishioners. In this chapter, we present the responses to these questions and some reflections about the meaning of these responses for sex in the parish.

SEXUAL ATTRACTION

A few pastors said they have never been attracted to a parishioner, or that it happened only once or twice and never again. Several responded to our question asking whether they had been attracted to or had fantasies about a parishioner with a blunt no. One said, "no, except for very fleeting thoughts on rare occasions." One woman explained that while she has experienced a *collegial* relationship in which there was attraction on both sides, she has never been attracted to a *parishioner*. Thus, a small minority reported that they had experienced attraction to parishioners either not at all or rarely.

The vast majority, however, said that they had been attracted to parishioners or had had sexual fantasies about a parishioner. "Yes, several times" and "There always seem to be one or two" were common responses. One suggests that, especially early in ministry, there is always someone "with whom you connect on so many levels so well." Some thought the answer was obvious: "If I hadn't, I'd be dead. We are sexual beings after all." "Over thirty years, are you kidding?!" Thus, for most of our pastors, just as sexuality is a normal and accepted part of what it is to be human, so sexual attraction is an accepted and expected phenomenon.

One pastor explained the phenomenon at some length:

> I've been sexually attracted to a member of my congregation numerous times. Mostly it has arisen in small groups and individual counseling situations, several instances in out of town intensive workshops where I am removed from the reality of my ordinary world. In small groups in the church setting, it has been true in both youth groups and adult groups. In counseling, it has

been more true with adults, not youth. It is most likely to happen in counseling when there is intimate sharing, which of course is mostly on their part but some on my part as well.

This pastor points to two sets of issues that affect the dynamics of desire. First are the structures of work within the church. The intimacy generated in pastoral counseling, settings where one is divorced from one's normal environment, working intensely with parishioners over time—all these and other factors peculiar to pastoral work contribute to occasions for desire to arise and to be expressed.

Indeed, Robert Carlson argues that ministers, among all the helping professions, are perhaps especially vulnerable to sexual involvement with their clients.[4] The loneliness of clergy, the close relationships they enter, the fact that they have intimate access to people's homes and bedrooms, the privacy and isolation of their own office settings—all these factors can be conducive to sexual desire and can contribute to the temptation to act on that desire. As one male pastor put it, "For the pastor there are more situations, more opportunities to act out sexually. If you're not clear about your sexuality, you're going to act on your fantasies."

The first important factor, then, is opportunity and work structure. While we think there are some particular factors here for clergy, still we note that clergy are not alone. In *Sex in the Forbidden Zone*, Peter Rutter notes that 80 percent of the women he spoke with had stories to tell about sexual approaches by doctors, therapists, pastors, lawyers, or teachers.[5] He concludes that sexual violation in professional relationships of trust is an "epidemic, mainstream" problem.[6] A poll conducted by the research department of *Christianity Today* found that 23 percent of clergy—or nearly one-fourth—said they had engaged in some form of sexual behavior that they considered inappropriate. Of these, 12 percent reported having sexual intercourse with someone other than their spouse; 18 percent said they had engaged in other forms of sexual contact such as passionate kissing, fondling, or mutual masturbation; and only 4 percent said they were found out.[7]

Just as the structures of work settings contribute to the dynamics of desire, so do interpersonal dynamics of sexual arousal and the use of sexuality in interpersonal relations in this culture. It is these that will occupy our attention in this chapter and the next, as we look at what pastors do and why.

Consonant with what we found in chapter 1 about the positive aspects of sexuality, several pastors suggested that these instances of sexual attraction added an important dimension to life. "The sexuality added to the richness of the relationship although it took no form of physical or verbal expression," said one. "The attraction enlivens relationships, but I think in ways that have not been destructive," claimed another. "I have praised God that such vitality existed, and then let go of it," said a third.

RESISTANCE

Like these three respondents, most pastors draw a clear distinction between *being attracted* to a parishioner and *acting on that attraction*. Readers who are distressed by newspaper reports of sexual involvement between pastors and parishioners may find it encouraging to know that of more than fifty pastors in one of our surveys who said they had been attracted to a parishioner, only six moved into any kind of sexual involvement with that parishioner. And two of these ended in a covenantal relationship: "I married her." Thus, only a handful reported entering relationships other than covenantal ones. While the typical pastor accepts the fact of attraction as a "given," he or she also rejects the idea of acting on that attraction in anything other than honorable circumstances. Of course, some of our respondents may not have reported their activities accurately. Precisely because they experience such a strong taboo against pastor-parishioner sexual relations, they may simply deny that they have ever acted on their feelings. Nonetheless, the picture presented to us would indicate that most pastors are careful about boundaries.

Indeed, a number of pastors made comments akin to the following: "I have *very* strict boundaries as far as parishioners are concerned and have *never* crossed them." Many pastors seem to feel very strongly about the issue. Indeed, they may have felt so strongly about the wrongness of pastor-parishioner sexual contact that they deemed it unnecessary to offer any reasons for their judgment beyond their clear indignation.

However, some were more explicit. They offered reasons why involvement would be wrong. And in some other cases, we can "read between the lines" to discern the reasons operating. Three possible reasons emerged with some clarity.

For a number of pastors, it was a marriage commitment with its vows of fidelity and monogamy that would make a sexual encounter with a parishioner wrong: "To personally promote these thoughts would have been adultery." "My personal standards about sexual behavior are defined by my monogamous and erotic relationship with my sexual partner."

Indeed, the strength of a marriage had a great deal to do with how some pastors responded to their congregation. "I have had a solid marriage, and an enjoyable one." "Nothing came of it because I did not

want it to and because I was happy at home." Of
pastors who specified the reasons that they did not
get involved with parishioners, by far the largest
number mentioned their primary commitments to a
spouse or partner. Carlson notes that "having a good
marriage is a very important factor in maintaining
appropriate sexual behavior in one's professional
relationships."[8]

One pastor explained in some detail how his
marriage helps him set boundaries:

> By this time I've developed some well-practiced, non-
> thinking boundaries. They stem from the strong com-
> mitment that my wife and I have to a monogamous
> relationship. We've always had that, even in stormy
> times. We've also maintained openness, truthfulness,
> and commitment to our children and family life over the
> church. We have been married for 27 years. These
> commitments shape the way I draw lines with other
> people.

This pastor does not socialize with other women
unless his wife is present—and if the other woman is
married, her husband must also be present. Another
pastor, responding to the question about how to draw
lines, put it simply: "I process what I say and what I
do through the eyes and ears of my wife . . . if I would
not like for her to see or hear what I am doing then I
stop."

Thus, those who offered a reason for why sexual
involvement with a parishioner would be wrong most
often mentioned their marriage covenant. This leaves
us wondering whether they would think sexual contact wrong if neither pastor nor parishioner was
married; we will return to this question in chapter 8.
Moreover, Carlson notes that many clergy marriages
suffer the strains of the time demands on the minister,
and are therefore under stress and not strong; while

they may be an effective bulwark at times, even a good marriage "does not inoculate one against being attracted to, or even falling in love with, another person."[9]

Marriage covenants, as important as they are, are not a sufficient guarantee against improper sexual relations. First, not all clergy are married. Second, not all clergy who are married experience joy in their marriages; loneliness experienced there may contribute to their tendency to seek another relationship. And third, even the best of marriages does not keep people from falling in love or from acting out sexually. It is important to see, then, what other reasons kept clergy from becoming sexually involved with parishioners.

For some, marriage or a previous covenanted relationship was not the central concern. Rather, their sense of personal and especially of professional identity was at stake: "It would have destroyed my sense of identity if I had gotten sexually involved." "It is simply not professional to get involved with someone with whom you have a professional relationship." "I do not want my pastoral relationships destroyed by my gonads." A few said they work deliberately to maintain separation between personal and professional lives, for example, "It is and has been my policy not to date members of the congregation." For these pastors, it is not just a personal commitment that makes the potential sexual encounter wrong, but an understanding of what is at stake professionally.

Several explained why they consider sexual contact with parishioners unprofessional. One says, "Just a few moments reflection on what it could do to damage the other person's spiritual journey and abuse their understanding of God is enough to put the attraction in proper perspective." Here, fostering the parishioner's spiritual journey and maintaining trust in God was the reason for avoiding sexual contact. Another centered his reasons in his understanding of what the church is supposed to be: "The church must be a safe place for people. When pastors are having sex with their parishioners, the church is not a safe place." Thus, the purpose of the pastoral role, centered in the nature of the church and in the parishioner's spiritual needs, can also be a reason for avoiding sexual contact with parishioners. We will return to this question when we look at pastoral power.

One pastor combined marriage and professional ethics in a brief statement: "My sense of fidelity to my spouse, my sense of values and my commitment to my ordination serve to guide me in my relationships." Personal and professional issues come together in this claim.

For yet others, it is past experiences of pain that have formed their sense of appropriate boundaries. "Attraction led to an unprofessional relationship that ended with some hurt," explained one pastor. One woman spoke of being very careful about boundaries now because she had experienced a pastor who transgressed boundaries with her. Thus, some pastors draw not simply on their understanding of pastoral role nor on their primary covenantal relationships, but on their own or others' experiences of pain.

While these three reasons—previous commitments, professional obligations, and past experiences—emerged to ground some pastors' views, most did not specify a reason for rejecting involvement with parishioners as wrong. They wrote simply of sexual attraction as a "temptation" to be resisted (". . . lead us not into temptation"), or of not letting things get "out of hand" or of maintaining "self-control." By far the majority simply said, "nothing happened," and left it at that. One pastor sums it up by saying "there is from the beginning of any relationship an internal boundary check." These pastors were clear on the limits they set but did not articulate the reasons for choosing those limits. It is almost as if they simply understood the pastor-parishioner relationship to be a "forbidden zone" in which there is no need to spell out the grounds for their caution.

THE "RADAR" SYSTEM: WARNING SIGNS

If attraction is a common phenomenon, and pastors find it enlivening their ministries yet do not want to act on it, then they must develop a "warning" system of some kind to determine what levels of attraction are acceptable and when they are approaching the limits of acceptable intimacy. We asked pastors, How do you decide when you are reaching the limits of acceptable intimacy with a parishioner? What alerts you to the possibilities that an inappropriate boundary might be crossed? With these questions, we hoped to gain some sense of whether pastors bring a preformed notion of what is right and wrong, and what informs their judgment about the appropriateness of various kinds of contact with a parishioner.

Language itself becomes a problem at this point. The term "intimacy" is used to mean a variety of forms of contact. Several pastors made a clear distinction between "intimacy" and sexual contact. One declared flatly that there should never be limits to "intimacy" with a parishioner: "Always seek greater intimacy with communicants. There should be no limit to the intimacy." However, he clearly distinguished intimacy from sexual contact: "If sexuality limits the intimacy, the sexuality is inappropriate." Sexual relations inhibit rather than foster the true intimacy of pastor and parishioner in the view of this pastor, and it is precisely their blocking of genuine intimacy that makes them wrong.

In a similar vein, another writes: "The question of my sexuality is only part of the larger issue of personal intimacy. . . . It has been my experience that some persons use sexuality to *avoid* being intimate." Here again, sexuality is clearly distinguished from intimacy and is even seen as one possible way of avoiding genuine intimacy.

Thus, when we asked about limits to acceptable "intimacy" in our questionnaire, we may have created problems for pastors who believe that *sexual* (genital) intimacy between pastor and parishioner is wrong and who yet want to uphold the notion of a genuine *pastoral* intimacy as always appropriate. Some would probably even say that spiritual intimacy, which always has elements of the sexual in it, is always acceptable, but that genital expression of that spiritual intimacy is wrong. Language can be confusing in this arena and the term *intimacy* can have several possible meanings. The different responses that we received may therefore have something to do with the language that we used.

Most pastors, however, understood "intimacy" in this context to imply genitally oriented sexual intimacy. Thus, they responded in terms of what they would see as the proper limits on a sexually oriented relationship between pastor and parishioner. Most offered at least some indication of what signals they use to know where the limits of sexual contact are and when those limits are in danger of being transgressed. Let us turn, then, to the ways that pastors decide when they are approaching the limits of acceptable behavior.

We have already mentioned the pastor who said he processes things through the eyes of his wife and feels that anything he would not want her to see or hear is not appropriate. Other pastors also appear to use a "test of publicity" to determine acceptable limits. In her study of the morality of lying, Sissela Bok proposes that a "test of publicity" asks which lies would survive the appeal for justification to reasonable persons.[10] The test of publicity is designed to challenge privately held assumptions and hastily formed conclusions by requiring that arguments for one's position must survive the test of public scrutiny. One pastor simply limits all physical contact to public encounters, "never in private." Another argues that any hug that could not be given in a public setting is inappropriate. One says bluntly, "The limits are defined by what is publicly acceptable behavior." Others speak of "convention" or of not letting a relationship affect other relations in the church in a negative way. All these appeals are to the public arena as the test of legitimacy.

However, by far the most common appeal was not to the public arena but to the private. Most pastors spoke simply of what "felt right" or what their "instinct" or "intuition" told them. "I tend to go with what feels comfortable and appropriate." "My own comfort zone tells me a lot." "I judge by my feelings." "I try to let feelings (whether they are ones of wanting to get closer or ones of wanting to avoid) be an indication of my state of being." "Intuition." "Instinct." "If I begin to feel uncomfortable." "The best sign for me is an *inward feeling.*" One said flatly, "You just know."

These responses appealing to instinct, intuition, and their own comfortableness were by far the most common response to our question asking pastors how they decided when they were reaching the limits of acceptable intimacy.

This is not surprising when we consider that most pastors score high on the "feeling" category in the

Myers-Briggs Type Indicator.* This personality inventory assesses the way people perceive and process input. Those who are "feeling" oriented (as opposed to "thinking" oriented) tend to trust not in argument but in inward signals as a mode of decision making. In a recent study published by the Alban Institute, Roy Oswald and Otto Kroeger found that, of 1319 pastors studied, fully 68 percent fit the "feeling"-oriented category.[11] Indeed, they found that not only are 68 percent (more than two-thirds) of pastors feeling-oriented, but that 44 percent of pastors are both feeling-oriented and "intuitional" (compared to only 12 percent of the general population). Thus, it is not surprising that clergy, male and female alike, would tend to trust their "intuition" or "instinct" or "feelings" to tell them when something is going wrong.

That this is a common approach among clergy and that it fits their basic personality type does not, however, make it a good mechanism for determining when boundaries are being reached. Notice that one of the pastors quoted said he trusted his feelings to tell him whether to seek *more* intimacy as well as *less* intimacy; intuition can be a mechanism not only for drawing back, but also for deciding when to approach someone. Intuition or instinct works both ways, toward greater involvement as well as away from greater involvement.

Moreover, intuition is not infallible. What we often call "instinct" has large cultural elements in it. Indeed, what we call intuition or instinct or "feelings" is largely socially conditioned. As we will see in later chapters, our "instinctual" responses in the sexual arena are heavily influenced by our sexist and heterosexist culture and therefore are not altogether dependable. We will return to this question in the next

---

Myers-Briggs Type Indicator® is a registered trademark of Consulting Psychologists Press, Inc.

chapter when we assess the failure of limits and look at the social context of ministry.

THE GENITALIZATION OF FEELINGS

One response was common—and striking—among male pastors, but lacking among female pastors. This was the dependence on physical response and specifically on sexual arousal as a warning system. Quite a few men said they know they are approaching the limits of what is acceptable "when I sense sexual arousal in myself," or "when I'm so sexually aroused that biologically I have a desire to move toward intercourse," or "if our conversation is causing me to become sexually aroused." "A physical response," said another. "When I have bordered on sexual arousal, I sense danger signals." "Sexual arousal is certainly a warning indication." Many male pastors would agree with the one who said, "The limits for me are marked by what is going on inside my body."

In short, a number of male pastors use sexual arousal, particularly erection, as the sign that they are moving toward unacceptable intimacy with a parishioner. The "feelings" that they are trusting to help them set limits are specifically sexual feelings, and they are feelings that tend toward intercourse.

Recent studies of male and female sexuality and personality help to explain this phenomenon, which occurred among male pastors but not among female pastors. Nancy Chodorow's ground-breaking study of socialization demonstrates that in cultures where child rearing is done almost entirely by women, boys learn to define their gender identity primarily through separation from the mother.[12] Men then tend to associate "maleness" with "separateness" or autonomy. Intimacy, therefore, is always to a certain extent a threat to male identity, since that identity is dependent upon autonomy and separateness. Hence, as James Nelson puts it, there is always a tension for men between masculinity and intimacy. Nelson proposes that most men have a "precarious grip" on their masculinity.[13]

Men thus tend to define themselves in terms of separateness rather than in terms of relationality and intimacy. Feelings are suspect, and logic and rationality are prized. Because intimacy and feelings are less easily accommodated into the male personality, strong feelings cannot be expressed directly as emotion. Culturally, the display of emotion by men is suppressed and discouraged. Strong feelings will therefore tend to be genitalized—to come out in the form of sexual attraction, and specifically in the form of genital arousal. When men feel strongly about women, then, they tend to move toward genital involvement. This is also true of men's feelings for other men, and explains some of the homophobia that characterizes our society in general. Indeed, Nelson proposes that this is one reason that men develop both weak friendships and strong homophobia: they are afraid that strong feelings for men will result in genital attraction, and they therefore relegate friendships to joint activities rather than in-depth sharing of personal feelings and put strong constraints on sexual relations with other men.[14]

Male sexuality then becomes dissociated from emotion and expression of intimate feelings, and becomes focused on the phallic, on the sexual act, on penetration. Male language reflects this: things are "up" when they are going well and "down" when they are not; "hard" data is trusted while "soft" data is not; and so on.[15] The male world is a world in which feelings are not dealt with directly as strong emotional attachments, but are genitalized and turned into sexual attraction. Rutter notes, for example, that women's desire for deep union and women's expression of passionate feelings is often nonsexual, but that "cultural messages encourage [men] to believe that relief from inner pain is inextricably interwoven with sexually consummating a relationship."[16] Hence, when a man seeks union, he seeks *sexual* union. Indeed, as we saw with our pastors, his sexual feelings may be the first clue that he is seeking union at all.

Because male pastors use feelings as a mode of decision making more than the typical male population does, they may differ from the typical male response. But they are not free from the general male tendency to genitalize feelings. This is demonstrated in the responses that identified sexual arousal as the warning signal for inappropriate conduct. Some male pastors do not even know they are having strong feelings until they become sexually aroused. Nor are they sure of having another forum in which to deal with their strong feelings. Thus, sexual—genital—involvement is always a danger, because the dynamics of socialization in our culture do not permit other modes of male response to the strong feelings that can be elicited in the sharing of intimacy.

Because male pastors use feelings as a mode of decision making more than the typical male population does, they may also think that they are fully in touch with their feelings and that their feelings are a good guide to ethical behavior. In the next chapter, we challenge this assumption.

FANTASIES

In addition to sexual arousal, warning signals mentioned by pastors included heightened energy, their desire to seek out the parishioner, the temptation to direct the conversation to sexual subjects, and their own fantasies. "The limits of intimacy with a parishioner are stepped over when sexual fantasies abound." "When I begin to think of that person as a potential sexual partner—not just a very dear friend—then that boundary has been crossed." "When that person is in my thoughts inappropriately in intimacy with spouse or in daydreaming." "If I sense heightened energy levels within." "If I am seeking the parishioner out." "Another warning indication is the desire to do more and see more of a parishioner than is actually necessary." "If it begins to occupy/preoccupy me too much." "When I find myself inclined toward making suggestive comments." "If I am tempted to ask questions of a female counselee which would encourage her to give more sexually explicit details." The direction of their *thoughts*, not simply physical response, is a warning signal for some pastors.

While many pastors took the direction of their thoughts to be a warning signal, it was also clear that most thought nothing was wrong so long as they were only "thinking" or "fantasizing" and not "acting" or "doing." Many pastors clearly adopt the understanding that *fantasies are acceptable, so long as they are not acted out*. For example, the woman pastor who had been attracted to a co-worker declared: "Being open and honest about our caring for one another helped us through this time and allowed us to understand but not act out the fantasies." Another pastor said, "fantasy sufficed, and being attracted to these individuals was sufficient without acting on the attraction."

Most pastors clearly made an effort to keep fantasy at the level of fantasy and not turn it into a reality. "I enjoyed the fantasy but left it there." "Yes, but nothing happened." "Yes, trusted it as a fantasy." Most were very clear that to act on the fantasy or attraction would have been wrong.

Some indicate that they have gained in ability to

deal with attraction over the years. One said he "trusted it as a fantasy—at least in more recent years." Another said, "It was a matter of grave concern when I was younger. I now feel it to be fairly normal—not to be acted upon but not to be feared or to be ashamed of."

Thus, the common approach would seem to be acceptance of the fantasy for what it is coupled with a strong sense that it would be wrong to turn fantasy into reality. This view gets support in the literature on professional ethics. In *Sex in the Forbidden Zone,* Peter Rutter declares: "As long as the line is firmly drawn between imagination and realization, sexual fantasy is not invasive."[17] He later adds that "looking a woman over is not in itself inherently exploitative if a man can keep this instinctive activity to himself."[18] It is a common—almost universal—view today that fantasy is acceptable so long as it is contained and not realized.

Yet there is a rare voice who finds even fantasy problematic. One pastor spoke of an occasion when he permitted himself to fantasize about a woman because he knew of a previous affair that she had had, and thus the fantasy seemed "safe" at the time. However, he calls it a "tragic" mistake and notes that nothing happened, and that it was the only time that he indulged his fantasies about a parishioner. This pastor would seem to suggest that fantasy is not always innocent or "harmless," and that there is reason to attend to it as an ethical issue in professional practice.

Because fantasies are a common phenomenon, the question of their meaning and of their place in an ethical framework for pastoral practice needs further consideration.

First, there are dangers in shutting down fantasy. Because sexual attraction is a powerful force in human life, to try to shut down all one's sexual fantasies about others can result in repression. When this happens, the sexual energy does not go away. It simply surfaces in another guise or form—and possibly not in a healthy one. As Rutter puts it, a person should not be condemned simply for having fantasies.[19] In fact, Rutter suggests that fantasy is such a central element in the psychological life of men in this culture that it often "captures the man's interest more than the real woman who stands before him."[20]

Second, fantasy has a good role to play in human life. Imagination, play, and fantasy are closely related to human creativity. Fantasy can be a way of prefiguring reality and therefore of planning for contingencies or generating necessary energy and creativity. For example, the pastor who fantasizes on Saturday night how well received her sermon will be on Sunday morning is giving herself a "trial run" in a safe environment.

Such imaginative playing with reality fosters creative interaction and can help channel energies into helpful modes. The pastor may walk into church on Sunday morning full of good feelings for the congregation and confidence in herself. This use of fantasy is healthy, helpful, and closely linked to creative aspects of human spirituality. Similarly, the single pastor may use fantasy to explore behavior which he finds limited by his profession or by the decision he has made not to be sexually active. Fantasy has a positive role to play in bringing options into view and helping us to imagine a new reality.

Given the strength of sexual attraction and the positive role of fantasy, it might seem, then, that there is no reason to urge caution about sexual fantasies. So long as they remain at the level of fantasy and are not acted out, is anything wrong?

The pastor who called his fantasizing a "tragic mistake" did not specify why he judged it this way. But there are several possible reasons to be concerned about fantasy and to see it as something other than a harmless daydream.

First is the possibility that fantasy will turn into reality. "When will and fantasy compete," quips Carlson, "fantasy always wins."[21] Recognizing how compelling the sex drive is, he cautions that erotic and romantic longings "almost always win precedence over rational thought." Indeed, he suggests that "If our minds were read, we'd be revealed as having often, in our fantasy at least, crossed over that line into inappropriate behavior."[22] Precisely because fantasy has a role as a precursor to reality, as a "trial run" for the real world, it also can tend to be enacted in the real world. Thus, the first danger is that fantasy may get turned into reality, particularly when it is fantasy in the sexual arena.

But two other dangers are not always recognized. Even if fantasy is not turned into action, it may yet be harmful. The second reason to be cautious about fantasy is what it does *to the one fantasizing*. Fantasy can become all-consuming. It can distract from necessary chores. It can distort judgment. When this happens, it becomes the "lust" of which the New Testament speaks. It becomes the new core or center of the person's life and thoughts. In short, fantasy that gets out of hand can undermine professional practice not because it is acted out directly but because it distorts judgment and distracts from other, healthful, activities. Fantasy involves not just "my thoughts" and another person about whom I think, but a "vector" toward the world. While a good fantasy can make me alive, energetic, creative, and ready to deal with reality, a warped fantasy does exactly the opposite. It drains energy, turns me inward, and ultimately makes me less able to deal with reality.

Fantasies can even become addictive. One respondent identified himself as a sexual addict, addicted to pornography. In describing his struggle with porno-graphic material and thoughts, he says:

> I have known what I have done has been wrong, against my values, but I was powerless, just as if I were addicted to alcohol. I would tell myself I will not do that again, and then literally be unable to stop myself. I would hate myself and feel shame afterwards but repeat the pro-cess—until I was treated. I have been in recovery for a year, and my life is totally different. Thank God.

While this pastor is not describing fantasy per se, there is a strong link between fantasy and addiction to pornographic material. He says that he shares this story "to say that my theology was unable to prevent me from acting out." The one who becomes addicted will find that not even theology is a sufficient bul-wark. While fantasy has a normal role in human life, it can also become addictive and is then destructive.

Finally, we add a third caution. Those who believe in the power of prayer, as most Christians do, believe that what we hold in our hearts can also directly affect the outside world. While the mechanisms for this affecting of reality are mysterious, and Christians would disagree about the efficacy of "faith healing," for example, most would agree that the channeling of energy in prayer can have *some* effect on the world.

If this is true, then Christians are saying that what we think and hold in ourselves can affect other people and even the course of history ("faith that moves mountains"). This means that we should also ac-knowledge the possibility that fantasy will affect the person about whom we fantasize, even if we do not move directly to turn fantasy into reality. Minimally, we recognize that because I fantasize about someone, I will probably relate differently to that person. To at least that extent, their reality will be changed.

Moreover, fantasies have content. Even when men

think they are just having a "healthy fantasy," they may be objectifying women in their thoughts. For instance, the pastor who said he allowed himself to fantasize about the woman because he knew of her previous affair with someone had to a certain extent objectified her. He was treating her in his thoughts as a sex object, not as a person. As Rutter cautions, "The sexual act [if it occurs] makes clear the degree to which the man has already, on a psychological level, been using the woman as an impersonal object in his own inner world."[23] Such objectification cannot but affect the way the man deals with women in reality in both sexual and other spheres. If objectification of people is wrong, then fantasy may not be the innocent pastime or the "natural, unavoidable, and harmless" activity that it is often taken to be.

Finally, the pastor who spends time fantasizing about a parishioner is dealing with that person in terms of the pastor's needs, not in terms of the parishioner's needs. This is a violation of professional ethics. For all these reasons, we concur with the pastors who saw the development of sexual fantasy as a warning signal that an inappropriate boundary might have been reached.

TALK, TOUCH, AND SUBTLE SIGNALS

A related signal for some pastors is the temptation to direct conversation toward their own interests and to lose focus on the parishioner's agenda. "Am I being tempted to 'talk' about our relationship?" "When the conversation becomes sexual in nature, focusing on the parishioner or me, which is not the major topic of the counseling session." "When the focus of our relationship begins to move away from the individual's concern, problem, task and begins to center on whatever may be happening 'between' us." "It would be inappropriate if the gesture of affection was 'romantic' or more to meet my own need than the parishioner's." Thus, when pastors begin to focus on their own desires and needs rather than on the parishioner's needs, this is a warning signal.

Other warning signals come not from the pastor's own feelings or actions but from parishioners' actions. A number of clues were mentioned by our pastors. Perhaps the most important one is the parishioner who wants to dominate the pastor's time: "when the phone rings too often or that one comes by the office too frequently"; "if he is finding reasons to spend time with me alone"; "need for counseling sessions beyond normal"; "do they seem to idolize me, dominate my time, etc." The parishioner who appears too needy becomes a red flag for many pastors.

As one pastor explains, members who are hurting "frequently become attracted to the pastor." While this has clearly been the experience of a number of pastors, one pastor suggested that he is wary of certain groups of people whom he considers to be at special risk for wanting inappropriate intimacy. He is wary, he says, of those having difficulties in their marriages and of the recently widowed. Thus, he exercises special care in those contexts.

Other clues from parishioners included verbal and physical ones. "If a hug lasted too long," suggests one pastor, that would be a sign. Others mentioned touching "that seems to be something other than casual." One admits that "extended touching, hugging, or 'looks of passion' scare the hell out of me." This pastor was not the only one to mention being scared. Two others said their primary mechanism for knowing when they are reaching the limits of intimacy is "when I get scared."

Some mentioned that parishioners have said "I love you" in ways that seem inappropriate. Others just talk about "verbal hints" or "suggestions." Parishioners' overtures, whether through touching, hugging, or eye contact, are a signal for many pastors. One pastor sums it up by saying, "alerts or red flags I see are body language that is provocative, especially an eye contact that implies sexual promiscuity, language, subject content, and requests for privacy."

Other pastors focused on overall behavior patterns or overt advances. One suggests that "any sort of erotic stimulus that is mutually acknowledged is inappropriate." Others said that any "overt" sexual advances from either side are clearly inappropriate. Another said that "it's a fairly obvious difference in behavior if one is relating to a pastor or a lover."

THE CHECKLIST FOR DESIRE

In short, pastors use a range of signals to tell them when they are getting into trouble. The full list of such signals might include the following:

the "publicity" test: what would others think?
physical arousal—one's own or the other's
inordinate sexual fantasy
sexual gestures or body language
sexual innuendo in verbal exchange
intuition, instinct, or not feeling right
wanting to share intimacies that are not called for
a parishioner wanting too much time or attention
wanting to shift the focus to sexual subjects

Not all these signals function on the same level. Some are internal mechanisms for foreseeing trouble. Others are tests that can be used after an initial "feeling" alerts the pastor to the fact that something is wrong.

Most pastors appear to use a variety of clues in order to sense when they are approaching a danger zone or an unacceptable arena. One pastor offers an additional caution: "I have enough respect for the nonrational dimensions of sexual attraction and for its potency in taking over despite one's self-discipline that I remain fairly guarded about allowing myself into situations that might lead to getting out of hand."

In this chapter we have looked at how the "typical" pastor sets limits to sexual contact with parishioners. Most pastors experience sexual attraction to at least some parishioners during their time in ministry. Pastors who are attracted to parishioners but do not wish to act on that attraction use a range of resources to help them avoid contact when they deem it inappropriate. While some suggest that they are not sure they have handled attraction well in the past or that they may not always handle it well in the future, most pastors seem to feel that they have this issue well controlled. They do not transgress the boundaries that they set.

But crucial to the entire equation, then, is the question of how pastors know what the limits should be. Unless they know what the limits are, they will not know when to draw on their resources in order to avoid inappropriate contact. They may not transgress the boundaries they have set, but have they set the boundaries correctly in the first place? And do they have an adequate mechanism for knowing when they are approaching those boundaries?

Here, we found that some pastors use standards of publicity or other mechanisms to help them decide, but most trust their own developed capacity to sense trouble. Most pastors depend on internal criteria related to intuition, instinct, and feeling. Even those pastors who specify a list of verbal and nonverbal clues often trust their "instinct" to tell them when a touch is wrong or a word inappropriate. In the next chapter we will offer a case history that raises some questions about the adequacy of this approach and adds some dimensions to our perspective on sex in the parish.

3
The Failure of Limits

In the first two chapters, we have largely listened to the voices of pastors and tried to understand sex in the parish from their perspective. We have seen the positive side of their affirmations of the role of sexuality as an energizing, creative, bonding force that links us with an incarnate God. We have also seen the ambivalence and sense that there is a need for limits and boundaries in the expression of sexuality within the church and within professional life.

We turn now to the development of an ethical framework. We will continue to attend to the voices of pastors, but we will add more theoretical considerations. In this chapter, we will look at what some of the literature on psychology and social psychology adds to our pastors' perspectives. In the next chapter, we will add some more sociological and political dimensions to the framework for analysis. As we go, we will also be attending to theological and ethical resources. All these tools must be used in order to get an adequate perspective on experience and to know how to interpret it in developing an ethical perspective on sex in the parish.

SEXUAL INDISCRETIONS

We saw in the previous chapter that most pastors are indeed sexually attracted to parishioners at one time or another. Most think they keep this attraction within proper perspective. Yet we raised questions about whether the trust that pastors place in their "instinct" or "intuition" is always well placed. In this chapter, we want to present some evidence for why there may be dangers in this dependence on private notions of feeling, intuition, and instinct.

First, while most pastors do not seem to become sexually involved with parishioners, some do. Our own survey suggests that roughly 10 percent became involved sexually with a parishioner. The survey presented by the research team of *Christianity Today* presents a higher statistic: nearly one-fourth of all pastors have engaged in some sexual behavior with a parishioner that they consider "wrong." It is possible that our statistics are lower because they are focused primarily on sexual intercourse, and not on other forms of sexual advance or involvement. Moreover, in another informal survey of one denominational locality, we found that roughly 9 percent of pastors become genitally involved with parishioners at some time in their ministry. Whether the higher or lower statistics are adopted, it is clear that some pastors do become sexually, even genitally, involved with parishioners.

For example, one pastor said that he has always been attracted to at least one woman in his congregation who is active in the church, creative, committed, and "brings out the best" in him. One of these women convinced him that "secondary sexual relationships enhance the primary," and he had an affair with her. He writes: "I felt seduced for years with all of this, was very angry about it, and only came to resolution when I left the church I'd gone to after leaving that one."

This pastor did not specify exactly when this incident occurred. But he makes clear that it was early in his ministry. Judging from his age and the length of time he has been in ministry, we would guess it occurred in the late 1960s or early 1970s, during the time of the so-called sexual revolution and arguments for "open marriage." He is not the only pastor to indicate that he was swayed at that time by arguments for multiple sex partners and only later came to question both his own judgment and the nature of the arguments presented to him.

Another pastor says he tried for years to deny that he was sexually attracted to anyone in his parish, but finally capitulated to his feelings when a woman to whom he was attracted approached him at a time when his ministry was at low ebb. He writes, "I felt a tremendous amount of guilt and remorse about this, but the whole situation helped me deal with my own fallibility and sexuality." Their mutual attraction remains but is not acted out today.

Interestingly, for this pastor the incident provided something of a breakthrough in his marriage. Discovering that he was attractive to other women caused his wife to deal with some of her sexual inhibitions. Ultimately, their marriage was strengthened. "All in all," he writes, "it was a positive, although extremely stressful, experience for all concerned." Thus, his own evaluation of the incident is more mixed than the first pastor reported above.

Another writes that he acted on his fantasies once and had an affair. It never became public knowledge, but "was finally dealt with in my marriage." With the perspective of hindsight, he calls it "a foolish and self-indulgent act." And he notes that although he enjoyed it tremendously at the time, he has since learned that the potential damage far exceeded the potential benefits.

Several other pastors indicate that they have not yet become involved but are not sure they would always keep appropriate boundaries. One writes that he does not know of any "graceful" way to deal with attraction to parishioners. Sometimes he has withdrawn in fear. Sometimes he has talked it out with the person. And he writes, "I have not yet chosen to become involved with a parishioner, but fear it might happen someday." Another says that he once made a "modest advance" toward a woman who rebuffed him gently but firmly. Although that ended any possible relationship there, he queries, "Who knows what might have happened if she had allowed it to continue." Both these pastors intimate that they may yet succumb and seek sexual involvement with a parishioner.

Thus, although most of our pastors have set clear limits and adhered to them, a few have not. Some appeared to be unsure of where the limits should be, and others simply did not manage to adhere to the limits they had set. These occurrences suggest that pastors may yet be in jeopardy. Indeed, there is reason to think that we have seen only the tip of an iceberg: since it has become known to denominational bodies that we are engaged in this research, we have been told of more sexual indiscretions in the parish. At this point, our experience indicates that virtually every denomination in every region in the United States has dealt with or is struggling to deal with some instance of sexual indiscretion or abuse on the part of a pastor.

One pastor agreed to tell his story at some length. We share portions of that story here because we think it is indicative of the experiences of several others and because it is suggestive of areas for further concern. It has elements that help to illuminate aspects of others' stories. And it sets the stage for the ethical framework that we wish to develop for sex in the parish. We have tried to keep the basic structure of the story intact, but we have changed some details in order to prevent identification of the parties involved. All names have been changed.

ROBERT'S STORY

We will call this pastor Robert. Robert is now the pastor of a moderate-sized church in a suburban neighborhood. He is considered a good minister by his congregation and peers alike. The story we are about to tell is not generally known. At no time during Robert's ministry has his sexual history "blown up" in his face or threatened his continued work in ministry. Yet that history has elements in it that are potentially explosive for Robert. It might have blown up at some time—and indeed it still might.

Robert's own family background was not a happy one. His parents divorced when he was very young, and his mother remarried. She also had an addiction—he does not specify to what—and was sexually active to support her habit. Robert remembers walking in on her and one of her lovers; he also remembers that there were unusual sexual practices that were not talked about. Robert attributes some of his current "liberal" stance on sexuality to this early childhood exposure to different sexual practices.

Robert married young and he and Adele began a family immediately. His marriage was in difficulty almost from the beginning. Both he and Adele sought counseling—he from a counseling center, and she from their pastor, Karl. It was Karl who encouraged Robert's interest in ministry, securing a job for Robert during his seminary years and then inviting Robert to be his associate at a church on the West Coast. Karl became Robert's mentor in ministry.

Shortly after Robert became his associate, Karl confided to Robert that he was in love with a woman from the congregation and was considering a divorce in order to marry her. Robert was pleased to be taken into Karl's confidence and honored Karl's request for secrecy. He trusted Karl's judgment and believed in Karl's honorable intentions.

In the meantime, Robert's own marriage continued to deteriorate. He and Adele had never had the kind of relationship either wanted; no matter how hard they tried, it seemed there was something missing. Robert plunged into his work with energy, often spending sixty or more hours a week at the church. To meet his intimacy needs, he found himself latching onto other people, especially other women. Because all his time was spent in the church, the women he met were from the church, and particularly from the counseling he did. He began a sexual relationship with one of his parishioners.

Since the senior pastor was also sexually involved with a parishioner, there was no model to indicate to Robert that his behavior was unacceptable. Karl offered no condemnation of Robert's behavior nor any serious questioning of it. This incident took place during the early 1970s, when "open marriage" and the so-called "sexual revolution" made standards of sexual behavior more elusive for many. Both within the church and without, there seemed to be an acceptance of "liberal" attitudes toward sexuality. If Robert felt that his affair was wrong, he did not dwell on this, either at the time or in retrospect.

However, a crisis came: the senior pastor's affair and intended divorce became known in the church. As often happens in such a case, some church members were outraged. At first, Robert defended Karl. Indeed, he claims that he was a staunch defender— perhaps partly to justify his own affair, and partly because of his great admiration for the man who had encouraged him to enter into the ministry.

But then something happened to change Robert's position. Adele took him aside and disclosed that she had been having an affair with Karl off and on for some nine years, ever since seeking counseling with him early in her marriage. Robert was devastated—not so much, he claims, by the fact of his wife's infidelity, but by the blow to his image of the man who had been his idol in ministry. He explains: "I was probably less demolished by what she had done than by what happened in terms of my relationship to him, my idea of ministry."

Robert was angry and hurt. He knew that Karl's affair had not been divulged to the church, but Robert expected that he, at least, was privy to the whole story. Robert had thought that Karl was being open and honest at least with him. Indeed, he had enjoyed being Karl's confidant. To discover that Karl was not altogether honest with him was a devastating blow: "I lost all respect for that man."

Like his mentor, Karl, Robert had fantasized about leaving his wife and marrying the woman with whom he was having an affair. He now decided to end the affair. He also confronted Karl, and he began to learn of other affairs that Karl had had, both during this ministry and in previous settings.

However, Robert admits that "I don't know if I learned everything I needed to learn because of that. I still haven't resolved a lot of things personally." The shock of this experience may have changed Robert's immediate decisions about his marriage and other relationships, but it did not change some fundamental patterns.

In his next parish, Robert also had several affairs—first with Sandy, the woman who later became his second wife, and then with at least one other woman during the time of his second marriage. Both were women with whom he worked in a counseling setting. Thus, early in his ministry, Robert clearly exhibited a pattern of having affairs with women from his church, and particularly those with whom he counseled in an intimate setting.

For Robert, neither the fact of a marriage commitment nor his own painful experience of marital infidelity and loss of faith in his mentor was sufficient to help him set limits on his involvement with parishioners. These factors do not always suffice to prevent a pastor from entering into sexual relations with a parishioner, as Robert's circumstances show. While the hurt that Robert experienced from learning of Karl's involvement with his wife made an immediate change in his behavior, neither that nor either of his marriage commitments was enough to help him break the pattern of involvement with women in his parish.

Why not? What factors created and sustained the impetus for Robert to become sexually involved with the women he counseled in his churches?

ADDICTIVE PATTERNS

Let us begin with some factors in Robert's family background. Reflecting on why his pattern of involvement with parishioners persisted, Robert mentioned his own unhappy childhood and the sense of having never been wanted as a child. He spoke of being the little boy who always wanted to "rescue" the girls on the playground.

Significantly, Robert also spoke about his mother's addiction. Here, the studies of addiction conducted by Anne Wilson Schaef and her associates are helpful. Most of us have learned about addiction to substances such as alcohol and drugs. But Schaef's argument is that many things, not only substances, can become addictive. She proposes that there is an "addictive process" that takes various forms, of which addiction to substances is only one.[1] Among the other kinds of addiction are "process" addictions such as workaholism and addiction to relationships.

One such process addiction is often called "co-dependence." The co-dependent typically is the child of an addictive or dysfunctional family system. Co-dependents grow up trying to please the addictive parent. They develop low self-esteem, are oriented toward the opinions of others, try to take care of others and control things, and deceive themselves and others about reality. They have a difficult time with intimacy because "in order to be intimate, you need a self" and they have really lost themselves.[2]

The co-dependent clings, is dependent on the opinions of others, structures his or her life around what others will think and therefore tries to do what will please, has a hard time saying no, gets depressed easily and is therefore on an emotional roller coaster, personalizes situations, and needs to rescue hurting people. "Co-dependents," says Schaef, "are relationship addicts who frequently use a relationship in the same way drunks use alcohol: to get a 'fix.' "[3] Indeed, in her recent work titled *Escape from Intimacy*, Schaef suggests that "much of what we have previously described as co-dependence is probably relationship addiction."[4]

This description of relationship addiction would fit the pastor we quoted in chapter 1 who called himself a "sexaholic." Recall that he said that arousing sexual attraction and being told that he was attractive was his "drug of choice." What he describes is classic co-dependent behavior: needing to be reassured and seeking relationship in order to feel good about himself: "If I'm feeling bad . . . [I] find a woman and have her tell me, 'Oh, you're good.' " While few of our pastors described themselves in such blunt terms of sexual addiction, there is a possibility that forms of sexual or relationship addiction are more widespread among pastors than is generally recognized. Thus, many pastors may unwittingly be caught in an addictive web that has not as yet been well named or recognized.

A number of factors suggest that pastors are so caught. First, in their study of addictive organizations, Schaef and Diane Fassel suggest that "our society itself is an addictive system."[5] That is, addiction is not simply a problem of some individuals. Society is permeated with addictive patterns and behavior. "By virtue of the fact that we live in this system," they argue further, "we carry many of the characteristics of the addictive system unless we are actively recovering from it by means of a system shift."[6] In other words, many if not most people are addictive, and pastors are not immune.

Second, pastors are part of the "helping professions," and the helping professions attract people who are particularly prone to some co-dependent characteristics. "People in the helping professions tend to be non-recovering co-dependents," declares Schaef.[7] Indeed, many people enter the helping professions in order to continue taking care of others. The little boy who wanted to rescue the girls on the playground becomes the grown man who wants to rescue the physically, mentally, or spiritually sick.

We see this in Robert's story. As a little boy, he wanted to "rescue" the girls on the playground. As a man, he entered a "helping" profession. As a minister, several of his affairs were with women who came to him for help. One of those was a woman whose husband was possibly sociopathic and who needed a great deal of support. Robert tried to rescue her from her abusive situation.

Third, many pastors are workaholics. Schaef and Fassel argue that "workaholism" is the most prevalent addiction of co-dependents, and that many of those in the helping professions exhibit co-dependent characteristics, particularly workaholism.[8] Because workaholism is more socially acceptable than is alcoholism, it is harder to detect and to treat. But it is a form of addictive behavior nonetheless.

Schaef and Fassel argue that the church actively promotes workaholism: "Theologically and in practice, the church puts before us the picture of the good Christian as one who works hard."[9] It is clear from Robert's story that he was pouring energy into his work to the neglect and denial of problems at home during the phase when he first began to have affairs with women in his church. This pattern could have been a warning signal to Robert and should be one for other workaholic pastors as well.

Fourth, Schaef and Fassel argue that the church's theology can promote co-dependence: "The society's concept of 'good Christian martyr' is the perfect co-dependent," they claim.[10] The person who is always giving to the other, neglecting her or his own needs, is seen as a "saint" in Christian tradition, but this is also the description of the co-dependent who organizes her or his life around the needs of the addict. Co-dependents are attracted to professions that allow them to spend time taking care of others or "rescuing" others. The ministry is one such profession.[11] We see this in Robert's admission that he had always wanted to "rescue" those who are hurting; it is reflected in the fact that it was primarily women who came to him for counseling about problems with whom he became sexually involved.

Finally, we noted in the previous chapter that Oswald and Kroeger found that 69 percent of pastors are feeling-oriented and 44 percent are both feeling- and intuitional-oriented on the Myers-Briggs Type Indicator. Intuitional, feeling-oriented people bring many gifts to ministry: they are empathetic, charismatic, often excellent at communication, and so on. But, like all personality types, they also have liabilities. The characteristics of intuitional, feeling-oriented personality types include needing to rescue people, wanting everyone to like them and thus having a hard time saying no, personalizing situations and taking things personally so that often they experience an emotional roller coaster, and having a hard time saying goodbye, hence fostering dependency. They are also prone to discouragement when not praised, and they often avoid conflict by going along with others.

These characteristics of 44 percent of pastors are reminiscent of the characteristics of the co-dependent described by Schaef. This is not to suggest that all intuitional, feeling-oriented people are automatically addictive personalities. Since Schaef and her associates claim that we are an addictive society and that most people exhibit some characteristics of addiction, it is to be expected that all personality types will exhibit some co-dependent or addictive characteristics. But it may be true that intuitional, feeling-oriented people are drawn into the helping professions that are so well suited to co-dependence. While co-dependents are rarely addicted to primary substances such as alcohol, they are often addicted to food, work, or processes such as romance, sex, or relationship. As Carlson puts it, "we work hard not to upset people. It is that very need to please that puts us at particular risk with people who come talking of their lack of fulfillment, their longing, and their hurt. We want so much to be able to fill that void."[12]

ADDICTION AND TRUST IN FEELINGS

The importance of this analysis of the addictive process for our purposes lies in the effects of addictive processes on feelings. Remember that most of our pastors, and this includes Robert, depend to a large extent on what "feels right" or what their "intuition" tells them in order to determine what is acceptable behavior. To trust feelings as a guide to ethical behavior is not altogether wrong, and we shall examine aspects of this mode of decision making further. But the studies of addiction, and especially the suggestion that addictive patterns are prevalent among those in helping professions, give us pause when it comes to trusting feelings as a guide to ethical behavior.

Schaef and Fassel argue that most addicts "are almost totally out of touch with their feelings, intuition, and other similar sources of information."[13] Indeed, one of the primary characteristics of addictive people is separation from their true feelings, and one of the characteristics of an addictive society, in their view, is to foster people who are out of touch with their feelings. To the extent that we live in an addictive society that creates addictive personalities, therefore, most people will *not* be in touch with the deepest level of their feelings or with what we discussed in chapter 1 as the deep form of the erotic that puts us in touch with God.

We noted above that what we call intuition or instinct is itself socially conditioned. When our society is warped, the intuitions that it fosters will also be warped. For example, in one organization studied by Schaef and Fassel, a male supervisor was accused of sexually harassing women staff and clients. When apprised of the situation, the executive director of the organization appealed to the women not to bring suit against the supervisor, arguing that to do so would undermine the agency at a "critical" time. The women, say Schaef and Fassel, were taken in: "What the executive director was asking felt 'right' to some of these women—they had grown up with [such] rules and saw them as normal."[14] In short, the women readily capitulated to permitting the wrongs to continue in the system because they were so enmeshed in an addictive system that they had lost the ability to feel healthy outrage. Our feelings can be distorted by living in a society that encourages addictive and co-dependent behavior. Something that is in fact wrong can "feel" right.

For this reason, we are uncomfortable with the heavy reliance of pastors on what feels right to them. One pastor was quite blunt in suggesting that feelings can go either way: "I try to let feelings (*whether they are ones of wanting to get closer or ones of wanting to avoid*) be an indication of my state of being" (emphasis added). Feelings can be used not only to set limits on intimacy, but also to encourage intimacy. Only if we know that our pastors are healthy, nonaddictive people whose feelings and instincts do not reflect addictive patterns in the culture would we be inclined to trust their feelings as a guide to ethical behavior. It seems likely that most pastors are caught in an addictive system and therefore are not as much in touch with their true feelings as they might like to think.

When we remember that the studies of Chodorow and Nelson suggest that men are out of touch with their feelings and tend to genitalize emotion, we have extra reason to urge caution about trusting the "instincts" of male pastors in particular to tell them where the limits are. Patterns of child rearing that include both dominant nurturing by women and also addictive and co-dependent patterns in families and in society at large suggest that trusting to "feelings" as a guide for ethical behavior is questionable at best. As Robert's story indicates, his own best "feelings" were not a sufficient guard against unethical behavior.

In short, the research of Schaef and her associates

on addiction and co-dependence suggests that it is risky to trust pastors' feelings because pastors are caught in an addictive system in which it is likely that they exhibit co-dependent characteristics, including lack of contact with their own deep feelings. This research is sobering and suggests that the church has serious problems that may be contributing to the failure of limits for some pastors.

SOCIOCULTURAL FACTORS

As is already clear, addictive patterns are not simply "personal" attributes any more than the male tendency to be out of touch with feelings is just a "biological" phenomenon. These factors, which we often take to be personal or biological, are also socially constructed: they are at least in part determined by cultural and social forms, such as child-rearing patterns and family dynamics. In speaking of the addictive process to which most helping professionals are prone, "it is of utmost importance," says Schaef, "to be aware that this underlying addictive process is culturally based and learned."[15] We tend to think of addictions as personal problems, but they are socially and culturally structured.

At one point, Schaef and Fassel consulted with a church whose pastor was a sexual addict. They comment, "because the church frequently functions as an addictive organization, especially in the way it handles issues like sexuality, it often attracts men like this minister."[16] When churches become addictive organizations, they attract men with addictive and co-dependent problems.

Although Robert did not see himself as a sexual addict, two of the pastors we interviewed did, and a third had been sufficiently interested in sexual addiction to read some literature on it. Not all pastors who become sexually involved with a parishioner are sexual addicts. But sexual addiction is not unknown in the church. And while some pastors may not be *sexual* addicts, they may be *relationship* addicts—codependents who will tend toward involvement in order to get the "fix" of feeling good about themselves.

Indeed, Schaef argues that the church contributes to sexual and relationship addictions through its attitudes toward sexuality, romance, and marriage. By limiting acceptable sex to marriage, the church contributes to sexual repressions that can get acted out as obsessions or addictions. It also contributes to the attitude that one "must" get married (and must also stay in destructive marital relationships): "In the church, people are not considered normal unless they are coupled."[17] Thus, instead of offering a genuine covenantal notion of relationship, the church, she proposes, "has often settled for the 'normal' addictive relationships of the society."[18] Along with other institutions, the church may be actively promoting unhealthy ways of relating; it therefore provides a home for those from addictive backgrounds who readily fall into process addictions such as sexual and relationship addictions.

OTHER FACTORS

We have put some stress here on addiction because we see it as one of the significant cultural patterns that affects people in ministry. It therefore must be accounted for in an ethical analysis of sex in the parish. But addiction is not the only social and cultural factor that played a part in Robert's perpetuation of a pattern of involvement with parishioners. Several other factors merit attention.

Robert mentioned his own liberal posture toward sex, and cultural pressures toward "open marriage"

and "loving more than one person at a time." Robert
entered ministry in the late 1960s. This, along with the
early 1970s, was a time when the culture was in flux,
and a new sexual ethic of "free love" abounded. It
was a time when arguments were made for "open
marriage" and for the "enhancement" of primary
relationships by having secondary ones. As noted
above, at least one other pastor from our survey was
directly influenced in his sexual ethics by such arguments. Since Robert readily admits that he always had
a "liberal" sexual ethic, he may also have been easily
convinced by such arguments. Without clear standards for sexual behavior, he was more amenable to
arguments—and rationalizations—for involvement
with more than one person at a time.

While Robert found opportunities for sexual involvement in the church, "I didn't go into ministry
looking for that opportunity," he says. It was something that he fell into later, he claims, because of
"situational factors." A look at three stages in his life
when Robert was *not* involved with parishioners is
instructive of the interplay among personal, cultural,
and situational factors.

The first stage in which Robert was not involved
with parishioners was early in his career. He served a
church during his seminary years and did not get
sexually involved with women in that church. Many
situational factors may have contributed to his noninvolvement. In the early years of his marriage there
was perhaps more hope for the marriage. As indicated above, happiness and sexual fulfillment in the
pastor's marriage may be an important factor in
determining whether the pastor will yield to temptation. Robert's marriage was not fulfilling for him, and
the stresses of his marriage may have been a significant factor in his later pattern of having affairs with
women in the church.

The second important situational factor that explains the discrepancy between his earlier behavior and his later pattern was the presence in the later stage of a senior colleague who was actively involved in an affair with a parishioner. This senior colleague was the man who encouraged Robert into the ministry and was his "role model." Karl was Robert's mentor, and to a certain extent Robert idolized Karl. On some level, Robert may have thought, "well, if it's all right for Karl to do this, then it's all right for me." Peter Rutter postulates that one reason sexual indiscretions are not punished more swiftly by institutions is that other men are secretly envious and would like to engage in forbidden-zone relationships themselves.[19] The influence of a mentor's example could be quite powerful. Moreover, Karl offered neither rebuke to Robert nor any genuine confrontation about what Robert was doing. So Robert did not get the kind of supervision that would have militated against or even counseled caution about involvement with a parishioner.

Thus, we see that at least two situational factors may be very important: the strength and quality of the pastor's primary relationships such as marriage, and the behavior of role models or mentors.

The second break in Robert's pattern came during his second marriage. Robert left parish ministry for a few years to direct an alternative form of ministry. In this other setting, he says, he could never step out of his public role, as he could in the parish. His life and ministry were "too open" and the secrecy necessary for an affair simply was not possible.

In this alternative ministry, all those situational factors that Carlson names as crucial for establishing the privacy and intimacy out of which parish pastors work were missing. There was no pastoral counseling in a private office to provide "the occasion for a sense of privacy that can enable things to develop that wouldn't in a more public setting."[20] The "maximum of acquaintance with a maximum of opportunity"[21] that exists in the parish simply did not exist in the alternative ministry.

In his study of pastoral ethics, Gaylord Noyce suggests that "there is no more frequent and painful a ministry-wrecking blunder than sexual involvement growing out of cross-gender pastoral care."[22] The frequency of this blunder is due at least in part to situational factors that encourage intimacy between pastor and parishioner. In *Professional Ethics: Power and Paradox*, Karen Lebacqz argues that dependence on the character of the professional to establish behavioral guidelines is not enough. Situational factors in the organization of institutions are as determinative of behavior as are professional training, good intentions, and personal character.[23] Indeed, situational factors may be more determinative of behavior than are these other factors.

We see this mirrored in Robert's story. Here was a man who was prone to deep emotional involvement with parishioners. He was probably an intuitional, feeling-oriented person, according to the Myers-Briggs Type Indicator, and he was certainly a co-dependent with some relationship addictions. He was also a man who tended to genitalize his deep emotional involvements and turn them into sexual involvements. He therefore developed a pattern of sexual contact with female parishioners with whom he did pastoral counseling. In Marie Fortune's terms, he was a "wanderer." Unlike the "offender," who is at root sociopathic and will manipulate, deceive, and coerce, the "wanderer" is simply a minister who falls into relationships at times when things are not going well. He thereby seeks to bolster sagging esteem or replace something that he feels is missing in his life.[24]

Yet this "wanderer" did not always act out sexually. Situational—and particularly institutional and structural—factors were important. Robert's history demonstrates that some changes in the institutional structures of parish ministry could be important. One family therapist quips, if more pastors did family counseling in which at least three people are always in the room at the same time, there would probably be a lot less sexual involvement between pastor and parishioner! Robert's affairs were always with women whom he saw in counseling settings. The privacy of those settings contributed to his giving rein to his feelings and also provided a cover under which an affair could be conducted.

BREAKING PATTERNS

The third break in Robert's pattern—and the one that seems to have changed his pattern on a more fundamental level—came later still. During his second marriage, Robert discovered that his wife, Sandy, had entered another relationship. In spite of his own affairs and his presumably "liberal" stance toward loving more than one person at a time, Robert found that he could not deal with this.

The gap between theory and practice hit him hard. As he puts it, he needed a firmer foundation for his point of view, or his relationships were not going to work! Robert and Sandy spent six months working out their commitments and understandings. While they remain open in theory to the possibility of other close involvements, since that time neither has been seriously—or sexually—involved with anyone else.

Reflecting on this time, and the marital crisis that precipitated it, Robert talks about a watershed in his own ability to trust that he is loved and lovable. "She never gave up on me, and I never gave up on her," he says of his marriage. In spite of the fact that both Robert and Sandy retain a theoretical freedom to be sexually involved with others (the "liberal" stance in theory), neither has chosen to act on that possibility. Robert argues from this experience that change must come from deep within, and particularly from being loved and affirmed as a person.

The change that precipitated this last break in the pattern for Robert appears to have involved a "systems" change. The gap between theory and practice is significant here. Robert's theory—his liberal notions of sexual involvement and their meaning and place in human life—was not adequate. It did not provide a framework that could give him what he needed and wanted most, which was intimacy.

In *Escape from Intimacy*, Schaef argues that relationship addicts always appear to want intimacy, since they seek constantly to be in relationship. But in fact, they are not seeking intimacy, but the opposite of intimacy—control, appearance, security. Genuine intimacy always involves growth, change, and risk. One is not in control.[25] Significantly, one of the changes that Robert described in his own counseling after he went through this third break in the pattern was a change in the nature of his counseling relationships with women. He no longer seeks long-term, "intimate" counseling, and—perhaps more significant—he now understands that he cannot control what will happen in their lives. He has given up the pseudo-intimacy of control and is seeking genuine intimacy and growth with his spouse instead.

The move from addictive relationships to genuine intimacy involves what Schaef calls a "systems shift." To accomplish this shift, Schaef recommends a twelve-step program (patterned on the twelve-step program originally developed by Alcoholics Anonymous) for nearly all professionals so that they can come to terms with process addictions (including sexual and relationship addictions) and substitute a systems shift toward genuine intimacy. In a similar vein, one pastor said: "Someone who is a pastor or therapist should be involved in a twelve-step program. There are enlightened people, a few, who don't need it, but everyone else should be. Everyone has an addiction of some kind." While not everyone may need a twelve-step program in order to accomplish a systems shift, the crucial thing is to recognize that a systems shift is in order.

To argue for a systems shift is to argue that our very perspectives on sexuality, what it means, how to approach it, must be changed. Our very perspectives on intimacy, what it is, how to approach it, must be changed. In later chapters, we will be exploring some aspects of the systems shift that we believe is necessary in order to have an adequate professional ethic for sex in the parish.

Robert's history is an instructive one because it includes both episodes of involvement with parishioners—particularly with those who sought him out for counseling—and it also involves periods of noninvolvement. By learning what happened and why, we might learn something of help to other pastors who are struggling with difficulties in their marriages, with attraction to parishioners, and with changing cultural mores.

However one assesses Robert's pattern of sexual involvement with parishioners, it is clear that the pattern results not simply from some "failure" in Robert himself. The failure of limits here is the result not of lack of character in the pastor, but of enculturated patterns—patterns of child rearing, of family relating, and of understanding the meaning and place of sexuality in human life. When we see sexual acting-out in ministry, it is always tempting to blame the individual pastor. Certainly we concur with Marie Fortune and Peter Rutter in putting *responsibility* for maintaining boundaries squarely in the hands of the professional, and we will discuss this further in chapter 5.[26] But to argue that the professional carries responsibility for boundaries is not to say that the professional alone should carry the blame when boundaries are crossed.

The pastor does not stand alone. Pastors are affected by their cultural and particular settings, and by the social structures that surround them. Patterns of male and female sexual relating influence how they experience and respond to sexual desire and temptation. Patterns of cultural reward and permission influence how pastors experience and respond to sexual desire and temptation. There are pitfalls in professional practice, and these pitfalls are not simply personal failings. They are also structural and institutional issues.

Reflecting on his history, Robert says, "I know a lot about what the pitfalls are—having been a pitfall myself!" Among those pitfalls, Robert lists the following.

First is the fact that churches provide no means for resolving problems of sexuality within the church. When problems arise involving the pastor, says Robert, churches try to "hush it up" or keep it quiet. They sometimes recommend counseling for the pastor, assuming that sexual misconduct is a one-time matter and that proper therapy will resolve the issue. Robert's own experience suggests that individual counseling is not an adequate response, for several reasons. First, pastors do not always tell everything to the therapist. Second, therapists do not always raise ethical questions, but often deal simply on the level of feelings and of "what works." Third, sexual misconduct is not always a one-time matter, and the assumptions on which therapy is based may not be adequate to patterns of sexual misconduct.

So the first problem is a structural one: churches need a more adequate structure to deal with the question of sexual involvement between pastor and parishioner. The tendency to hide what is going on, or to refer it for counseling that in fact is ineffectual, merely permits sexual relations to go on undercover.

A related pitfall is the pastoral role itself. Robert notes that his own behavior was different when he was in another role that did not permit the latitude for privacy and secrecy, nor the expectations of rescue and involvement, that are routinely understood for pastors. When counseling with parishioners now, he does not try to be as much of a "therapist" as he was before. He remains more focused on the spiritual dimensions of parishioners' troubles and does not open up the full range of past history and psychological dimensions. Above all, he no longer thinks he will be the one to "save" the parishioner. He also is careful to limit counseling to short-term issues. In any extended counseling now, he suggests, he would begin by clarifying the nature of the interaction and the role he is to play.

Finally, another pitfall is the all-too-human tendency to rationalize our actions. "You can know intellectually all you want," says Robert, "but you are informed by basic messages from life." When people want to do something that they really think they should not do, they will simply rationalize it by claiming that "this time, it's different. This time, I'm in love and I'm going to marry the woman."

At root, suggests Robert, self-esteem gets in the way. To admit to anything that appears to undermine one's self-esteem is very hard. Therefore, we tend to rationalize. There is, he argues, a certain fantasy level in all of this: the pastor is trying to secure something that he fantasizes as both possible and as better than reality. Until we learn to understand what true relationships are, we do not give up our fantasies. Pastors and parishioners need to be better trained both in the realities of relationships and in demythologizing cultural messages, so that they do not so easily rationalize their actions or buy into messages that say "secondary sex enhances the primary."

Thus, Robert's own experience has led him to develop some sense of the pitfalls in ministry. He locates these pitfalls in the basic structures of the church, in the particular structures within which ministry is practiced, and in his own personal needs and tendencies. Yet Robert also admits that if he were propositioned today by someone he found attractive, he is not sure what would happen. "I remain to be seriously tested," he says. Like several other pastors mentioned at the outset, Robert is not sure that he would avoid patterns of involvement in the future.

Our experience of Robert is that he is a man in search of ethical guidance. He is deeply reflective on some aspects of his experience. He offers no excuses and tries to look honestly at himself. Yet he seems unclear as to what would make a pattern of behavior right or wrong. While he criticizes typical therapy for offering nothing other than reflection on "feelings" and on "what works," Robert himself did not really go beyond those categories in his own reflections. He is isolated in his ethical decision making, he does not know what to trust, and he therefore has no firm rooting for his behavior. His career has exhibited a pattern of sexual involvement with parishioners. While that pattern is no longer evident in his current practice of ministry, there is no guarantee that it will not recur.

Robert—like many other pastors—needs a theological and ethical framework on which to hang his hat, or at least his sexual self. In the next chapter, we begin to develop that framework by looking at the pastoral role.

4
Pastoral Power

We have seen that most pastors consider sex to be one of the joyful aspects of human life. They affirm sexuality as a part of who they are. Yet they hesitate about interpersonal expressions of sexuality and think clear limits are necessary. But most rely on their feelings to set limits. They have not developed an explicit ethical framework.

The purpose of this chapter and the next is to develop that framework. Is it wrong for pastors and parishioners to become sexually interested or involved with each other? If so, why? Although there has been traditionally a fairly strong taboo against pastor-parishioner sexual relations, the grounding for this taboo needs articulation and examination. The first part of such a grounding lies in an examination of the role of pastor, and that is the subject of this chapter.

PASTORAL ROLE VERSUS THE BODY OF CHRIST

We asked pastors, "Do you think that being in the pastoral role has anything to do with deciding about appropriate sexual boundaries?" We also asked them to distinguish pastoral from personal intimacy. The answers to these questions provide the first forum for understanding why sex becomes a problem in the parish and what an ethical framework for sexual intimacy in that setting might be.

A few pastors said they did not think the pastoral role has anything to do with setting appropriate boundaries. Several answered our question about pastoral role with a flat no; one said, "I don't really think there is a difference." But most elaborated on the reasons for this judgment.

For some, their negative answer was based on a desire to avoid double standards for pastors and parishioners. "The Bible has the same standards for every man and woman." "There is not a double standard." "I believe every Christian is commanded by God to maintain sexual boundaries that will prevent him or her from committing sexual sin . . . . The role of pastor requires no more, no less." "I think it's no different than for any responsible mature Christian person."

While several recognized that clergy are in a "public" role, this still did not make a difference in terms of the ethical standards they would apply: "clergy are more public, yet accountable to the same standards as the general population." "I think the boundaries between Christians are about the same whether lay or clergy." Thus, for some, *all* Christians, whether lay or clergy, should be held to the same standards. There are no special standards for pastors, no double standard in the church.

For some of these pastors, then, the key to sexual ethics lies not in the pastoral role, but in the personal standards of the role-holder. Pastoral ethics is then a matter of *personal ethics:* "It is personal—and the person in and out of the pastorate must be on guard to keep himself away from questionable intimacy"; "sexual boundaries are always drawn in a personal manner . . . pastoral intimacy is an outgrowth of one's personal mores concerning intimacy." Some simply felt that no boundary exists: "there is no real boundary between personal and pastoral intimacy." Pastoral ethics then becomes a matter of personal integrity.

Given the stress on character and personal integrity in church evaluations of pastors, it is perhaps not surprising that many pastors see sexual ethics in the church as primarily a matter of personal integrity and personal ethics. In the national study *Ministry in America,* David Schuller and his associates found that across denominational lines, churches consistently seek pastors with primary attention to personal qualities. "While the expectation of ministry or priesthood in North America includes competence in functions," they assert, "it is also highly sensitive to the character and spirit of the person who carries out these functions."[1] Indeed, four of the top five qualities sought in pastors had to do with matters of character. In light of this emphasis within the church, it is not surprising that pastors, too, would come to place emphasis on personal integrity and personal ethics. For some, this may account for a stress on personal ethics rather than professional role.

For others, *all* Christians are to be seen as pastors, and hence the standards should be the same for all. " 'Pastoral' and 'Christian' are basically synonymous in that pastoral is a Christian function, so I'm not sure the pastoral role has any greater value-setting power than any dedicated Christian role," said one. "The *pastoral* role in the Bible is for *every* born-again believer," said another. These ministers point to the fact that ministry is the function of all church members, and that it is not only the ordained person who provides "pastoring." Therefore, any standards that apply to those in "pastoral" settings would apply to all church members. Here, the stress is not on the personal integrity of the pastor, but on the equality of all Christians in the eyes of God.

About one-fifth of our pastors, therefore, would have no special standards of sexual ethics for clergy. Either because they believe that pastoral ethics simply grow out of personal ethics, or because they believe that all Christians are called into the responsible sexuality that should typify a "pastoring" role, they reject any double standard for sexual ethics in the church.

THE PEDESTAL

Yet even these pastors who resisted the notion that there could be a double standard nonetheless sometimes articulated a sense that being ordained to the pastoral ministry sets limits, and that there is a clear difference between professional intimacy and personal intimacy.

The pastor quoted above who thought that every Christian is commanded by God to maintain sexual boundaries and that the role of the pastor requires no more and no less went on to elaborate some grounds for a possible difference: "But since the pastor's role makes [the pastor], in the public's eye, the model and example of the faith, [the pastor] must be consciously circumspect and cautious about stepping over appropriate sexual boundaries." And he summarized with the adage, "if gold rusts, what will iron do!" In short, although he rejected *in principle* any difference between the sexual mores of ordained and lay people in the church, *in practice* he recognized that clergy are often seen as models or exemplars, and that this makes a difference.

The business of being a model or example of the

faith plagued many pastors. And for most, it provided grounds for seeing a different ethic for those in the ordained pastoral position. "As shepherd of a flock, one of my duties is to set an example." "I believe pastors are called to be models for appropriate relationships between people." "When you accept the role of minister, you are an important example." "The pastor is a leader and leaders help set standards." For many pastors, being in the pastoral role brought with it some responsibilities as a model or example of ethical behavior. It fell to them either to set or to follow standards.

In short, these respondents pointed to some modern remnants of the old notion that the pastor is somehow on a "pedestal," expected to be better or to behave better than others. Pastors are role models, like it or not. Pastors must adhere to high standards, like it or not. For all of the stress in Protestant tradition on the "priesthood of all believers," it remains true that the shepherd of the flock is expected not merely to stand "apart," but sometimes also to stand "above." It is partly this that causes confusion and concern for our pastors.

Even those who wanted no double standards, or who see pastoring as the role of all Christians, sometimes pointed to something special about the role of the pastor. Some saw no difference in personal and pastoral intimacy per se but felt that the public nature of the role of clergy was a factor in determining stringent adherence to boundaries. The *boundaries* would be the same, but *adherence* to them would need to be more strict because of the public nature of the role.

Thus, some spoke of the community's *expectations* as important for determining strict adherence to ethical standards on the part of the pastor: "for the sake of the community I am more conscious of boundaries"; "the expectations for sexual behavior are more rigid for a pastor." The sense that high standards are either expected by the community or called for by virtue of the role itself was a common perception. "Pastoral and/or counselor intimacy calls for a high standard of ethical (moral) behavior," said one woman pastor. And another undoubtedly spoke for many when she said, "whether you choose it or not, you play that role." Whether pastors choose it or not, something of the pedestal attaches to their role.

We argue that the role of the pastor is morally relevant to determining appropriate sexual ethics in the parish. Indeed, the power that attaches to the pastoral role is the key ingredient in ascertaining what is proper for the pastor to do. While none of our respondents made the argument as clearly as we might wish, many of their responses include elements of this concern. We will begin with a review of their insights, and then summarize with our own argument about pastoral power and its relevance for a sexual ethic.

PASTORAL POWER: FREEDOM AND ACCESS

What is so special about being in a pastoral role? Is the proverbial pedestal simply a remnant of days gone by that should be eschewed in the modern church? Or does it point to something important and give clues to the development of an adequate sexual ethic in the church?

Many pastors both recognized the existence of the pastoral role with its pedestal implications, and also resisted its meaning. One woman wrote of her sense of confusion and frustration about the demands of the role. We quote her at length because her answer points to two central issues—freedom and mutuality:

I do think that being in the pastoral role has something to do with deciding about appropriate sexual boundaries. And even as I say that, I balk. I know that because I am a pastor, people have expectations and I'm supposed to be a model. But I think every Christian is supposed to be a model. I think I always do try to live according to my faith—as a disciple—and my sexuality is part of that discipleship. I resent the double standard that is applied to me because I am a pastor.

I think there is a much greater degree of mutuality in a personal intimacy. Yet I believe that the best pastor is the most intimate one—one you can be close to. At the same time, the pastor is in a role as pastor and there is a freedom that is missing. Yet I think the best pastor is one who is free. It's confusing.

This pastor reflects several paradoxes that emerged from our respondents' answers. She thinks there is something "different" about being a pastor, and yet she also thinks there should not be a double standard. She thinks mutuality and hence intimacy is limited for those in the pastoral role, and yet she thinks intimacy is crucial to good performance of that role. She thinks pastoral freedom is limited by the role, and yet she also thinks that in order to be a good pastor, one must be "free." Can these paradoxes be explained?

We think so, and we further think that they provide a clue to intimacy ethics for pastors. If there is something special and different about the pastoral role, it may have to do precisely with questions of freedom and of mutuality. Both of these point to the *power* that attaches to the pastoral role, and to the *vulnerability* of parishioners. While few pastors spoke directly about power issues in this context, many spoke about freedom, mutuality, and vulnerability. These issues may set the stage for understanding why the good gift of sexuality becomes problematic in the pastoral setting.

The woman pastor quoted above thinks that the pastoral role *limits* freedom, because the mutuality of personal intimacy is missing. Because the pastor is in a role, there are things that are not appropriate for the pastor to do. This applies not only to professional relations but even to personal sexual mores. For example, one minister noted that because of his role as pastor he could not live with the woman he loves as another single person might be free to do. Thus, he experienced limits in his personal intimacy because of his public role as clergy.

Yet this very role that limits freedom in some ways also gives *more* freedom in other ways: "as a pastor, it is more appropriate to hug and be alone with the opposite sex." Pastors are permitted a kind of intimacy that those in other roles might not be. "My lower class parish," writes one pastor, "only sees men or women as sexual partners and assumes this is the only way the two relate." She deliberately hugs her parishioners in order to break through this stereotype and offer them a new model of collegiality and new ways of seeing men and women in relationship. This is a freedom she has as a pastor that she might not have otherwise. Similarly, a male pastor talks about the ninety-six-year-old woman in his parish who said to him, "Reverend, you're the only person who kisses me." Many pastors think that the role of pastor gives them more *access* and more *freedom* in relating to parishioners than they would otherwise have.

Part of the pastoral role, then, is precisely that it fosters a kind of intimacy between pastor and parishioner. As Marie Fortune puts it, "The pastoral role by its very nature gives the pastor access to people's lives on a very immediate and intimate level."[2] This intimacy in some ways means more freedom for pastors—more access to people, an ability to hug or kiss or provide friendly physical gestures to incarnate and

symbolize their caring. If intimacy means closeness—
being able to see, touch, and experience the other's
presence[3]—then the pastoral role is intended to permit deep intimacy, for the pastor has access to the core
of the other person—his or her soul.

This very access and intimacy creates problems.
Several pastors considered the amount of intimacy
permitted those in the pastoral role to be a *danger*.
"The pastoral role," said one, "gives a reason/excuse
to be together, and talk about personal, intimate
things. This can be easily abused." Another con-
curred: "It is very easy to cross the boundary from
being pastorally caring and intimate into sexual intimacy. People are so vulnerable in crisis situations and
can be easily led." This pastor further cautions that
women may see him as a man even when he is trying
to be a pastor and that therefore even a "pastoral"
intimacy can be misunderstood as personal intimacy.

Dangers are perceived from both sides. On the one
hand, the pastor can easily abuse the intimate setting.
The parishioner, especially one who is in crisis or
despair or grief, is vulnerable and is likely to trust the
pastor. The parishioner's guard is down, and it is easy
for pastors to step over appropriate limits. Moreover,
the very vulnerability of a female parishioner may
itself be arousing to a male pastor. As Peter Rutter
puts it, "I discovered at first hand just how passionate
and dissolving the erotic atmosphere can become in
relations in which the man holds power and the
woman places hope and trust in him."[4] There is, he
suggests, an "intoxicating mixture" of timeless freedom and timeless danger in such encounters. Thus,
caring and intimacy can easily lead the pastor or other
professional into inappropriate sexual expressions.

On the other hand, the parishioner may misread
pastoral signals and think that an offer of human
caring is an offer of sexual interest. Just as vitality and

human energy in general connects to sexual energy, and therefore the two may sometimes be confused, so human caring can be confused with sexual or romantic interest. The pastoral role fosters intimacy, and if both pastor and parishioner are not careful, that intimacy can be confused with other forms of deep human intimacy, including sexual intimacy.

Indeed, one pastor considers it dangerous to use a rhetoric assuming a difference between pastoral and personal intimacy, as it allows pastors to hide what they are doing behind a professional mantle: "I feel that some pastors have hidden behind the thought that there is a difference between pastoral and personal intimacy and have used the office to fondle or seduce women," he says. He points to the problem that assuming the legitimacy of pastoral intimacy may not merely create freedom for pastors to relate more caringly but may also create license for pastors to abuse their parishioners. The very fact of increased pastoral freedom can also mean increased possibility of abuse.

The freedom brought about by the pastoral role, therefore, is seen by most pastors as necessitating *limits* on intimacy. While there may not be written rules, pastors nonetheless often feel as though there are stringent and special internalized expectations requiring great caution in intimacy with parishioners.

What lies at the heart of these perceptions and expectations is the recognition that mutuality is missing in the pastor-parishioner relationship. The pastor has power, and the parishioner is vulnerable. The very freedom of access to parishioners' lives means that pastors are dealing with people who are often extremely vulnerable. The core of professional ethics lies in the recognition of this power imbalance between the pastor and the parishioner. It is this that makes sexual contact problematic.

MUTUALITY VERSUS VULNERABILITY

Few pastors mentioned power explicitly. But many pointed implicitly to it when they spoke of the vulnerability of parishioners. For a number of pastors, the key issue in intimacy ethics lies in the dependency and vulnerability of the parishioner. Pastor-parishioner intimacy is not the "two-way street" that personal friendship or intimacy can be. The parishioner shares deeply with the pastor, but the pastor does not share personal matters with the parishioner. As is the case with most professionals, the client can become dependent and the professional must be careful not to abuse the vulnerability of the client. One party is more vulnerable and therefore responsibility lies on the stronger party.

One pastor expresses this cluster of concerns succinctly:

> The pastor/parishioner relationship is different from other relationships because of the dependency which some members can develop on the pastor. It is also different because of the possibility of transference. A pastoral kind of intimacy can result when a member trusts the pastor and feels "safe" sharing deeply personal issues. The member trusts that the pastor will not unfairly use his/her position to exert sexual influence on a personal level. In a pastoral role, I am more careful and intentional about defining sexual boundaries.

Here, the pastor identifies dependency and the need for safety in order to share deeply as key to pastor-parishioner interaction.

In a similar vein, another pastor defines "pastoral" intimacy as "providing comfort in the face of painful vulnerability." The readiness of the parishioner to be vulnerable is a pastoral trust that "ought not to be violated." For many pastors, therefore—particularly

for male clergy—the key to the special ethic for
pastors lies in the vulnerability of the parishioner and
the fact that pastoral care (perhaps especially pastoral
counseling) is not a two-way street. Instead of the
mutuality that characterizes personal intimacy, the
pastoral setting is characterized by the dynamics of
vulnerability versus power. In Peter Rutter's words,
in the professional relationship the professional
"holds in trust the intimate, wounded or undeveloped parts" of the client, in this case, the parishioner.[5]

Because of these dynamics, issues of *trust* and of
safety were crucial for many pastors: "when a member
trusts the pastor and feels 'safe,' " as the pastor quoted
above put it. These themes emerged frequently.

One male pastor said, "I see myself as a father-
figure or an uncle, as a trusted male member of the
tribe to whom some will turn." This pastor felt that
"sexual intimacy destroys the pastoral role" because it
destroys that trust. Another claimed that "the old
Gospel hymn, 'I would be true, for there are those
who trust me,' has been a wonderful constraint when
my own virtue might not be sufficient to avoid
entangling situations." Another says that "boundaries must be maintained for the sake of trust." The
notion of trust was prevalent. For these pastors, trust
is central to the pastoral role, and anything that might
undermine trust is wrong. As one put it, coital
intimacy "forfeits" the pastoral role.

One male pastor and several female pastors likened
the violation of trust by one in a pastoral role to the
violation of trust that occurs in incest: "There is an
incestuous quality to every violation of trust by pastor
or counselor when sexual intimacy is involved."
Marie Fortune argues that because the church is often
seen as a family, incest is indeed an appropriate
model in this context: "The parallels to incestuous
abuse are disturbing."[6]

This incestuous quality is related to the numinous dimension of the pastoral role. One woman pastor put it this way: "To be their savior and then to cross sexual boundaries is devastating to people." Because clergy represent God, Christ, and the church, to be violated by a member of the cloth is to feel violated by God, Christ, and church. Thus, one pastor concludes that intimacy in this context "does not wholly belong to the pastor," but that boundaries must be maintained "for the sake of trust." In short, to be in a representative position means that one's actions have symbolic import far beyond one's personal intentions. This symbolic import is crucial for setting limits to behavior.

Many pastors spoke of the need to provide a "safe" environment. "The church needs to be a safe place for people," said one. Another noted that at critical moments people are likely to blurt out anything, including sexual dysfunction. "You carry bedroom secrets," as he puts it, and "that wouldn't happen if they believed it was an unsafe intimacy." Another suggests that pastoral intimacy emerges *only* "when a member trusts the pastor and feels 'safe' sharing deeply personal issues." Thus safety is a prerequisite to developing the kind of intimacy necessary for pastoral functioning. For this safety to exist, he argues, the member must trust "that the pastor will not unfairly use his or her position to exert sexual influence on a personal level." For this reason, he is more "careful and intentional about defining sexual boundaries" in the pastoral role.

Indeed, far from regretting the "asexual" image of pastors, one pastor found it a decided advantage: "People can approach them more closely with less fear of being sexually abused." The traditional pedestal expectations of pastors' exemplary behavior thus help to establish a context in which parishioners can feel safe and trust can emerge. Ironically, that same sense of safety can come from new wrinkles on the old pastoral cloth: one woman noted how appreciative women in her congregation were of having a female clergyperson with whom they could discuss personal matters!

However the sense of safety is attained, it is clear that the sense of safety to share intimately is crucial to pastoral work. The "freedom" and power of the pastor to deal intimately with people's lives brings with it the increased vulnerability of the parishioner. Or, to put it the other way around, it is precisely because of the vulnerability of parishioners, and the lack of mutuality in the pastor-parishioner relationship, that important kinds of freedom can emerge and that certain kinds of ministry can happen. But for vulnerability to be present, there must be safety and trust.

Indeed, the violation of trust and safety that occurs when appropriate sexual boundaries are crossed led some pastors to suggest that doing so undermines ministry as a whole. One asks himself, "Will it negate not only my ministry, but the total credibility of the church? Will it weaken, rather than strengthen, relationships?" For some, this was expressed in terms of a pastor demonstrating clear commitment to biblical values of monogamy and fidelity: "Being a pastor makes one more committed, I hope, to biblical and ethical standards of monogamy, marriage, and fidelity." Not all would set the standards in exactly this manner, but most would agree that trust and safety are crucial to pastoral ethics, and that the vulnerability of the parishioner makes transgressions of sexual boundaries unethical.

PROFESSIONAL ETHICS

Some pastors expressed this idea in general terms. They made reference to concepts of being *professional* or exercising professional leadership. One said, "professional ethics taboos sexual intimacy with those who lay their lives open. It is a matter of professional trust." Another said, "in pastoral ministry you need to be able to discuss intelligently with a parishioner their sexual lives without becoming sexually involved with the parishioner. You need to be professional." Another replied, "there is a professional ethic which definitely governs relationships." One said, "the pastoral role is professional—you have ethics and a code of honor." All these responses point to the notion that ministry is a *profession* and that there are therefore stringent expectations of the pastor as there would be for any professional person.

Several articulated these expectations in terms of a *distance* or *objectivity* expected of one in the professional role. "There is detachment in the pastoral role," said one. The professional role is not to be confused with the "total abandonment" that characterizes personal intimacy. One pastor defined pastoral intimacy as a kind of "tough love" that is able to be both forgiving and confrontational. It is, he said, "engagement but with a professional distance."

Another spoke of times when friends from the parish say to him, "I need you to be a pastor for the next two hours." He interprets this to mean "that they need me to listen, to give them straight feedback." He continues, "There's a kind of clear objectivity they're asking from me that requires stepping back from the friendship." Thus, being professional in part means keeping enough distance to be able to make helpful judgments; too much intimacy might threaten this ability. Sexual intimacy certainly might undermine the pastor's ability to exercise judgment, and therefore would undermine what some take to be the core of professional practice: good judgment.

Many pastors argue that, even if the *boundaries* for sexual intimacy are the same for pastor and lay person, the *responsibility* for maintaining those boundaries falls to the professional person. It is he or she who must establish and keep those boundaries. "I believe a clergyperson—as a professional—has more responsibility for keeping the boundaries safe than a lay person has"; "I believe it is my responsibility to keep the boundaries clear and firm." Another suggested that pastoral intimacy is more "structured" and that "there is some sense in which the pastor is the person responsible for the relationship." Here, the assumption seems to be that the pastor is the stronger party in the relationship and therefore must take more responsibility. Here, our pastors echoed Peter Rutter's conviction that because the professional is the keeper of trust, it is the professional's responsibility, no matter what the provocation or apparent cause, to assure that sexual behavior does not take place.[7]

In short, the mere fact that the pastor is a *professional* already sets some boundaries for many pastors. It means that the pastor must adhere to professional codes and be honorable in his or her dealings with the parishioner, and above all it means that it is the pastor's responsibility to set limits.

PASTORAL ETHICS

While professional ethics in general appeared to provide a framework for some pastors, others articulated the difference between pastoral and personal intimacy in terms of the specific demands of *pastoral* intimacy. That is, the pastor is not simply a professional but is a particular *kind* of professional. James Lowery suggests that a pastor is (1) a person—born, (2) a Christian—baptized, (3) a professional—licensed, and (4) a cleric—ordained.[8] The pastor is not like every other Christian, who is baptized but not ordained. Nor is the pastor like every other professional, who is licensed but not ordained. It is ordination that makes the difference. As one pastor put it, "There are boundaries beyond which I would not go because I am ordained." But what exactly is this pastoral or clerical difference brought about by ordination?

For some respondents, it is the *goal* or purpose of the role of pastor that makes the difference. "Pastoral intimacy," said one, "has in mind a different outcome than any other kind of intimacy—the healing, caring, bringing-to-wholeness of the other." Another said, "Pastoral intimacy comes out of the office which allows a certain intimacy that has its own accepted guidelines and has the goal of the parishioner's well-being." For many pastors, pastoral sharing focuses on the healing and growth of the other in a way that personal sharing might not.

The ordained office, then, sets limits on appropriate behavior in that office. One pastor was quite clear that if the goal of pastoral intimacy is the growth and healing of the parishioner, sexual involvement is not appropriate because it could never foster this goal: "Sex is not a means of therapy or healing." Others spoke of focusing on the parishioner's needs: "I'm there for their needs, not my own"; "pastoral intimacy meets the need of the other while personal intimacy meets the need of the pastor." Part of what would be wrong with sexual intimacy between pastor and parishioner for these respondents is that it would be a violation of the goals of ordained ministry. Specifically, it would violate the goal of healing the parishioner's wounds.

Several spoke not merely of a goal of healing for the parishioner, but of the specific element of *spirituality* or *God-talk* as central to pastoral intimacy. While many professional relationships focus on healing or helping, what is distinctive about ministry is its focus on God. "Pastoral intimacy focuses on the relationship with God. How is God present in the current moment in the life of the parishioner?" Personal sharing is the exchange of joys and sorrows; pastoral sharing tries to be consciously aware of God's presence and purposes in what is happening.

One woman pastor illustrates this focus when she reflects about a pastoral visit: "What that woman yesterday needed desperately was for me to be a pastor. She needed to talk about issues of faith and God and I needed to keep raising those issues." Personal intimacy does not focus on the spiritual dimension in the way that pastoral intimacy does: "pastoral intimacy entails receiving confidences in order to provide spiritual guidance." What legitimates pastoral intimacy is its purpose of bringing growth and spiritual direction to the parishioner; it is this very purpose that limits the kinds of intimacy that a pastor may seek.

One pastor who counsels as a trained psychotherapist in addition to being a pastor spoke of the difference between the two roles as follows: "In my pastoral role (as opposed to my professional counselor role) I see things in biblical, ethical perspectives in addition to the psychological." Thus, the dimension of *God* or Scripture is a central and distinguishing part of the healing role of pastor and helps to determine appropriate forms of pastoral intimacy.

This dimension of God-talk or spirituality is sometimes called the numinous dimension. Numinous refers to the divine, the holy, the spiritual, the "supernatural," the mysterious. "I believe that, always, we who are clergy carry a certain invisible mantle of authority or spirituality or human embodiment of the spirit," said one pastor. This invisible mantle of authority placed on clergy means that "we are more to most parishioners than we desire or usually recognize."

Because of the authority and the numinous dimension of the pastoral role, it is difficult if not impossible to escape the role: "Even when socializing or playing or being involved as people of the same community, we are being received and perceived as their minister." Pastoral intimacy, therefore, "functions within self-proscribed or community-determined boundaries." No doubt it is in part this sense that clergy mediate the divine in human life that leads to the so-called "pedestal effect." Even pastors who are uncomfortable about the pedestal and the double standard that it implies recognize that they are bearers of a special quality that goes with being ordained, and that this special, numinous quality makes a difference.

This numinous dimension of relating the congregation to the divine is clearly linked to the expectations that the pastor be exemplary in moral behavior. It also means that pastors have tremendous power over parishioners. As Peter Rutter puts it, the power of the pastor over the congregant is tremendously enhanced by his authority, if he wishes to exercise it, to describe to a woman her status with God.[9] The power to define a parishioner's status with God is a power that comes with the particular role of minister. It is therefore both a professional and a clerical or pastoral power.

Some pastors expressed this same sense of the numinous or of something special about ministry by pointing to the representative nature of the role: "In the pastoral role you represent authority—the church—even God." "Like it or not," said one, "the pastor is called or sent into a 'representative' ministry." Thus, while one pastor preferred to think that at root there is no qualitative distinction between pastoral and personal intimacy, he nonetheless believes there is "a difference between the amount of intimacy tolerable from a pastor due to this representational aspect of ministry." Another pastor also points to the representational nature of ministry as central to determining appropriate sexual boundaries: "The office of the pastor is representative of the Body of Christ. Intimacy in that context does not wholly belong to the pastor—boundaries must be maintained for the sake of trust."

Clergy often are seen to represent not only their profession but also the church and even God. As one pastor put it, "I see myself as an example of what Christ would do in many behavior areas. Sexual behavior is one of them." Since he represents Christ, "being a pastor places a greater constraint on my sexual activity."

In later chapters, we will examine what happens to this representational role when the person in ministry is a woman or gay or lesbian. Issues of representation and concomitant "numinosity" or power may be different for men and women, or for any of those who have not traditionally had power in society. But the bulk of current ministers, who are male, stand in a role in which they represent the power of the divine dimension in human life. This adds to the power that they would have as professional people.

Most of our pastors, therefore, found a wide range of reasons for thinking that the pastoral role is relevant to determining sexual ethics. For some, being in the role simply requires more stringent adherence to standards that are otherwise applicable to all Christians. For most, however, there is something—however difficult to articulate—about being in the role that makes a difference.

That difference lies in the power gap between pastor and parishioner. Parishioners are vulnerable. They share, risk, trust. It is the pastor's responsibility to set limits so as not to take advantage of the vulnerability of the parishioner and so as not to destroy the precious trust of the relationship.

Yet the very vulnerability of the parishioner is related to the numinous and representative dimension of the pastoral role. Sexual ethics in the parish must be developed with attention to role dynamics. The role of pastor and the power that it connotes is crucial for determining an ethical framework for sex in the parish. It is to this framework that we turn next.

5
An Ethical Framework

The reflections of our pastors on power and vulnerability are important for setting the ethical framework within which pastors must operate. The ethical framework that we shall develop here draws on the insights offered by the pastors in our study but supplements those insights with a more systematic understanding of the role of the minister and the implications of power and vulnerability for professional ethics.

We say professional ethics here rather than sexual ethics because it would be a mistake to assume that all sexual contact is a matter of sexual ethics. Rape, for example, is largely an act of violence rather than a sexual act. The appropriate ethical analysis of rape will therefore utilize a framework appropriate for dealing with violence. Similarly, some sexual contact between pastor and parishioner has little to do with sex and a great deal to do with the display and garnering of power. A framework is needed, then, for professional ethics, not for sexual ethics alone.

Two approaches to understanding the importance of power and vulnerability have been taken in the literature. In *Sexual Violence: The Unmentionable Sin* and later in *Is Nothing Sacred?* Marie Fortune argues that sexual contact requires mutuality and consent, and that gaps in power render consent invalid. Sexual contact between professional and client, including clergy and parishioner, is problematic because the power of the professional undermines consent.

In *Sex in the Forbidden Zone,* Peter Rutter argues that sexual contact between a professional in a position of trust or mentoring and that professional's client or protégé violates a "forbidden zone." His argument is based not on consent per se, but on an understanding of the centrality of trust to the professional relationship: "the forbidden zone is a condition of relationship in which sexual behavior is prohibited because a man holds in trust the intimate, wounded, vulnerable, or undeveloped parts of a woman."[1]

While there is a slight difference in emphasis between Fortune's work and Rutter's, both locate the problem squarely in the professional role. With this, we agree. We will build on their insights to develop a framework for understanding why sexual contact between pastor and parishioner is generally wrong, and whether there can be any room for exceptions. Our framework involves understanding the impact of power and vulnerability on matters of consent, the significance of the trust required in the professional role, and the special vulnerability that attaches to sexuality in our cultural setting.

CONSENT

In Christian tradition, any sexual contact that is morally acceptable must be loving. And to be loving, it must be genuinely consensual. This basic principle is articulated in both Protestant and Catholic sexual ethics. In its recent preliminary study on human sexuality, the United Church of Christ declared: "Sexual acts that are characterized by loving motives and intentions will exclude all acts that are coercive, debasing, harmful, or cruel to another."[2] Similarly, the Catholic Theological Society of America argues that God's gift of sexuality has been "seriously abused" wherever "sexual contact becomes personally frustrating and self-destructive, manipulative and enslaving of others, deceitful and dishonest."[3] Acts that are coercive, manipulative, or deceitful are not consensual. By implication, therefore, both Protestant and Catholic statements appear to put consent of both parties at the root of ethical sexual contact. While neither would think consent alone is sufficient for ethical sexual contact, both see it as a necessary condition.

This is in fact precisely the argument that Fortune presents in *Sexual Violence: The Unmentionable Sin.* Fortune proposes that for consent to be genuine, the relationship must be able to give an affirmative answer to several questions. Among those questions are: Is power shared equally? and, Do both parties freely and with full knowledge choose to interact?[4] Where power is not equal or the parties are not acting with freedom and full knowledge, the consent would not be valid.

Fortune cites equal power, full knowledge, and freedom as the prerequisites of consent. We can elaborate these requirements for valid consent by drawing on the literature in medical ethics, where the requirements for valid consent have been developed in considerable detail. In the arena of professional ethics in medicine, valid consent is understood to require four components. Each of these is applicable as well to the question of sexual contact between pastor and parishioner. And each suggests why some forms of sexual contact between pastor and parishioner should be considered suspect. We will illustrate these difficulties with reference to two cases: Robert's story cited in chapter 3, and the story of Rev. Peter

Donovan presented in Fortune's *Is Nothing Sacred?* Rev. Peter Donovan, as Fortune calls him, was a single man about forty years old who had been in the ministry for some fifteen years when he came to First Church of Newburg, a middle-sized mainline Protestant church. Six women eventually made formal, written allegations of sexual misconduct by Donovan. A look at these allegations will illustrate how the concept of valid consent can be used to illuminate problems with pastor-parishioner sexual contact.

The first requirement for valid consent is that the person be "informed." In the medical context, this refers primarily to being informed of the risks of any procedure proposed. In the pastor-parishioner context, it would mean being informed of risks and not being deceived or having important information withheld. As the Catholic Theological Society of America puts it, deceitful or dishonest sexual contact is not ethical.

If the allegations against Donovan are true, then he clearly was unethical. He lied and made false promises to many of the women in order to get them into sexual relationships, for example, telling them he would marry them and telling each she was the only woman in his life.[5]

Not only do such obvious lies constitute a breach of the requirement of informed consent, but also, before any consent to engage in sexual relations could be valid, the parishioner must be told clearly that she or he will now lose her or his pastor and must make other provision for her or his spiritual direction and counsel.

The second requirement for valid consent is that the person consenting must comprehend the information given. It is not enough to be told of risks; the person must have some understanding of what these risks mean, so that he or she can make decisions based on them. In the medical arena, to be told about risks in technical medical language that the patient does not understand would not constitute adequate grounds for consent; the patient must comprehend the risks. Those with diminished mental capacity who cannot process and utilize information are by definition not able to give a valid consent.

This requirement raises serious questions about the validity of any consent given by people who are in shock or grief or experiencing any extreme distress, even if temporary. A bereaved parishioner may be experiencing too much grief to be able to process and fully appreciate risks. Several of Donovan's alleged sexual liaisons were with women who were experiencing times of particular vulnerability: several had just lost a loved one, one had had a mastectomy and was struggling with her sense of self, and so on. The pastor used their grief and vulnerability to gain sexual access to them. It is questionable whether they were really in a position to exercise judgment about any information given.

Robert's situation probably falls into a borderline area. It is clear that several of the women with whom he entered affairs had come to him specifically for counseling and that at least one of them was experiencing an abusive and explosive situation at home. It seems probable, then, that several of them had diminished capacity to consent when they entered a relationship with Robert, and we would probably judge their consents to be invalid.

The third requirement for consent to be valid is that the person must be legally competent to give consent. Children, by definition, are not legally competent to give consent to risky medical procedures, nor are those who are mentally retarded. Procedures for "proxy consent" are designed when the patient cannot give a legally valid consent.

All sexual relations between a pastor and a child would be, by definition, unethical, since the child cannot legally give consent for such relations. While none of the women who made written allegations against Donovan was herself a minor, he had started an affair with one of them when she was just above that age, and there were reports that he had propositioned minors.[6]

The fourth requirement for consent to be valid is the most important for our purposes. It is that the person giving consent must truly be free to consent. Indeed, this element is so important that we prefer not to use the common term "informed consent," but to speak instead of "free" or "valid" consent. The information component of consent should not be emphasized to the neglect of freedom. Valid consent requires that both parties not only be informed and knowledgeable about relevant risks but also and above all be free to consent.

Freedom is a difficult concept, however. Since all of us are socially conditioned and bounded by our cultures, there is a sense in which all of us lack freedom. How do we distinguish ordinary limitations on human freedom from those limitations that would render a consent invalid?

Here, it is helpful to distinguish a range of factors that can undermine the freedom to consent. On one end of the spectrum is overt coercion. Coercion involves a threat of harm or actual physical force. For example, "Rev. Katie Simpson" reported that Donovan pushed her down on a couch, forced his finger into her vagina, and tried to rape her.[7] Clearly, under such circumstances, there is no consent at all, and the sexual contact is unethical.

But direct coercion is not the only possible factor that can undermine freedom to consent. In addition to declarations of love and of marital intentions, Donovan promised "Bernie Mitchell" a promotion in her job. This promise cannot be considered coercion, since it does not involve a threat of harm or direct force, but rather the offer of a reward or benefit. Nonetheless, it can undermine the person's freedom to consent or refuse sexual contact. For example, if Bernie Mitchell wanted that job desperately, if it was crucial to her sense of her own status and integrity that she be given the promotion, then to offer the promotion in exchange for sexual favors constitutes "undue influence" on her decision. The promise of reward weights the factors in the decision unfairly and undermines the rationality and validity of her consent. Similarly, a pastor who offers time and attention to a needy parishioner in exchange for sexual contact is unduly influencing that parishioner's decision and therefore the consent is not valid. This may possibly have been true in Robert's situation.

Most important when considering the question of freedom to consent is whether freedom is undermined by being in a position of unequal power. When there is a power gap between professional and client, or pastor and parishioner, does this power gap itself undermine the freedom of the parishioner and therefore render the consent invalid?

We think so. Inequality of power can restrict the capacity for voluntary action. If being in circumstances characterized by unequal power compromises a person's freedom to consent, then there is reason for caution in the sexual arena when two people have unequal power.

We argued in the previous chapter that this is in fact the case where pastors and parishioners are concerned. Pastors have power as professionals. They also have the power of the numinous dimension of human life. In addition, if the pastor is male and the parishioner female, then he has the power of men in a sexist society. (We will deal further with this in the following chapter.) Thus, there is a power gap between pastor and parishioner. This power gap undermines the validity of consent because it means that the two parties do not come as equals.

Consider, for example, the case of "Kristin Stone," who simply submitted in stunned silence when Donovan began to disrobe her. "She felt overwhelmed by him," reports Fortune.[8] Disbelieving that her minister would ask anything wrong of her, she simply did not exercise the resistance and caution that she otherwise might. Here we see clearly that it was precisely his role not only as professional, but *as minister* that made her unable to protect herself. She trusted him, she did not believe he would do anything wrong, and her acquiescence in their sexual contact derived from being immobilized by shock and disbelief. It could not be considered a genuine consent. Donovan did not have to coerce her because his role as pastor had effectively undermined her capacity for normal self-protectiveness.

For this reason, Fortune proposes that some relationships, "by nature of the roles of the two persons involved," simply do not exhibit the qualities necessary for sexual relations grounded in love and justice.[9] In reflecting on Donovan's situation, she concludes that his violation of the women lay in the fact that " he initiated sexual activity within a pastoral relationship and that he used coercion and deception."[10] We will return to the question of coercion and deception. Here, what is significant is the suggestion that no sexual relationship can be acceptable when it happens between people who are in certain roles, including the role of pastor and parishioner. Similarly, Peter Rutter appears to consider the roles of professional and client to prohibit any acceptable sexual contact. He declares the professional relationship of trust to be a "forbidden zone" in which any sexual relations are simply exploitive and inappropriate.

TRUST AND VULNERABILITY

But now we have a problem: If pastor and parishioner have unequal power, and if unequal power undermines the validity of consent, then it would seem to be the logical conclusion that no parishioner could ever consent to anything requested by a pastor! If freedom is necessary for consent, and if freedom is compromised by positions of unequal power, then why isn't freedom compromised in all arenas? Is there something special about the sexual arena that makes the consent problematic here when it is not problematic elsewhere? Surely we do not want to say that no parishioner can ever consent to anything asked by a pastor! But if consent can be valid in other arenas, then why is the sexual arena different?

Indeed, we could imagine Robert asking this very question. Robert appeared to operate on the assumption that the women with whom he became involved were competent adults. He might even have thought it insulting to suggest that they could not give an informed, knowing, voluntary consent. If it was all right for them to consent to join him in educational programs or other activities that he suggested at the church, then why was it not all right for them to consent to being sexually involved with him?

We argue that there are some special vulnerabilities in the sexual arena that put parishioners at particular risk here, whereas they might not be at particular risk in other areas of their lives. Indeed, vulnerability is part of the essential meaning of sexuality.[11] Our sexuality is linked to our vulnerability in a special way. It is often the place where we experience part of the "core" of ourselves—our maleness or femaleness, our femininity or masculinity. Because of this, it is easy to feel insecure and to have questions about one's sexual desirability and adequacy, and such vulnerability in the sexual arena cuts deep into the soul. Such questions can underlie a host of other issues brought explicitly to a counseling session or raised in the course of pastoral care.

Because of the special vulnerability in the area of sexuality, sexuality can become a particularly explosive and potentially painful arena for the abuse of power or the failure of consent. Thus, to our general concern about the power gap between pastor and parishioner, and whether it undermines genuinely valid consent, we must add some concerns about the special vulnerability of sexuality in human life and its relationship to trust in the professional role. We believe that this vulnerability is one of God's good gifts. It brings tremendous capacities for growth. But it also carries tremendous pain and the possibility of shutting down future possibilities for growth.

Here, Peter Rutter's analysis is very helpful. The client or parishioner brings into the forbidden zone "the intimate, wounded, vulnerable, or undeveloped" parts of herself or himself. For women in particular, these wounds can include wounds from sexual or psychological invasion experienced in childhood.[12] The woman hopes for acceptance and nurturance that has been missing elsewhere in her life. What she hopes for, above all, is to be treated as "special," without being treated as the sexual object that she has been taken for so often. In other words, she brings a legacy of pain and of hope into the relationship, and some of that pain and hope centers on how she has been treated and how she hopes to be treated as a sexual person. What she wants is a nonsexual value: to be held as special. But she may accede to sex as a way of maintaining a relationship that has come to have extraordinary importance for her.[13] When she does that, however, she is repeating old patterns of being told that her only value is as a sexual object. Thus, there is tremendous vulnerability for her in the sexual arena. What happens to her sexually symbolizes much more than mere genital contact.

Rutter suggests that women who have not been supported in their sense of self—a typical experience for women in a sexist culture, and one that we shall explore in the next chapter—will seek support "on virtually any terms" from a powerful man who offers a semblance of special recognition.[14] Thus, when the woman begins to hope for a special connection to this powerful man, she reveals more and more of herself. "Even a woman with a firm sense of boundaries in other kinds of relationships," says Rutter, "may well stop guarding them so that her core may be seen and known by this man."[15]

In short, when a male professional and a female parishioner are involved, she may not make a fully informed or voluntary choice to enter into sexual relations with him. While she may appear to consent, in fact she is being unduly influenced by the circumstances—by her hopes for deep connection with someone of power who will heal the wounds of her past experiences with men. She is particularly vulnerable in the arena of sexuality, for that is where so many of her wounds have been.

In the next chapter, we will raise the question of whether the tables are turned when a female professional and a male client are the parties involved. Certainly, the man brings into the pastor-parishioner relationship his unhealed wounds. Rutter argues that men's quest for healing "usually takes the form of seeking sexual contact."[16] He quotes one therapist as saying that, for men, the importance of having the erect phallus accepted by woman should not be underestimated: "the acceptance of our sexual selves is like an acceptance of our total selves."[17]

Like women, then, men experience particular vulnerability in matters of sexuality. However, it is a different vulnerability. The man seeks healing through sexual desire and acceptance, whereas the woman seeks healing apart from sexual desire. In fact, Rutter argues, sex in the forbidden zone does not provide healing for either the man or the woman. For the man, it keeps him from dealing with his own need to get in touch with the feminine part of himself. For the woman, it revictimizes her, repeating patterns from her past, and keeps her from recognizing and claiming her own strength apart from a man.

The point for our purposes is that sexuality is often the locus of particular vulnerability: of past pains and future hopes, of illusions in which a woman gives to a man or a man gives to a woman more control over her or his life and destiny than anyone should have. Thus, even the parishioner who can easily consent to other activities with the pastor cannot give a valid consent to sexual contact because there is too much vulnerability and too heavy a hidden agenda attached to the sexual arena.

The power of the pastor and the vulnerability of the parishioner undermine the mutuality needed for genuine, valid consent to engage in sexual relations. Thus, there is good reason to question whether consent to engage in sexual relations is ever valid when such relations are between a pastor and a parishioner. Since nonconsensual sex is wrong, most sex between pastor and parishioner will be wrong.

In short, it is the power of the pastoral role that makes the difference for sexual ethics. The pastor has power not only as a professional person, but as an ordained person. The pastor has a numinous dimension, representing not only a profession but also God. The pastoral role is also one of trust. While this is true for most of the helping professions, we would note that the pastor works with the spirit of the person, with what is closest to the person's core. In addition, sexuality is a particularly vulnerable arena for most men and women. Thus, the vulnerability of the parishioner is great and safety in the church setting is very important. It is because of the power of the pastor, the vulnerability of the parishioner, and the lack of conditions for valid consent that we would see sexual contact between pastor and parishioner to be generally wrong.

Even Lisa Mainiero, who generally supports romance in the workplace, offers cautions where the partners are not equal. "Romantic relationships between hierarchical levels should be avoided," she argues.[18] Indeed, she adds that they should be avoided "at all costs." The reasons for this prohibition lie in the risks to the parties, especially to the party with less power. "Romantic relationships between bosses and subordinates are problematic," she suggests, "because it is only across hierarchical levels that sex can be traded for power."[19]

Mainiero's concern is that a sexual involvement, no matter how innocent or genuine, will be seen by co-workers as a power play. Here, she picks up the delicate link between sexuality, vulnerability, and power to suggest that the good gifts of sexual involvement are subverted where the power base between the parties is not equal. Her argument is based more on utilitarian concerns about risks to the parties than on concerns about adequacy of consent. Nonetheless, it fits the general outlines of the cautions raised by Fortune and Rutter and by our own analysis. All these considerations taken together suggest that sexual contact between pastor and parishioner is suspect at best and unethical at worst.

THE "NORMAL NEUROTIC"

And yet, we are troubled. Fortune argues that Donovan's violation was "that he initiated sexual activity within a pastoral relationship *and that he used coercion and deception.*"[20] What if the women had *not* come seeking explicit counsel from Donovan? What if he had *not* used coercion and deception? What if they had simply been pastor and parishioner, working together in the context of church and finding themselves attracted to each other in an open and aboveboard manner?

Indeed, we argue that Donovan was not engaging in genuine sexual contact at all, but was using the sexual arena as the arena in which to gain power and control over women. Genuine sexual attraction between pastor and parishioner is not the same thing as the use of sexual attractiveness as a weapon. Thus, we are not inclined to see Donovan's behavior as belonging properly to the realm of sexual ethics.

But what about the question of sexual ethics between pastor and parishioner? If no coercion or deception is used, if the pastor is not manipulating or unduly influencing the parishioner, is there room for a genuinely loving and acceptable sexual relationship between pastor and parishioner?

Some think not. Rutter declares flatly that the pastor-parishioner relationship constitutes a forbidden zone in which sexual contact will always be a violation of trust. Fortune sometimes appears to adopt a similarly blanket prohibition: "the matter of sexual contact by clergy in a professional, pastoral relationship [is] a professional issue of misuse of power and authority which is by its very nature abusive and exploitive."[21] Here, Fortune appears to assume, with Rutter, that any sexual contact between pastor and parishioner is automatically exploitive and a violation of the pastoral role.

Yet at other points, as we have seen, Fortune adds some qualifications: Donovan's violation was that he was in the pastoral role *and* used coercion; the problem was that he was a pastor *and* the women came seeking explicit counsel; and so on. These statements appear to suggest that it is not the pastoral role per se that is problematic, but whether there is an explicit relationship of counseling established, or whether abusive and exploitive methods are used.

Is the pastor-parishioner relationship always a forbidden zone, or is it only problematic when certain elements are present, such as an explicit counseling relationship? Is it the fact of the pastoral role that makes consent impossible? Or is the consent problematic only when pastoral power is misused? What about pastors who fall in love with a parishioner and get married?

In a survey of one denominational region, we found that of twenty-one male pastors who became sexually involved with one or more parishioners, ten of those relationships ended in marriages. Thus, nearly half of the pastors ultimately married a woman whom they met in what Rutter calls the "forbidden zone." Either these marriages are founded on an unethical base, or there must be some room made for valid romantic and sexual interest between pastor and parishioner, including valid consent to sexual intimacy.

Is it possible that a parishioner might face a pastor as a strong, competent woman facing a man who happens to be a minister? Is it possible that his role as minister will not leave her unable to exercise judgment and self-protectiveness?

We are very cautious about answering yes to these

questions. Certainly, the kind of egregious behavior reported of Donovan would make us tend to tip the scales in the other direction. And yet, we have ample evidence from our own circle of friends and acquaintances to suggest that it can and does happen that pastor and parishioner can meet as equals, become romantically and sexually involved, and enter solid, committed relationships. How, then, do we account for this in the framework developed here?

First, we note that underneath Rutter's absolute prohibition of sex in the forbidden zone lies an assumption of a special relationship of trust and vulnerability between the professional and the client. This is certainly true in the psychiatric practice that forms the base for Rutter's argument. In psychiatry, above all, the client bares her or his soul to the practitioner. As Rutter himself puts it, "This is a sacred and dangerous condition. Her spirit reaches out to him, and his to her."[22] This would certainly be true in any situation where a parishioner has come seeking particular counsel from a pastor, as Fortune notes. Here, there is a soul-baring, soul-reaching relationship that requires the element of sacred trust of which Rutter writes.

But not all pastoral practice is like this. Ministry differs from some other professional practices. Some parishioners never come to the pastor for private counseling. Some simply worship, work together, and support the church and its ministry as colleagues. Such a parishioner does not necessarily hold the pastor in awe nor lose the ability to exercise judgment and perspective in consenting to relationship. As Fortune notes, ministry is more prone than other professions to a blurring of roles in which the pastor does become friends with parishioners as well as being in a professional role.

Thus, it is possible that not all parishioners are in a situation of particular or distinctive vulnerability, in spite of the power of the professional role.

Moreover, not all pastors would use techniques of coercion or deception. Fortune considers Donovan to be an "offender."[23] Offenders are manipulative, coercive, controlling, predatory, and often violent. They are sociopathic; they have little conscience and are willing to use others for their own ends; they tend to lie and to deny their behavior when confronted.

But not all pastors who enter sexual relationships with parishioners are offenders. As noted in our discussion of Robert above, Fortune suggests that there is another category: the "wanderer." The wanderer is not a sociopath or a predator. Typically, the wanderer is a minister who is not functioning well personally or professionally and who experiences conflict, inadequacy, and anxiety. The wanderer falls into relationship to bolster his flagging self-esteem and because he has difficulty retaining boundaries.

But we think there is yet another category. We would call it the "normal neurotic." This pastor does not wander from parishioner to parishioner nor from church to church looking for relationship. This pastor is not sociopathic but has a well-functioning conscience—hence, our designation: "normal neurotic." This pastor knows that developing a sexual relationship with a parishioner is suspect and tries diligently to guard against any inappropriate behavior. But this pastor falls in love. And sometimes—like the ten out of twenty-one pastors in our survey—the pastor marries the parishioner.

Our framework will be inadequate if it is based only on instances of abuse or malfunction, of offense or of wandering, and does not make room for healthy patterns of human relating. While we are cautious and skeptical, we do believe that there are pastors who exhibit such healthy patterns. We acknowledge the possibility of a genuinely loving, consensual relationship between pastor and parishioner, where the parishioner might meet the pastor as an equal and the pastor's own behavior is professional and ethical.

Even so, we would exercise two cautions. First, the numinous power of the pastor should not be underestimated. The pastor preaches and has the power of the pulpit. The pastor administers communion and has the power of inviting people into the presence of God. The pastor stands in front of the congregation week after week, invoking the blessing of God with arms raised. Representing God, the church, and the divine dimensions of life is built into the rituals of the pastoral role. The power of these rituals is immense. While we make room for the "normal neurotic" pastor who might enter a genuinely consensual relationship with a parishioner, we would put the burden of proof on the pastor to demonstrate that it is such. We will discuss structural protections that might be provided in chapter 8.

Second, the situation of pastoral power is complicated by the dynamics of sexism in this culture. Even the most mature and competent of women will not have the same power as a male pastor, both because of his role and because the sexism in the culture gives him more social power in general. She is not likely, then, to stand as his equal who can give valid consent.

The ethical framework for pastor-parishioner sexuality presents a mixed picture. On the one hand, the power of the professional person undermines the possibilities for valid consent. Special vulnerability in the sexual arena makes this a place where professional trust carries extra significance. In general, then, there are few circumstances in which parishioners can be said to give truly valid consent to engage in sexual relations with their pastors. Most of those relationships we would judge to be unethical.

And yet, ministry is both like and unlike other professions. Not all parishioners face their pastors with special vulnerabilities, and not all pastors use devious or unethical means to secure sexual access to parishioners. The power gap between pastor and parishioner should always put the burden of proof on the pastor to demonstrate that the parishioner is genuinely free and equal and can give valid consent. But there are cases in which a "normal neurotic" pastor genuinely falls in love with a parishioner or develops an honorable relationship with a parishioner. An ethical framework must be able to account not only for instances of abuse of parishioners by their pastors but also for those instances of honorable intention.

The framework provided here takes seriously questions of consent and trust and of the particular vulnerabilities that people may experience in the sexual arena. It nonetheless allows for the possibility of good experience of pastor-parishioner sexual contact. That contact must be placed within limits, and it must be done within structures that are intended to protect the parishioner. These will be addressed further in following chapters (see especially chapters 8 and 9). Here, the point is to suggest a framework that allows for a modulated response to the question of whether pastor-parishioner sexual contact can ever be ethical. We believe it can.

However, we also believe that any attempt at ethical pastor-parishioner sexual contact is fraught with dangers, and we therefore offer significant cautions. Some of those cautions have to do with the impact of sexism on our experiences of sexuality, and it is to these questions that we turn in the next chapter.

6
Women in Ministry: Sex and Sexism

"Women and men in ministry are as different as night and day." This declaration from one of the women respondents is only one of many signals that the perspective women pastors bring to issues of sexuality is unique. The temptations of ministry, the power issues, the understanding of the pedestal and of pastoral role—all these undergo subtle and not so subtle changes as we turn to look at the plight of women in positions of leadership in the parish.

AGGRESSION VERSUS PROTECTION

Perhaps the most striking difference in the material we received from men and women was in response to our question asking pastors how they know when they are reaching acceptable limits of intimacy with a parishioner. Almost invariably, male pastors answered this question by attending to how they know when *they* want to step over the line:

> What alerts me to inappropriateness are my feelings for that other person. When I begin to think of that person as a potential sex partner—not just a very dear friend— then that boundary has been crossed.

When I begin to catch myself being tempted to share data with this one (about myself or someone in the parish).

I can feel the attraction.

Almost invariably, female pastors answered this question by attending to how they know when *the other person* wants to step over the line: "Extra squeezes on the hand, hugs where one of their hands is placed near my breast (on the side) or slides down a little towards the rear." While there were male pastors who spoke of being approached or propositioned by women in their parishes, and female pastors who spoke of their own attraction to male parishioners, by far the more common patterns are those represented by the quotes chosen randomly above. *Male pastors are concerned about protecting female parishioners from unprofessional advances. Female pastors are concerned about protecting themselves.* The difference is striking.

This difference is a key to the impact of sexism on sex in the parish. In a sexist culture, men and women do not experience their sexuality in the same way, they do not experience their professional roles in the same way, and they do not experience questions of intimacy in the same way. The ethics of sex in the parish must reflect these differences. Just as the socialization of men that leads to the genitalization of feelings must be understood in order to develop an adequate framework for intimacy in the parish, so must the socialization of men and women that leads to differences in the experience of power, vulnerability, and sexuality.

One obvious difference between male and female experiences of sexuality in this culture is that men are generally understood and expected to be the aggressors sexually. "Drawing the line" has traditionally been left to women. Men's cultural training, suggests

Rutter, encourages them to challenge women's boundaries.[1] Thus, women in general in our culture have been forced to take a more self-protective stance when it comes to their bodily integrity and sexual self. In a culture in which men are expected to "make moves" on women and women are expected to be in a responsive mode, it is no surprise that men would think in terms of their desires to approach women, whereas women would think in terms of the need to protect themselves from male aggression. These general cultural patterns are reflected in the responses of our male and female pastors.

In short, the expression of sexual attraction is experienced differently by men and women in this culture, and that difference emerges in the responses of our women and men pastors. In a culture in which women and men are not raised to be equal sexual initiators, men will think in terms of initiation of sexual activity and women will think in terms of response to initiation from outside. This pattern is what we find among our clergy. It is the first indication of the pervasive influence of sexism on the patterns of male and female sexuality in the parish.

HARASSMENT

But there is a more troubling side to this pattern. The concern of the women pastors for their own protection is well grounded. One of the questions we asked was "have you ever been sexually harassed by a parishioner or a colleague?" Harassment is difficult to define, and we deliberately left the question vague, so that respondents could fill in their own meaning. This vagueness makes it difficult to compare figures exactly. Nonetheless, it is striking that less than 10 percent of men spoke of being sexually harassed, whereas fully 50 percent of the women said they had been harassed or gave examples of harassing experiences.

Of eighteen women in one of our surveys, nine said they had been harassed. Two others said "no" or "nothing I couldn't handle," but their responses at other points in the survey included instances of dealing with aggressive sexual advances in circumstances that would fit definitions of harassment given in the literature.[2] Thus, the figures from this study suggest that at least 50 percent of women clergy have experienced sexual harassment either on the job or during training for ministry. This figure may seem high, but it is consonant with the 40 percent figure offered by the Coordinating Center for Women in the United Church of Christ. Our figure cuts across denominational lines, whereas theirs is drawn from the United Church of Christ alone.

The incidents of sexual harassment described by our respondents included everything from inappropriate touching or persistent seductive behavior to deeply intimate involvement with a person in a position of power over their lives. One spoke of a seminary professor who made promises to her and with whom she became involved. Another spoke of two men on her ordination review board who implied that she would not get ordained if she failed to cooperate sexually. Another described a church officer who would not leave her alone. Yet another described a campus minister who tried to rape her while she was a student. Others spoke of parishioners who made passes or suggestive comments. One spoke of two parishioners, two pastoral colleagues, and a denominational official *all* of whom offered to "service" her sexually, on the assumption that as a recent widow she was hungry for sex!

These kinds of harassing incidents were not described by any of the men. Although several men also mentioned instances during seminary training of an older person (usually a male teacher or field supervisor) making sexual advances, or spoke about being approached, even aggressively, by women parishioners, their experiences were of a different order. Men spoke of women in the parish who said, "I love you" or even made direct propositions, but none had had experiences like the following ones proffered by the women respondents:

> A man in the congregation said to me once in front of a bunch of people, "Boy, you have great thighs." "I beg your pardon?" I said. "Boy, you have great thighs," he said again. "I beg your pardon?" I said again (irritation rising). "You have great thighs," he said a third time. I couldn't believe it. I have had to set limits with him constantly. I don't think men have to deal with such overt sexual come-ons.

> One time a parishioner stopped by my office (he had been stopping by often) and he asked me how I was. I told him I had a cold. He asked what I was using to treat it. I told him vitamin C and juice. And he said, "I'm really good at rubbing Vicks on chests."

> I received a flashlight shaped like a penis from another staff member.

While men spoke of women flirting or dressing in sexy attire to get their attention, few mentioned the kind of direct sexual imagery or suggestion that these women experienced. Male pastors spoke of receiving gifts from parishioners (male and female), but none had been pressured, coerced, threatened, or continually approached in the ways described by these women. The men pastors had sometimes experienced situations that were distressing or uncomfortable, but they had not experienced situations with the same level of fear, threat, and potential loss as those described by nearly half of our women respondents. In almost all the instances involving male pastors, a rebuff was accepted by the other party, putting an end to the approach. Thus, the men did not lose their power in the exchange.

This issue of power is central to the dynamics of sexual harassment and is also central to the dynamics of sexism. Therefore, it must be attended to in order to develop an adequate ethic for sex in the parish. Not until we understand the subtle dynamics of power in sexuality will we have an adequate ethical framework.

For instance, a sexual approach can be inappropriate without necessarily being classified as harassment. A female parishioner might invite a male pastor to bed. Her invitation may be inappropriate, given their roles, but it is not sexual harassment per se. What differentiates sexual *harassment* from mere sexual *approach* is a question of power. Sexual advance becomes sexual harassment when the party making the advance uses power over the other to manipulate or control the situation, takes power from the other, or represents a threat to the integrity (personal or professional) of the other.

If the female parishioner who approaches the male pastor is a very powerful person in the parish (such as chair of the board or the pastor-parish relations committee) with power to make or break his career in the church, while he is a young and inexperienced pastor, then her advance takes on the character of sexual harassment. Harassment is a sexual advance by one who is in a position of power and where there is either explicit or implicit in the advance a threat to use that power in some form.

There has been considerable discussion of sexual harassment in feminist literature. Feminists distinguish between coercive harassment, which involves either a threat of punishment or a promise of reward, and noncoercive harassment, such as the use of lewd nicknames to refer to a woman.[3] Both kinds were reported by the women respondents. However, what these forms of harassment have in common is not simply that they are "unsolicited, unwelcome, and generally unwanted" by the women,[4] but also they imply and utilize the greater power of the perpetrator in ways that are either directly or indirectly threatening. Thus, we concur with Rosemarie Tong that "sexual harassment is not so much an issue of offensive behavior as of abusive power."[5]

This link between sexual harassment and power makes clear why it is difficult (although not impossible) for female parishioners to harass male pastors sexually. Given the dynamics of power outlined in the previous chapter, it is clear that clergy have both professional and pastoral power. Parishioners lack both. Thus, it is hard for a parishioner to challenge the pastor's power, and even an annoying sexual advance from a female parishioner does not generally threaten the power of the male pastor. She does not have power over him, she cannot easily take away his power, and she does not generally represent a threat to his professional or personal integrity. Of course, any lay person can create a scandal or damage the reputation of the pastor by spreading rumor or innuendo. Pastors are understandably self-protective in the light of such possibilities. This "power" is indirect power, however, and depends on the ability of the parishioner to convince others of the inappropriate behavior of the pastor. Marie Fortune demonstrates in *Is Nothing Sacred?* that convincing others of the inappropriate behavior of the pastor is no easy task. As awkward and uncomfortable as the situation may be for male pastors who are propositioned by female parishioners, so long as they hold the greater power in the situation, they are being annoyed but not harassed.

SEXISM AND POWER

But since women pastors are also professionals who hold both professional power and pastoral power, why would the situation be any different for them? Judging by the analysis of professional power in chapter 4, they should also have significant power. Are the women pastors who said they have been harassed genuinely harassed or were they simply approached? If it is nearly impossible for female parishioners to harass male pastors, then is it possible for male parishioners to harass female pastors? Does professional and pastoral power always give the pastor the edge?

In *Office Romance,* Lisa Mainiero asserts that women are *not* at greater risk than men. It is power, not gender, that matters. "Women who are powerless can be used as the pawn of men," she declares, "But those who have power cannot."[6] While she readily acknowledges that "sex in the office *is* a power game," she believes that contemporary women, at least executive women, have enough power not to be manipulated in this game. It would seem, then, that the woman pastor has as much power over a parishioner as does a male pastor, and that professional power always gives the pastor the edge over the parishioner.

We disagree. We hope for a day when women genuinely carry the power that should attach to their professional roles. But that day has not as yet arrived. Sexism introduces distortions into the power of men and women in various kinds of relationships. Sexism affects women in professional positions as well as women in nonprofessional positions.

In sexist culture, men have power generally. They have more earning power, they hold more positions of social and political power, and they have more power to define what is "normal" and what is aberrant. Men are not only the initiators in the arena of sex; they are the ones with power generally and therefore with the power to initiate, to determine, to effect or block change. The sexual arena is but one of the arenas in which the power of men is felt. (It is, however, a very important arena, and one in which the power of men is keenly felt.)

It is precisely the dynamics of power that led one woman to identify a chasm between men and women in ministry:

> I think there's a real difference between the power that women and men have in the ministry. With men, people easily get Pastor, God, and Father all mixed up together. There is much more possibility for a blind breach of boundaries than between two women or a woman pastor and a male parishioner. It's just not the same ingredients that go into it. . . . As a woman pastor you just don't carry as much sexual weight.

Because women are not as powerful in general in our society, even the power they have as professionals and as pastors pales under the influence of sexism. A woman may have professional power as a pastor, but she is still a woman, and she still lacks cultural power in a sexist society. Even her professional power will therefore be distorted: she will not have the same numinous dimension that a male pastor will have, and she will not carry "sexual weight" in the same way.

Thus, for example, the men who were sexually approached by women—and even by other men—did not lose power in the exchange. Their refusal was honored. Their consent, or lack of consent, was taken as definitive. The same is not always true for women, as the stories told by our respondents make clear. While most of the women clergy were able to control the harassing situations, their refusal was not always taken as definitive, and often they had to refuse again and again. Almost all experienced a sense of rage, frustration, and loss of power to some degree. The one who had rebuffed a church officer said she found incest to be a powerful analogy: "it helped explain the depth of my anger, which was very similar to that which incest victims feel."

Some sought outside help and found that their perspective was not honored. For example, the woman who reported that she was given a flashlight in the shape of a penis by a staff member reports: "He was brought to staff-parish [committee] for a hearing and then dismissed. The issue was very difficult for folks to comprehend. It was not seen as sexual harassment and was never clearly identified by the group." Here, the woman's own perspective was not understood by the group in the church from whom she sought support, justice, and rectification of the situation.

Nor is she alone. The woman who sought counseling from her campus minister and was then sexually approached and almost raped by him reports that when she tried to blow the whistle on him, "no one wanted to listen—no one wanted to believe that he would do such things." The sad result was that she lost her community of friends in campus ministry "because everyone resented the fact that I made such accusations."

The unwillingness of those around ministers to believe that they would "do such things" is all too common. In *Is Nothing Sacred?* Marie Fortune documents the disbelief that surrounded the revelations about "Rev. Peter Donovan." Not only did people in the church disbelieve the stories told by the women who brought allegations against the pastor, but the women were threatened by church members. Several even received death threats.

SOCIALIZATION OF WOMEN

Partly because sexual gestures and approaches so often work by indirection—by suggestion and image rather than by explicit invitation—it is sometimes difficult to identify them as "harassing." Indeed, the subtleties of sexual signals in our culture work in several ways to make clarity elusive. One woman described a man in her parish who was attracted to her and indicated so directly. She notes, "at first I was very pastoral with him, and he thought that meant it was OK to continue." Being "pastoral" is often understood to mean being supportive and accepting of the other person, no matter what. It can be difficult for pastors, male and female alike, to reject a sexual advance without running the risk of appearing to reject the person. These dynamics are complicated, however, for women pastors for at least two reasons.

First, women are trained to be nurturing and are culturally conditioned in particular to build up male egos. Thus, it is often difficult for women to say a direct no. To do so appears to hurt the male ego, and this women have been conditioned not to do. Women are brought up to be "compassionate" and often find that this "compassion" means that they are inadvertently supporting the aggressive behavior of the other person. The pastor who rejected the male parishioner who was an officer of the church reported:

> Dealing with someone's attraction to me, also being a pastor, is tricky because I have to protect myself, too. This requires that I do some psychological maneuvering (or manipulating?) that might not be considered pastoral. For example, when this man came to me saying he was attracted to me, I said to him, "You don't want to act on this."

In this statement, the woman pastor reflects the dilemma of one who knows that she is entitled to protect herself, yet fears that to do so directly is to undermine her role as pastor. Thus, she must choose between her professional role and her own safety, or she must find some way to maneuver through the minefields.

Just as a direct rebuff might not be considered pastoral, so it might not be considered feminine. As Ann Douglas demonstrates, part of the "feminization" of women has been the rejection of direct forms of expression of power and the acceptance instead of influence and indirect power.[7] Women are denied direct power in American culture, and are expected instead to exert influence or indirect power. As one contemporary feminist puts it, "we exercise an indirect and mostly passive form of power."[8] To be considered adequately "feminine," therefore, women will often hold back on direct confrontation and try to do or say things indirectly.

Both these fears—of not being perceived as adequately pastoral and of not being perceived as adequately feminine—may make it difficult for the woman pastor to use directly the power that she does possess as professional and as pastor. This is why the woman quoted above feels uncomfortable about using her power to get a parishioner to stop harassing her.

Her discomfort may also be a sign of the tendency of women to assume they are *responsible* for sexual misconduct. Partly because the tradition tells women they must draw the line and set the standards for acceptable behavior, and partly because it also tells women they are seductive temptresses who lead men astray, it is often difficult for women to assign responsibility squarely where it belongs. Several of our respondents reflected this cultural pattern.

One wrote: "I was once grabbed and kissed by a writer whose play we were doing. Afterwards I agonized over what I had done to cause it—what signals I had been sending out." Another woman pastor said she would not be likely to seek assistance if she had been harassed because "I tend to blame myself for inviting this type of behavior." While in general we applaud the notion that clergy should always ask whether they have sent out mixed signals, we nonetheless concur with the first pastor's assessment of her situation when she finds it "sad" that she took responsibility on herself. Like many women, she tended to take responsibility even for a situation in which she was "grabbed."

This tendency may reflect the high levels of co-dependent or relational addiction in our culture. But it may also reflect what Margaret Adams calls "the compassion trap."[9] Because women are raised to be nurturing, even when they enter professions they tend to enter professions that require nurture of the other—the so-called "helping" or "caring" professions. Such professions are oriented toward the needs of others. Women then continue to adopt the stereotype of responding to others' needs instead of positing their own claims. Several women pastors expressed this difficulty when they wrote about qualms as to whether it was "pastoral" to honor their own needs. The tendency for women to meet others' needs at their own expense leads Adams to postulate that even professional women are still in "the compassion trap."

These cultural dynamics around blame, responsibility, and compassion provide the first nuances to the difficulties women experience in rejecting sexual advances, even when the woman is in a position of apparent power. The power of the woman professional is undermined by cultural patterns that give men power generally over women and place women in positions of nurturing men rather than claiming their own needs. It is easier for a man to say no than it is for a woman.

Second, it is easier for a man to get his refusal accepted than it is for a woman. Even when women say no clearly and directly, their refusal is not always honored: "I have had to set limits with him constantly," said the woman pastor of the man who remarked on her thighs in public. This is partly a reflection of power differences in general between men and women. But it is also a reflection of one of the most insidious aspects of sexist culture: the link between sex and domination, and ultimately between sex and violence.

SEX AND DOMINATION

In the arena of sex, the image of the "nice girl" who secretly wants sex but does not admit to liking it has not altogether left our culture. This image has left a treacherous legacy: an assumption that when women say no to a sexual advance, they really mean yes, and it is therefore acceptable for the man to continue. This may account at least in part for the fact that our women pastors had to say no repeatedly to men who made advances toward them.

But it has a more troubling result as well. In one study, over 50 percent of male teenagers and nearly 50 percent of female teenagers deemed it acceptable for a youth to force himself on a young woman, against her protest, if they knew each other, had been dating, or she had indicated interest and then withdrew.[10] Nor is it only teenagers who think it acceptable for men to force sexual contact on women: in another study, nearly 60 percent of "normal" American men said that if they could get away with it, they would force a woman to commit sexual acts against her will. When the vague phrase, "commit sexual acts against her will" was changed to the specific term "rape," 20 percent still said they would do it if they could get away with it.[11] In short, we are left with a legacy in which men and women both, but men in particular, think it is acceptable to force sexual contact on women, against their will. Our "normal" expectations around sexuality are not consensual and mutual, but involve male domination and even violence.

There are a number of reasons for this. The first is the myth that men are "out of control" and must "have" sex and therefore are not to be blamed for forcing themselves on women. Second is the myth that women are seductive and tempting and therefore men are not to be blamed for "wanting" them and even for "taking" them over their protests. As noted above, the cultural dynamics tend to place blame on women and to absolve men. Thus, the woman will have a harder time getting her refusal honored because she is at root held responsible for the basic dynamics of sexual interest and temptation.

But over and above those mythological levels, several other important social dynamics are also at work. One is that domination of women by men is considered sexy and sexually arousing. Studies of pornography demonstrate the eroticizing of domination in this culture. In pornography, the power of a man or men to make a woman do something that she does not want to do—generally something humiliating, degrading, or antithetical to her character—is used to create sexual tension and excitement.[12] While pornography may not reflect the active choices of all males in this culture, it is big business and reflects a significant dimension of the socialization of both males and females. Men are socialized to find male power and female powerlessness sexually arousing.

Thus, male dominance and female submission have

been eroticized not only for men in this culture but also for women. Women are attracted to powerful men and are trained not to be too powerful themselves. Men are expected to overpower women, and both men and women are expected to find this sexually arousing. It is no wonder, then, that many young people think it acceptable for a man to force himself on a woman: when he does so, he is merely being a man.

With these patterns in place, "taking" the woman who says no is not just an extreme form of sexual violence, but is normatively built into our expectations of sexual interaction and response. Women have a harder time than men getting their refusal of sexual encounter honored because the violation of a woman is sexually arousing. The man is supposed to initiate and the woman is expected to say no; her refusal is then additionally arousing, and he ignores it and "has his way with her" to his sexual satisfaction. Normal and expected patterns of heterosexual interaction include dimensions of men overriding women's refusal, and it is therefore difficult for women to have their refusals respected.

Rape is generally understood today to be an act of violence, not a sexual act per se. However, we agree with Hartsock[13] that a strong differentiation cannot be made: while brutal acts of rape may indeed originate in anger and not in sexual attraction, it is nonetheless true that much sexual attraction, as exemplified in pornographic material, draws on violence in order to titillate. Thus, the link between violence and sexual arousal must not be ignored.

Moreover, the link between sexual attraction and domination works both ways, albeit in altered form. Women are not expected or encouraged to dominate men nor to find such behavior sexually arousing. But they are expected and encouraged to seek out strong men and to be sexually responsive to the dominant and dominating male. "In 'normal' circumstances," writes Mariana Valverde, "men are sexy because they have male social power."[14] Women find powerful men attractive in this culture. Whether that power takes the form of the macho power of brute physical strength or the form of social power such as professional position and prestige, women are attracted to men who are powerful. They are attracted to men who are able to dominate aspects of the physical or social world. Domination and control add to a man's attractiveness. Men are expected to dominate and control, and this extends to the sexual arena. Romance novels are full of stories of women being "swept off their feet" or "carried away" by the hero. The implication is that it is all right for the woman to be sexually aroused so long as it is something that is done *to her* and she does not have to take responsibility for it. So long as she *says* no, she can in fact *enjoy* the actual act.[15]

The net result of these complicated patterns of expectation around sexuality is that women's refusal of sexual advances is not taken seriously. This result is well demonstrated in the adage that a man's word is his honor, whereas a woman's honor resides in her sexual purity rather than in her words. What women say is not believed, at least in part because they are expected to lie about their sexual relationships, saying no when they really want to be overpowered and dominated.

Ultimately, then, sexism not only distorts our sexual experience by introducing peculiar dynamics of dominance and submission into it but also undermines our trust in women's perspectives and statements. In short, sexism affects our processes of judgment. Women are not seen as authority figures partly because they have been underrepresented in the professions and therefore we have few models for seeing women's power in these roles. But even the introduction of more and more women into the professions has not eradicated a deeper effect of sexism that continues to undermine the authority of women in the professions: the effect of distrust of the woman's perspective. Part of the reason that women in ministry do not have the same "numinosity" that men do is that women are not typically seen as authority figures. Their words, their judgments, their definitions of the situation, are not traditionally understood to be definitive. And so, sexism ultimately affects not only the sexual arena per se, but also the entire arena of a woman's professional work and position.

In *Women Ministers*,[16] a number of women clergy describe their struggles over authority. Lacking role models in the pulpit,[17] women often question their own potency[18] or even their own worthiness.[19] Some women find the lack of models freeing and argue for the development of new models. "Freedom from stereotyped images tends to elicit responses that people might be more reluctant to share elsewhere," claims Brita Gill.[20] In a similar vein, one of our respondents noted that "I break all of their stereotypes . . . I create my own image . . . there's no mold for me to conform to." But almost all express some feelings of lacking the kind of automatic power that attaches to the ministerial role for men.

Part of this lack of power is having to work harder in order to have their perspective taken seriously. "Local churches are shaped by a long cultural and ecclesiastical tradition that has emphasized that women are persons who respond better than they initiate, who should be seen rather than heard, and who are passive rather than assertive."[21] One respondent suggested that "men have difficulty relating to women professionals." We are not used to seeing women as authority figures, and therefore women do not have the same power and authority in a professional role that men do.

Sexism changes the ethical picture. Although women are professionals with training and credentials, they do not generally have the same power as do men in professional positions. This is due largely to the dynamics of sexism in our culture. Those dynamics operate in a number of ways. First, they give power in general to men in our culture, so that a lay man may in fact have as much power as a professional woman. Second, they change the dynamics around sexuality and especially around sexual attraction. Men are expected to be the aggressors and women to be on the defensive sexually. Women's refusals of sexual advances are not taken as seriously as are men's refusals. Women experience a high level of harassment and find the sexual situation ethically "charged." The situation of men and women in ministry is indeed as different as day and night, as our respondent put it.

But if this is true, then it would seem that "a different ethic regarding intimacy applies," as she concluded. If power is central to professional ethics, as we argued in chapters 4 and 5, then where the power dynamics are different, the ethical analysis must be correspondingly different.

If women have less power in ministry, then it would seem that the power gap between the woman pastor and the male parishioner is less than the power gap between the male pastor and the woman parishioner. This might suggest, then, that there is more equality, and more possibility for an adequate and valid consent on the part of the parishioner to engage in sexual relations with the pastor. Thus, if a woman has a romantic interest in a male parishioner and wants to begin a relationship with him, she does not have the same power over him that a male pastor would have over a female parishioner. It might seem, then, that it would be more acceptable for her to approach him and to trust that his consent is a valid consent.

And this is true. However, it is also not the whole picture. In one of our surveys, we utilized a vignette in which a young, single woman pastor does in fact want to invite a young, single male parishioner to dinner and a movie. We said nothing about sexual involvement, but only specified that it was clearly to be a "date."

Moreover, as a professional woman, especially one in ministry, it might be difficult for this young pastor to find dates if she waits for the traditional male invitation. Precisely because men are not socialized to be attracted to powerful women, and especially in an increasingly "unchurched" culture, as an ordained woman she is not likely to be the recipient of many invitations. In setting up this vignette, therefore, we thought that our respondents would be sympathetic to her need for a social life and to her need to initiate that herself. We also thought that the power dynamics between men and women might make this situation less fraught with power imbalances than is the situation for the male pastor with the female parishioner. In short, we expected a sympathetic and supportive response.

To our initial surprise, many of our respondents raised serious cautions for the woman pastor. Some of these had to do with the fact that the parishioner would lose his pastor, and that there are risks to him. Some were simply uncomfortable with the idea that a woman might initiate a date, since this is an action traditionally reserved to the man. Some urged that she find ways to spend time with him in nondating situations before "upping the ante" into the possible emotional entanglements of dating.

But most of the cautions raised had to do with the

risks *to her* of taking this action. Precisely because she does not have power, even though she is the professional and the pastor in the situation, to take such an action is perceived by our respondents as very risky for her. She stands to lose. Indeed, some of our respondents cautioned that the woman almost always loses power in such a circumstance. Her job and even her career in ministry could be at stake.

We see in these responses the power of sexism at work in the culture. The woman professional certainly does not carry the same "sexual weight" as the man professional. Precisely at the point where we might think that power is equalized between professional and client and, therefore, consent to sexual involvement might be valid, we find instead that the woman professional's power is in such jeopardy that she is advised not to proceed! This makes sense only in light of the total effects of sexism on our culture. Remember that sexual advance is typically the male's prerogative, and that it is also understood as the man "scoring" against the woman. Under these circumstances, men gain power over women by having sexual access to them. For the woman to allow a man sexual access is therefore very risky for her because it means that he gains power over her in the eyes of the culture. What appears at first glance, therefore, to be a more equal and mutual relationship, in which she brings professional and pastoral power to an encounter with male power, in fact turns out to be a circumstance in which her power is readily undermined by the power of the man in sexist culture. We can begin to see that she stands to lose a great deal. It is no wonder that many of our respondents urged caution.

On the face of it, a simple analysis of the dynamics of professional power would seem to lead to the logical conclusion that it is more acceptable for the woman pastor and male parishioner to seek sexual involvement than it is for the male pastor and female parishioner to do so, since the power appears to be more equalized for the woman professional and male client. But a more complicated analysis of the dynamics of power in sexist culture leads us to the conclusion that the woman pastor is too much at risk in such a situation.

The caution that we raise here, however, is based largely on concerns about risks to the pastor, not on concerns about risks to the parishioner. There are risks for him, to be sure. He will lose his pastor if she becomes his lover. We would still think it inappropriate for the woman pastor to approach any male parishioner who has come seeking special counseling or who is in a particularly vulnerable position that might undermine his ability to give a valid consent. These cautions remain valid in the case of a female pastor and male parishioner, just as they are valid in the case of a male pastor and female parishioner. There are circumstances in which it would not be appropriate for the female pastor to approach a male parishioner because of concerns for his spiritual well-being and his role as parishioner.

But under other circumstances, the reasons for caution have to do more with the risks to the woman than with the risks to the man. Precisely because of the impact of sexism on our culture, the woman is at risk. Sexism distorts the dynamics of professional power and makes the exercise of professional and pastoral power a risky business for women.

7
God and Eros

We saw in the previous chapter that a woman minister stands in unique relationship to the power dynamics between pastor and parishioner. As pastor, she holds positional power; as a woman, her power is denied or usurped. Women's experience necessarily connects sexuality and power issues because it is sexual gender that has determined who holds positions of power in the social, political, and professional arena. Women have primarily experienced powerlessness, subordination, oppression.

Yet, ironically, it is the very women who have experienced so much oppression concerning their sexuality who are finding in that sexuality new resources for understanding God and for doing ministry. In order to understand how this could be so, we return briefly to Robert's story.

POWERLESSNESS AND INSIGHT

As indicated in chapter 3, Robert had a history of sexual involvement with parishioners, but there were several breaks in that pattern. One of these came about because external factors did not provide the privacy necessary for the development of affairs. But two of the breaks resulted from crises in Robert's life. The first was when he discovered that his first wife, Adele, was having an affair with their pastor. Robert was shaken, and he broke off his own affair at the time. He locates the cause of the break not simply in the infidelity of his wife but in his great sense of betrayal by his friend, colleague, and mentor.

The second crisis was when Robert discovered that his second wife, Sandy, was having an affair. In spite of his presumed "liberal" stance toward sexual ethics, Robert was not able to cope with this, and it caused him to take a harder look at his sexual patterns and personal needs. Ultimately, this crisis has led to his current stance of fidelity to his marriage and noninvolvement with his parishioners.

Both of these crisis points in Robert's journey were instances in which he was no longer in control. He was without power. He felt betrayed by his mentor in the first instance and insecure as a result of his wives' actions in both instances. His world—and the control he had always assumed he exercised within it— crumbled. Moreover, both were circumstances in which a sexual freedom that he had simply assumed for himself was being exercised by a woman. According to Robert, it was these events, in which he was confronted with his powerlessness and with the inadequacies of the framework he was bringing, that were the most influential in causing self-reflection and, finally, changed behavior.

Like Robert, most women entering ministry are capable, even charismatic individuals. They have personal presence and power. They also have professional presence and power. Yet, because of sexism, all women within this culture know the experience of powerlessness. What Robert experienced sporadically, they experience persistently and pervasively. And just as the experience of powerlessness led to self-reflection and challenge of previously accepted paradigms for Robert, so the experience of powerlessness has led to self-reflection and challenge of previously accepted paradigms for women.

Women have taken their experiences of harassment and oppression and have used those experiences as grounds for new insights and new theologies. Precisely because the dominant paradigms have *not* worked for them, they have sought, found, and created new paradigms.

"FEMININE" DIMENSIONS

In fact, while several women pastors thought that "my being female isn't an issue," the majority recognized that "it is still shocking to see a woman in the pulpit" and took some joy in the opportunities this gave them to model new ways of being in the pastoral role. A number spoke of using their femaleness as a definite resource: "I affirm myself as woman clergy and feel the feminine perspective which I can bring is a positive contribution," said one. "I celebrate my 'femininity' with colorful scapulars, references to my experience as a woman . . . and with my obvious joy at being married and doing mothering of two children," said another. "I'm clearly a woman and happy to be a woman," said another, adding later: "I express myself with my body. As I said earlier, I'm comfortable with myself as a woman." These women pastors are saying, "I'm happy to be a woman, and I find it a distinct resource for my ministry."

What is this "feminine perspective" or contribution that women make to ministry? For many, it is rooted squarely in their awareness of sexuality, and of the tangles and problems, but also the joys and possibilities, inherent in sexual encounter. "Women are more aware of sexuality," said one. Others concur. Precisely because women are so often treated primarily in terms of their sex and are seen as sex objects, they become sensitive to the dynamics of sexual energy and exchange. Recognizing that "men have trouble seeing women apart from their sexuality," one woman pastor watched the dynamics of male-female interaction carefully in her ministry. In one search process, she argues, "the women wanted a father and a lover. I watched them fall in love with the male candidate." She concludes, "It is no accident that we talk about the first year as the honeymoon."

Another mentioned similar sexual dynamics, this time concerning pastors who get divorced while in the church:

> When the male pastor I work with got a divorce, people got mad at his wife for not taking good enough care of him. The older women in the congregation started taking care of him—giving him larger portions of food at the women's group luncheons, and things like that. I know another man in the ministry who got divorced. His mistake wasn't getting divorced—it was getting remarried to a woman in the congregation. All the women started competing for him and wondering, "Why didn't he choose me?" Both of these men were so unaware of these sexual dynamics.

The attraction of congregation and pastor often has sexual dynamics within it. Precisely because they have had to develop a protective stance of being aware of hidden sexual dynamics in normal social exchange, women pastors consider themselves more aware of these dynamics than male pastors are, and they make use of this knowledge and awareness.

Women pastors often spoke, for example, about the importance and the delicacy of issues of touch in ministry. Because so many women grow up having experienced so much abusive touch, they are aware of the problem of "bad touch" and are often cautious about touch.

> I try to be real sensitive to how people feel about being touched—"positioning" myself for touch but letting them take the initiative or at least signal their willingness to be touched.

> Touch—I am open, but the other person needs to make the first move for a hug.

> I don't encourage hugging and am careful about too much one-on-one contact.

These pastors wanted to be sure that their touching of parishioners was not offensive or abusive to others. Their concerns were not so much to protect themselves from being misunderstood as to ensure that any pastoral touch was experienced as "good touch" by the recipient. They touch only where permission is given.

Yet even as women are sensitive to the problems of touch, they see it as a distinct resource that women can bring. One pastor spoke about intimacy and touch as special gifts that a woman pastor could bring that would not have been as acceptable from a man. While "shadowing" a woman minister during her training, she had observed the woman pastor put an elderly, ill woman to bed and "crawl into bed with her and read her a story." The trainee comments, "that is incredibly intimate!" and she notes that a man could not get away with it while a woman can. Based on this experience, the pastor has learned that nonsexual touching "is a strength that women can use," and, she says, "I use touch a lot in my ministry." Others also spoke about using physical contact: "I just hug 'em all the time." Women pastors also noted that women in the congregation were often glad to have a woman with whom they could discuss sexuality or intimate things that they might not have felt free to share with a male pastor.

The example of crawling into bed with a sick woman and reading her a story is, of course, reminiscent of the kinds of things that mothers do for their children. And, indeed, mothering is another resource used by women pastors. Women are more aware of the constant intrusion of sexuality into the dynamics of life not only because of being treated as sex objects but also because of their potential or actual role as mother. The rhythms and demands of menstruation, pregnancy, and birthing fall to women. The demands of child rearing also fall disproportionately on women. While these demands place special burdens on women, they also provide new resources.

Some feminists have argued for these experiences as a new source of insight or knowledge grounded in the fullness of eros in human life. In particular, mothering connotes images of a life-encouraging, life-protecting love in which power is used not to control and dominate, but to encourage the growth of the other—a "creative, nonpossessive love."[1] Mothering thus becomes the source of new knowledge of forms of love and therefore of ways in which God is present in human life.

This emphasis on the distinctive bodily experiences of pregnancy, birthing, breast-feeding, and mothering was mentioned by a number of women pastors. One said that her youthfulness, her married state, and her "mother-ness" tend to shape images of what she says and does in the church. Another claims that "being a parent has had more connotations for deciding on sexual boundaries than being a pastor." For her, her children's puberty was a particularly difficult and decisive time in shaping her own sense of herself as a physical person: "When my daughters began developing breasts I had a harder time showing them affection. I had to move through that." Thus, experiences of being a mother, both joyful and difficult, were decisive for some of our women pastors.

One spoke at some length about the importance of her pregnancy and its impact on her ministry:

> The congregation recently journeyed with me through my pregnancy, birth, and son's infancy. I often use illustrations which I would characterize as open to the developmental aspects of sexuality. It is not avoided as an area for discussion . . . . With my pregnancy it has been difficult if not impossible for folks to avoid my sexual side . . . . The major life-changing experience surrounding my theology of sexuality has been my son's birth. It has assisted me in seeing sexuality as a very dynamic force in my spiritual journey. It is no longer reified for me as genital expression.

For this pastor, pregnancy and childbirth has played a role in several ways. First, it has brought "sexuality" front and center in the church. Second, it has expanded the definition of sexuality from the genital alone to a broader understanding of the erotic dimensions of human life and the development of sexual response. Third, it has helped her to locate the importance of sexuality as a part of spirituality. We noted in chapter 1 that a number of clergy, male and female alike, are trying to draw links between sexuality and spirituality; for some women pastors, this link becomes a reality because of the particular sexual experiences of pregnancy and birth.

EROS AND POWER

The net result of this increased awareness of sexuality and of its negative and positive dimensions in human life is that women find sexuality a positive resource for their theology. The three characteristics noted above—the centrality of sexuality, the expanded definition of it, and its importance in spirituality—all emerge as themes for women pastors. Women see their bodies and physical processes as sources of knowledge and of pleasure. This physicality is turned into a resource for knowing life, goodness, the divine.

Thus, many women spoke of the centrality of sexuality and of their concrete sexual experiences as roots of their emerging understanding of theology and ministry.

> My own experience of a loving sexual partnership has increased my understanding and sensitivity to other partners, enriched my life, energized my ministry, increased my understanding of human connection.
>
> I know that my theology and my sexuality are totally compatible and comfortable for me. I would hope that being a better lover has made me a better theologian and vice versa.
>
> My experience has definitely changed my theology. Early in my sexual life I had sex with a man and I thought it was wrong. And I felt bad. But a few days later, I had this profound sense that I was loved by God though I no longer felt pure. It was my first very personal experience of grace. It made my theology more joyous.

Whether sexuality is experienced as providing the occasion for grace, or drawing/bonding people, or making us more forgiving, or simply adding joy to human life, for many women their concrete experiences of sexuality have had a significant impact on their theologies. Because of who they are sexually, they see God differently. As one woman pastor puts it, "People say of me that I theologize about everything. I am always looking for the God dimension. . . . Experience and theology are interrelated."

Women use their experiences of the broad dimensions of sexuality—not just genital sexuality, but motherhood, erotic energy, femaleness—as roots for a new theological understanding.

This new theological understanding has two primary dimensions. One is the affirmation of eros—of the primacy of bonding energy, of the goodness of bodies and of sexuality, of the life-giving and nurturing energy that flows from community and interconnectedness. "Eros connotes intimacy through the subjective engagement of the whole self in a relationship," argues Rita Nakashima Brock.[2] The "erotic" is that which connects people, draws people to be their fullest selves, engages their entire being. Many women clergy espoused such a broadened definition of eros or sexuality and saw it as central to understanding how God works in the world.

The second theological shift grows out of the first. Just as erotic love affirms the goodness of bodily connection, so it also affirms new forms of power. Erotic power is not the "power-over" of domination and submission paradigms. It is a power of mutuality and life-givingness. Erotic power is transformative and nurturing. It is beneficent, life enhancing, and liberating.[3] Erotic power is empowerment rather than "power over." The hesitancy that women clergy sometimes express about claiming their separateness as clergy comes in part from a hesitancy to claim "power over" and a desire to posit new forms of power in which friendship and mutual enrichment are the paradigms.

For many, this new theology rooted in and compatible with a healthy sexuality represents a radical break from their past:

> My personal Christian upbringing was repressive and guilt-producing, so where I am now—sexually and in

every other way, required me to overcome the harmful early effects and develop a whole new theology.

I now see the whore/goddess dualism of my Dutch Reformed background and am much more at ease with my own body simply as a *good*, functioning organism.

I hope that my theology helps form my sexuality—but my tradition as Church of the Brethren doesn't. It's a very asexual denomination even though we include touch (foot washing) in worship; we avoid real touching, take sexuality out of worship.

Women have experienced church tradition as oppressive not only of them as women but also of sexuality itself. In order to use their sexual experience as grounds for new theological insights, they must break with tradition.

THE ROLE OF EXPERIENCE

Often, what has led women to affirm new understandings of God over and against their traditional training and their personal experiences of sexual harassment and oppression is *trust in their own experiences* of the goodness of sexuality. This means that as women come to affirm new and expanded definitions of sexuality based in their experience, they are also positing a new epistemological framework. They are arguing in essence that in spite of the oppressions of the "system" as they experience it both in theory and in practice, there is something that they can tap in their own experience that is trustworthy and gives them a new understanding of sexuality and of God. Thus, the third dimension to the theology being created by women is a new understanding of the sources of knowledge about God and therefore about ethics.

We noted in chapter 2 that the most common response among clergy as to how they knew when they were reaching acceptable limits of intimacy was a response that trusted to "feelings" or "instinct." There, we raised some questions about the adequacy of feelings or instinct as a base for discerning acceptable limits of intimacy. While these concerns remain valid, it is now time to round out the picture.

Consider, for example, what it means to talk about "feelings" in the following context:

> I have not had sexual feelings *for* a parishioner, however I have felt male parishioners caring for me in a more intimate fashion. Extra squeezes on the hand, hugs where one of their hands is placed near my breast (on the side) or slides down a little towards the rear, extra long hugs, conversations that hint at their feelings . . . all these are *clear* signs to me that their actions need to be called to their attention and brought to a stop.
>
> The best sign for me is an *inward feeling.* If I feel uncomfortable with a parishioner sexually, I confront it so they know it is inappropriate.

We have used part of this quote in previous chapters. But when the quote is seen in its entirety, several aspects of it sparkle with insight.

First, this woman pastor is trusting her feelings at a point where *others are approaching her,* not at the point of her own desire to approach another. That is, she is trusting her feelings as a *protective* device, a defensive rather than an offensive maneuver. Oppressed people are often told by the dominant culture what to think, how to feel, how to react, what is "normal." Under such circumstances, to trust outside authority or dominant culture is to deny oneself. To trust one's own "feelings" can therefore be an act of self-affirmation and a way of getting behind cultural forms toward truth. As Mary Belenky et al. put it in *Women's Ways of Knowing,* "women's growing reliance on their intuitive processes is, we believe, an important adaptive move in the service of self-protection, self-assertion, and self-definition. Women become their own authorities."[4] Indeed, they suggest that the most common criterion for truth for these subjective knowers is "what feels comfortable to me," and they argue that this use of the interior voice is the hallmark of women's emergent sense of self, agency, and control.[5]

In short, trust in one's "feelings" or "intuition" may have a different meaning and a different valence depending on whether one is a member of an oppressed or a dominant group. We remain suspicious of trusting to inner feelings alone as a source for ethical guidance. Indeed, we note that Belenky and her colleagues are also critical of the "subjectivist" mode of turning to feelings. Although they consider this mode a very important step in the transition for women into claiming their own minds, voices, and selves, they also note some limitations of the "inner feeling" approach to knowledge: it abandons rationality and objectivity, isolates the "knower" from others, and ignores the fact that "no one's gut feeling is infallible."[6]

Nonetheless, women who need to be self-protective in a culture that is not protective of them may need to turn to "inner" voices that do not cohere with tradition or with received cultural forms and knowledge in order to find new sources of insight and knowing. It is also noteworthy that Belenky and her associates find that what lies behind this move to the internal voice is often the failure of dominant male authority. Specifically, what lies behind the appropriation of the inner voice is often loss of trust in male authority because of sexual harassment and abuse.[7] Thus, for women clergy who have experienced sexual harassment and come to find the dominant culture not trustworthy, affirmation of their own inner voice and perceptions is an important form of spirituality and of finding God in their lives. Trust in "intuition" may mean one thing when an oppressed person or group uses intuition as a protective device to guard against the advances of others and something different when those with power use it. Although we have raised cautions about pastors' trust in feelings, we recognize the significance and validity of this trust under some circumstances.

However, feeling is not all that is at stake here. The pastor talks about trusting her "inward feeling," but in fact she names a range of very concrete *behaviors* (hands near the breast or rear, extra hugs, prolonged hugs, squeezes, and so on) that are inappropriate. Thus, her "feeling" is well grounded in experience and can be communicated to others. What she calls a "feeling" here is more on the order of a conclusion drawn from accumulated experience and specifiable data. It is not in fact a purely "subjective" form of knowledge but is a conclusion based on experience and observation and open to the confirmation of other knowers. While this pastor would no doubt argue that truth lies hidden beneath the surface (the surface level of men's communication with her is not to be trusted, and truth must be ferreted out[8]), she also demonstrates careful observation and analysis as a ground for knowledge. Although she uses the *language* of feeling, in fact her mode of reasoning includes dimensions that go beyond the purely subjective implications of that language.

Thus, we note first that the use of inner voices and of the language of feelings may be more appropriate for those who are in positions of powerlessness and oppression than it is for the powerful, and second, that the use of the language of "feelings" is often a shorthand summary for what are in fact *judgments* well grounded in data that can be communicated to others. This sets qualifications on the use of "feeling language" alone. Although our pastor here may use a language that implies a purely subjective judgment, in fact her judgment is warranted, can be communicated, and her trust in her own internal processes makes sense in light of her oppression as a woman.

What this pastor shares with other women who use the language of feelings is the conviction that the most trustworthy knowledge comes from personal experience rather than from the pronouncements of authorities.[9] This sentiment is echoed throughout the women's answers to our questionnaire. At almost every point, they turn to personal experience as the ground for any conclusions drawn. For instance, one respondent, in speaking about the tools that help her to form her theology of sexuality, says: "I see how Scripture and theology have been used to bury any sexuality that has to do with partnership, not ownership or control. Experience, conversations with other women, my own sexuality and study have brought me to a belief that sexuality is partnership." Here, the fundamental theological theme of partnership and equality, rather than ownership and control, comes about not as a result of scripture or tradition, but as a result of personal experience and shared experience. Experience contradicts tradition, and it is experience that she has come to trust.

Another woman responds:

A lot of it I've had to think through by myself. . . . My spiritual direction has been great—really clearly illustrates the yin-yang of spirituality/sexuality. A very spiritual/sexual woman has a capacity for intimacy that can be nurtured in many ways. . . . I've been influenced by the modeling of other women . . . my own experience of prayer.

Here, the respondent draws on a range of experiences, from spiritual direction to prayer and the modeling of

other women, to argue for her new understanding of
the link between spirituality and sexuality, sexuality
and God.

Whether it is through direct experiences of sexuality
or through experiences of spirituality, women pastors
responding to our survey were of like mind in finding
personal experience the most potent source of new
knowledge about sexuality, spirituality, and God.
While some still found sexuality confusing and fearful,
and others found it a rich and trustworthy source of
insight, all drew on their own experiences and on the
shared experiences of other women for their insights
into the meaning and place of sex in their lives.

NEW MODELS, NEW VISION

Partly because of the tendency to trust experiences,
both one's own and others', and partly because of the
affirmation of "empowerment" or mutual enrichment, women were also likely to form support groups
in order to have places to share their ethical dilemmas
and theological insights. "If I am troubled about
relationships with individuals I talk with a close friend
and other colleagues," said one. Another noted that if
she finds herself attracted to someone, she talks to
some one "outside the situation" to help her defuse it.
One said that her women's clergy group was the place
for her to talk about sexuality. Another mentioned
that she had "deliberately decided to meet together
on a regular basis for the purpose of discussing
sexuality in ministry" with another woman clergy.
"We're a support group of two," she claims. Such
seeking out of colleagues and friends with whom
troubling and inspiring aspects of sexuality could be
discussed was a common maneuver for women—far
more so than for men.

The sense shared by all these women is that they

are modeling and mediating something *new*. They have broken stereotypes, the old rules about power and professional presence do not hold for them, and they must forge new ways of being. For most women, this means finding within their very "different-ness"—within their gender and their sexuality—new resources for understanding, approaching, and mediating God.

For some, it means that old language and forms no longer suffice. One woman put it eloquently:

> As a female pastor I have become aware that I have been trained to be a priest, but in actuality I am a priestess. I mediate Goddess, not God, and there are no guides within Christianity—no protections—no sanctions—that help me deal with Her power when it is unleashed. I feel as though I could spend the rest of my life exploring/rediscovering the art of being a priestess. Maybe then I could better understand the truest, deepest power of my own sexuality and the One who lies at the heart of it.

When one's very presence breaks all the stereotypes, and the general rules about power and professional presence do not hold, one is in the position of being a new kind of mediator. Women in ministry mediate God, but not the traditional God of patriarchal Christianity. They mediate "Goddess"—something new, something different. They realize that there are new forms of power that come from this incarnated mediation, new forms of power that come from their sexual and gendered presence in the church. It takes new skills to be a "priestess" rather than a priest. And it may take a lifetime to discover the new forms of power inherent in a recovery of eros and its meaning for mediating God.

These insights from women in the parish are profound. For our purposes, they have significance in two ways in particular. First, we have indicated that power is central to our ethical analysis. It is the power held by the professional person and the vulnerability of the parishioner that makes sexual contact problematic. Yet there are different ways of understanding power, different forms of being powerful. Women are seeking alternative forms of power and ways of exercising power that are mutually enriching rather than coercive. Women are seeking "empowerment" rather than "power over" another. We would caution that women should not forget the power over others that they may still have as professionals. Yet we also welcome new forms of power that would not present the same ethical difficulties.

Second, in chapter 3 some serious concerns were raised about using "feelings" or "instinct" as a guide to ethical behavior. These concerns need to be modified in accord with two aspects of women's reality. First, there is a difference between trusting feelings as a clue to aggression toward another (sexual advance) and trusting feelings as a clue to the need for self-protection. It is in the second sense that most women talk of trusting their feelings.

Oppressed people live with a constant denial of their own insights and perceptions. Others tell them what is real, what is trustworthy, how the world ought to be perceived. Often they refer to an "instinct" that says, "This is not right." Their own perceptions tell them that the received knowledge is not adequate—indeed, that it may be harmful. But lacking social power, it is difficult to offer an alternative view in any language other than the subjective-sounding language of feelings.

We would generally still urge clergy not to rely on the language of feelings, but to locate and specify the behaviors that are problematic. In fact, women clergy are doing precisely this. We would urge clergy to move into the arena of what can be argued as social policy, rather than remaining with the subjective language of what "feels right" on a personal level. However, we would also concur that the feelings of oppressed groups of people may be an important clue to what is going on ethically. When a man "feels" right about approaching a woman, we would urge caution. But when a woman "feels" wrong about an approach toward her, we would urge her to trust that feeling and to use it as a clue for ethical analysis.

Like the women in our study, we look for the day when we can affirm the positive meaning of sexuality in human life and in the church. We hope for the expression of the joy of sex, even in the parish. We seek a recovery of the fullest meaning of eros and its contributions to our understanding of God's activity in human life. But like the women in our study, we also recognize that sexual harassment, coercion, and abuse are daily realities, and that an ethical framework must take seriously not only the joys of sexuality but also the pains of sexism and their impact on our culture.

8
Single and Sexual

As the framework developed in the preceding chapters indicates, responsible use of the power that accrues to the pastor means that intimate personal relationships between pastor and parishioner are fraught with difficulty. With Marie Fortune and Peter Rutter, we believe it is a violation of professional ethics for the pastor to be both pastor and lover. The parishioner who becomes sexually involved with the pastor loses access to the pastoral role with that person. Although we may make room for the "normal neurotic" who develops an honorable interest in a parishioner, there are overall reasons for caution and for an initial negative response. The pastor who would develop an interest in the parishioner must be able to prove that the parishioner can give a valid consent.

We have been talking about pastors generally, as though being married or single is not the central issue. A pastor's sexual approach to a parishioner is not acceptable simply because the parishioner is single. The pastor still has the power of the professional role, and if the pastor is male, he also has cultural power. For reasons discussed in chapter 4, this power differential is ethically problematic and renders sexual contact between pastor and parishioner ambiguous at best. We recognize that women do not have the same power as men. We also recognize that the dynamics of male sexuality in this culture play a role in the sexual patterns of pastors. There are ambiguities. Nonetheless, there is reason in general to begin with a taboo against sexual activity between pastor and parishioner.

THE SINGLE SITUATION

But now we can hear the complaints from single pastors: "What do you expect of me? I work sixty or more hours a week; when do I have time to meet anyone except through my work? What if I'm in a small rural parish and there just aren't many single men or women available in my town—especially well educated and Christian singles?" Many single pastors would no doubt condemn sexual liaisons between married pastors and their parishioners but would argue that the situation is different when one is single.

And so it is. In some denominations, well over half the parishes are in small, rural churches. These are the parishes to which beginning pastors are often assigned or called. For the beginning pastor who is single, such a location presents problems: is he or she simply to have no sexual life at all? If he or she wants to date, who is available outside the parish? If she or he wants to marry, who better than someone who belongs to the church, sees the minister at work, understands what it means to be a pastor's spouse, and can become a true helpmate? The single pastor may have a legitimate concern about where to find suitable mates or partners, whether for dating or for covenanted relationship. It is understandable that many single pastors will look to parishioners for their social life.

And indeed, we all know pastors who have married a former parishioner and whose marriages are as "graced" as any we know. The authors of this book have known dozens of such cases. They appear to give the lie to all our cautions about the power of the pastor and the unacceptability of most pastor-parishioner romantic or sexual relationships.

And so, many readers probably think that as long as the pastor is single and the parishioner is single, and they intend a serious relationship that might lead to marriage, this would be the acceptable case of sexual relating between pastor and parishioner.

But is it the acceptable case? Is it acceptable for single pastors to date parishioners? Does the lack of opportunity for sexual expression justify an exception to the general conclusion drawn above? If both parties are single and hope for a covenanted relationship, does this fact change the ethical picture in such a way that we would find this relationship acceptable?

We have argued above that women do not have the same power in ministry that men do. If this is true, then there is not as great a power gap between the woman pastor and male parishioner as between the male pastor and female parishioner. It might seem, then, that the situation is different for single women in ministry, and that there is no reason to deny to the single woman minister the opportunity to date a parishioner. Is dating a parishioner acceptable for the woman minister at least? Do the special circumstances of being single make romantic or sexual interest in a parishioner acceptable for women in the parish?

To these hypothetical and actual queries from single pastors, we want to answer "Yes, but . . ." On the one hand, we have sympathy for the situation of single pastors who find their resources limited and see little hope for healthy sexual expression unless they can develop a relationship with someone in the parish. Each of the authors of this volume has known what it is to date—even to marry—someone within the circle of people who might otherwise be "forbidden." Thus, we do not want to say an automatic no to the single pastor's legitimate quest for a romantic and sexual partner, and we recognize the factors that may lead pastors to seek such a partner from among available parishioners.

At the same time, we are concerned about some of the dynamics that we have seen operating in our own circumstances and in the circumstances of others as well. Some of these dynamics have to do with issues that we have discussed above, for example, the male tendency to genitalize close relationships. We would remind our readers of some of these factors, but we will not rehearse them here.

THE PRESSURE TO BE COUPLED

Other dynamics have to do with the pressures on single people in general in this culture. There is tremendous pressure for people to "couple," not just in the sense of sexual coupling but in the sense of commitment, "relationship," or marriage. As John Landgraf puts it, this is a culture "where coupling is considered everyone's right and right for everyone."[1] In such a culture, to be normal is to strive for a primary relationship. With the exception of those committed to religious celibacy, we have assumed that sane adults never *choose* to be single, and that if they are single, it must be by accident or default.

In short, we are a marrying culture. We assume that marriage—or at a minimum, committed relationship and having a "significant other"—is the right way for adults to live. There is tremendous pressure on everyone, and on young people in particular, to get serious, to get engaged, or to get married. So coupling is not something that is simply natural or desired for personal reasons; it is also something that is culturally conditioned and socially requisite.

If this is true in the culture in general, it is even more true in the church. Churches have been slow to accept divorced pastors. They are skeptical of single pastors and wary of any possible promiscuity. As John Shelby Spong puts it:

> [T]he Christian church continues to assume that marriage is the norm of life and that singleness is either a sign of immaturity, or of sexual perversion, or of failure, or of extreme sadness, or of some tragic fate. Since singleness is not trusted save inside the rare vows of religious celibacy, the single person is regarded as a kind of loose cannon that threatens the marital fidelity of others. There is, therefore, a not-so-veiled negativity toward the "non-vowed" single person that emanates regularly from the voices and precepts of the church.[2]

The single pastor, whether young or older, is expected to seek covenanted relationship and to desire marriage. Precisely because the pastor holds symbolic meaning for the church, pastors are expected to embody covenanted relationship—and for most churches this means marriage. Precisely because the pastor holds symbolic meaning for the church, churches project onto the pastor a load of symbol systems, including the old desire to have both "father" and "mother" figures for the church, or "two for the price of one." Precisely because churches need to be a "safe space" for people to share, churches are wary of pastors who are single and might be "on the prowl."

Thus, the single pastor may not only *desire* to be coupled but may be under considerable *pressure* to be coupled. This fact alone gives us pause. While not all who seek partners do so out of pressure or out of a sense of being incomplete by themselves, some may. To seek relationship because one does not feel "whole" alone is not the best grounds for establishing the kind of relationship that genuinely exhibits covenant. As Landgraf suggests, nonmarried people can feel that there is something wrong with them, that they are single by "default," that they have failed or neglected to do something one is supposed to do.[3] Forming relationship out of a sense of failure is not the best grounds for clergy or anyone else.

Thus, even as we have sympathy for the desire of single people in ministry to find appropriate mates, we also caution against the social pressures that may lead clergy toward "coupling" too quickly or in inappropriate circumstances. It can be very tempting to think that normal cautions against professionals having relations with their clients do not apply so long as the professional is single and wants not just a "one night stand" but a genuine relationship or commitment.

In addition to some of these general concerns, there are special concerns about the situation of single women and men in ministry. Single women and single men face different issues in ministry. In order to decide whether there is any reason to make exceptions to the cautions offered above, it is helpful to look at each in turn.

SINGLE WOMEN

While all women in ministry face liabilities, single women (both heterosexual and lesbian) face particular liabilities.

First, in this culture, women's identity has traditionally come from being an adjunct to a man. It is harder for a single woman to hold on to a sense of her worth than it is for a single man. Cultural factors such as sexism and double standards for men and women not only increase the pressure on women for coupling, but also mean that having a sense of one's capacity and authority as a single woman can be difficult. John Landgraf puts it this way:

> Because of these cultural factors, singling women often experience a greater diminishing of their self-esteem than do their male counterparts. It is implied, or they may be flatly told, that in their singlehood women are double or triple failures: They have failed to prove themselves sexually attractive; they have been inadequate wives, homemakers, and mothers, the traditional badges of femininity; and they have probably not advanced as far as they might have in their professional careers. . . . In these and other ways, singling women in our society face a far more judgmental "put-down" than singling men.[4]

In short, a common societal message to single women is "there's something wrong with you; you are a failure; you are not feminine enough."

While Landgraf is speaking about single women in general in this culture, many of his clients over the years have been clergy. And his insights are supported by our respondents. One wrote: "I feel that I have to at times prove I'm attractive to the opposite sex. I feel I have to explain my singleness." Another respondent, who is divorced, said, "I am sometimes asked why I have not remarried." Being single, or staying single, are not seen as normative by churches, and therefore many raise questions about those who are in that state.

The first woman pastor quoted here thinks the problem is hers, not the church's. While she feels angry about having to "prove" herself attractive or justify her single state, she sees this as her own guilt. More accurately, it is an internalized attitude derived from the culture. It is therefore the church's problem as well as hers. In this culture, women are questioned if they do not do things in the approved and expected way, and that means marriage.

The questions raised of women run in two directions. On the one hand, the woman pastor may be under severe pressure to prove that she is not an old maid. The negative connotations of most terms reserved for never-married women—wallflower, old maid, spinster—indicate how difficult it is for women to maintain status as single people.

The single woman pastor will therefore feel pressure to marry, or at least to date, in order to demonstrate that she is feminine and attractive. Several women spoke of pressure from the congregation about their dress or hairstyle or makeup: "The congregation would like me to dress more 'feminine,' to wear makeup—to look like the 'genteel lady.' " The single woman pastor who does not appear sufficiently feminine is at a disadvantage in terms of social status.

Indeed, several of our straight single women pastors spoke of concerns that they might be viewed as lesbian if they did not date. "Since I am 'single,' some probably wonder about my sexuality and/or sexual orientation," said one. Behind this experience lies the cultural perception that *either* a woman will couple with a man *or* she must not be attracted to (or attractive to) men. One pastor had the experience of turning down an invitation from a man who then spread the rumor that she was lesbian.

These experiences of our women pastors reflect both sexism and heterosexism in our culture. They derive partly from assumptions that all women *want* to be coupled, and that no woman would choose to be alone. But they derive also from heterosexist assumptions that only a heterosexual relationship makes an adequate coupling. Combined, sexism and heterosexism lead to the assumption that women need to be identified with men in order to be full people. In this culture it is considered inconceivable that a heterosexual woman would choose *not* to be in the company of a man. Thus, the woman who so chooses will have her sexual orientation or her femininity questioned. Her sexual orientation is questioned because of heterosexism, which assumes that only heterosexual relations are normal and normative. Her femininity is questioned because of sexism, which assumes that a woman must be coupled in order to be sufficiently feminine. The combination of the two makes a powerful cultural force that moves many people to feel that they must prove their sexual orientation by being attached to or at least demonstrating that they are attractive to members of the opposite sex.

At least one of our women pastors was angry about these sexist and heterosexist assumptions and what they have done to her ministry: "I sometimes feel the need to assert heterosexuality, and then I feel angry and guilty about that," she said. She is angry and guilty because she does not like to adopt the cultural standards that she sees as discriminatory, yet she knows that she is not altogether free of them. Because social and sexual roles are socially constructed and culturally defined, she experiences limits in what will be accepted as an appropriate expression of her single, female self.

So, single women in ministry are under pressure to date in order to prove that they are heterosexual, feminine, attractive, *and* that they are "normal" women who intend what our society has long held as the norm for women—marriage. But there is a flip side of the coin. While single women who do not appear sufficiently attractive or feminine are at a disadvantage, so are those who do appear sufficiently feminine and attractive!

First, they may be labeled as "temptresses" or

"sirens," who are out to get men. While the woman who does not appear attractive enough may have difficulty establishing her authority, the woman who appears too attractive may have difficulty establishing trust with other women in the parish, who will worry about their husbands or partners, or be jealous of the attractive pastor.

Second, the attractive single woman may be thought of as "available" or easy prey: "Women are seen as neuter, or they are perfectly fine for other men, including male senior pastors, to violate." The attractive woman pastor who is single must deal not only with possible jealousy from other women but with sexual attention from men in the parish.

Thus, the problem of being single and female in the parish cuts both ways: women can lose status if they are *not* perceived as traditionally feminine, but they can also have problems if they *are*.

SINGLE MEN

Single women in ministry are not the only ones who are perceived as "available" or "easy prey." Several of our male respondents spoke of being approached by women who admitted that they were "husband hunting" or of having older women in the parish try to marry them off to favorite nieces or granddaughters. The single male pastor can be seen as a "catch" or prize. Thus, while single women in ministry may have a problem of not finding suitable partners for dating or developing romantic interest, single men in ministry may have the opposite problem: too many potential partners and too much interest in seeing them date.

Because of sexism, however, the dynamics of what it means for men and women to be "available" in this culture are not the same. The woman is "prey" in a different way than the man is. He is more likely to be considered "eligible" and sought after by parishioners as a marriage partner for themselves or for their offspring. He may gain status by being single, whereas she may lose it. He may gain status by being sexually active, whereas she may lose it.

Nonetheless, single men in ministry face problems with sexual expression. One male respondent summed up a complex of problems in talking about how he thinks his parishioners view him:

> Some are a little gun-shy because I'm single, dating, and have more room for error. Some admire me—they think I'm single and have it so together. Some feel sorry for me—because I'm not "getting any." Some have a fantasy that I run around town a lot—they get a vicarious thrill out of how they perceive my exploits.

Each of these phrases represents one of the problems single men can face in ministry, so we will consider each in turn.

"Some are a little gun-shy because I'm single, dating, and have more room for error." The single male pastor who dates may not be seen as "safe space" because it is understood that he may develop a sexual interest in women, even in women parishioners. Partly because of cultural assumptions about the irrepressible nature of male libido, and partly because of cultural patterns in which men learn to genitalize their feelings, the single male pastor may be seen as being "on the prowl"—not prey, but predator.

"Some admire me—they think I'm single and have it so together." Others may admire, or even be envious of, what they perceive as the male pastor's freedom as a single person. Because single males are under pressure to "score" in this culture, some will assume that no male is single without being sexually active. Here people may project onto the pastor societal images of the lucky bachelor or playboy.

"Some have a fantasy that I run around town a lot—they get a vicarious thrill out of how they perceive my exploits."

In fact, the single pastor may experience singleness not as a welcomed freedom but as a recipe for loneliness. Just as the single woman pastor who *enjoys* being single may be misperceived and pitied for not fitting the ideal of the married woman, so the single male pastor who does *not* relish his singleness may be misperceived as having the good life. Thus, on the one hand, single male pastors may be misunderstood because they are assumed to be sexually active, even playboys.

On the other hand, they may be misunderstood because of assumptions that a minister would be celibate. "Some feel sorry for me—because I'm not 'getting any.' " Some parishioners assume that the single male pastor, even if dating, is not sexually involved. They may pity the pastor they think is deprived of the normal sexual expressions of a male.

In short, single men in ministry can be misunderstood in several ways. The assumption that single male clergy are celibate may make it very hard for the pastor to develop normal dating or romantic relationships. He may feel that he has to live up to an image even if it does not match his own desires. For instance, one pastor said that he has developed a serious relationship with a woman, but it is not known to his congregation. "I would have more freedom now if I weren't in the ministry," he argues. "My behavior must be more discreet—in and out of the congregation." In particular, he notes that he cannot live with his lover "because of the pastoral role" and suggests that this would not be true for other professionals such as lawyers. For another pastor, a desire not to give the appearance of inappropriate personal intimacy has led him to curtail pastoral intimacy as well: "I tend to limit my pastoral intimacy (since I am a divorced single) at times in order to avoid the appearance of personal intimacy."

While the celibate image of pastors causes problems for normal dating and sexual behavior, the playboy image may cause distrust on the part of the church. The pastor who is perceived as a playboy, or even as a sexually active young man, will fly in the face of church tradition, which does not approve of sexual activity for singles, especially young, premarital singles.

Until very recently, all discussions of single sexuality in the church were framed as discussions of "premarital" sex. The designation "premarital" is itself a clue to the biases that are prevalent in the church. The term implies that the only people who are single are young people who have not yet married, and that they *will* marry. Clearly, these assumptions do not fit the realities of a world in which some people never marry, many are single in mid-life following divorce, and most are single at some time following the death of a spouse.

Thus, just as single women in ministry have special problems, so do single men. Both would appear to be caught in a "catch-22": they are condemned if they appear normal, attractive, and sexually active, and they are condemned if they do not. The exact nature of the catch-22 differs for men and women, but each has reason to understand that there are special vulnerabilities in being single in the parish.

SEXUAL ETHICS AND THE SINGLE PASTOR

Several single pastors indicated that they think the churches do not understand the real dynamics of human sexuality. "The church is out of touch with the real world of sexuality. They think that a heterosexual person meets someone, dates, gets engaged, and then has sex. . . . But that's not the way heterosexual people work these days." One of the realities that single people struggle with has to do with the complexities of romantic and sexual involvement. As this pastor indicates, few single people simply meet someone, date, get engaged, get married, and then have sex.

First, most single people will date around a bit. Thus, to date someone does not necessarily mean that the pastor intends marriage with that person. Second, most single people have some sexual contact, including genital contact, long before they decide to become engaged or married. Thus, the realities of the world are realities of sexual contact among single people who may have more or less commitment to each other.

Nearly every church group recommends that the level of sexual involvement should parallel the level of interpersonal commitment—and thus by implication, genital involvement would be only for those who are very committed, even covenanted. For example, the United Church of Christ in its preliminary study of human sexuality suggested that one principle for sexual morality should be that *"the physical expression* of one's sexuality in relation to another ought be *appropriate to the level of loving commitment* in the relationship."[5] But that is not the reality of single sexuality today. Both for young, never-married singles and for older, post-married singles, the cultural mores now include more sexual expression and more variety in sexual experience than some churches would permit.

Churches that expect single pastors never to experiment sexually, to be virginal until marriage, will appear to their pastors to be whistling in the dark. Fifteen years ago, Charles Rassieur declared that "any theological viewpoint out of touch with basic life experiences, including sexuality, should be questioned as to whether it is really Christian."[6] More recently, Bishop Spong in his controversial book *Living in Sin* argues that "the moral codes are today being rewritten in both practice and law, quite unaffected by the voices that seek to contain, control, or condemn."[7] Noting that people mature sexually earlier than they used to, and that marriages are often delayed until after a rather lengthy education, Spong asks whether cultural and moral norms can continue to insist that the only proper sexual outlet is inside marriage.[8] In this stance, he gives voice to concerns that were both explicit and implicit in the responses we received.

But the issue is not simply whether the church's traditional stance against sexual expression for single people is outdated. The issue is also whether it is theologically justifiable. Spong says, "Where sex enhances life, I am prepared to call it good. Where sex destroys or diminishes life, I am prepared to call it evil."[9] This statement is almost exactly paralleled by one of our respondents: "In my sex life, I am called upon to witness to my faith. I do that by trying to say "No" to things which are selfish or abusive. I say "Yes" to the joyous and to those moving toward covenantal relationships which are mutually self-giving." In short, there is a movement afoot in the church today to modify simple rules that deny sexual expression to anyone just because he or she is single and allow it only for those who are married. Many of the respondents would affirm this movement. As one woman pastor put it, "pastors are hungry to be healthy, whole, sexual people as well as Christian role models."

PROFESSIONAL ETHICS AND THE
SINGLE PASTOR

But even those who might affirm such a sexual ethic and find it acceptable for single pastors to be sexually active would not necessarily find it acceptable for single pastors to date or become sexually involved with their parishioners. "My theology," says one, "is more liberal than my practice." Another says, "It is and has been my policy not to date members of the congregation." That is, many pastors will differentiate a personal sexual ethic from a professional ethic concerning issues of sexuality.

With this, we concur. As indicated in chapter 5, it is never appropriate for a pastor to seek sexual relations with a parishioner or other person who has come seeking explicit spiritual or personal counsel from the pastor. This relationship constitutes what Peter Rutter calls a "forbidden zone." The special vulnerability of the counselee requires a pastor to have only one agenda: the needs of the counselee. To mix a personal sexual agenda is to cross boundaries into inappropriate arenas.

However, we have distinguished this case from the circumstance where there is no explicit counseling relationship. Where the relationship between pastor and parishioner is the more general one of two people who worship and work in a common context, but without the special vulnerability of counseling, there may be more equality between the partners. Even here, however, as we have already indicated, there are some reasons for the single pastor to exercise caution.

And there are other hazards as well. One is illustrated by a single pastor who told one of the authors that during his ten-year tenure as pastor of one church he had dated as many as fifty women. None of them, he said with some wonder, had remained in the congregation when the dating relationship had ceased. He appeared not to recognize that when a pastor begins a dating relationship with a parishioner, the pastoral relationship has been, willy-nilly, relegated to second place behind the potential of the dating relationship. The parishioner has lost her or his pastor. She or he cannot regain that pastoral relationship when the dating ceases, and therefore, in need of a pastor, will move to another parish. A pastor who is considering dating a parishioner should know at the beginning that loss of a church member is a real risk, should the dating relationship end in anything other than a committed or covenanted relationship.

The public nature of ministry makes it difficult for the pastor to have a private relationship of any duration without that relationship becoming the topic of parish conversation. Thus, to try to hide a relationship in some presumed "private" arena of life is very difficult for those who are in ministry.

Moreover, there are reasons based in professional ethics not to do so: a secret relationship leaves the parishioner vulnerable to the imbalance of power. For instance, in the case of "Rev. Peter Donovan" as reported by Marie Fortune, one woman believed that the secrecy of her relationship with the minister was necessary because of legal problems in his relationship with his former spouse. She later learned in conversation with another woman from the same congregation that the woman's daughter also had a secret relationship with the same minister. Similar promises were being made by the pastor to both women at the same time. Later, they discovered that even more women were involved with him. The secrecy that he required of each kept them from having the protective structures they might otherwise have had and from learning the truth.

We recommend several structural protections for the pastor who would date a parishioner. First, for the protection of the parishioner, the pastor and the parishioner should seek out another pastor who can fill the pastoral role for the parishioner, thus avoiding the dual relationship dilemma.

For the protection of both parties, but especially of the pastor, a church leader or pastoral relations committee within the congregation should be advised of the dating relationship. This person or group can help the pastor anticipate the reactions of the congregation and alleviate the aura of secrecy in any dating relationship between pastor and parishioner.

Also the pastor should be in ongoing relationship with colleagues who can be trusted to give honest feedback concerning the performance of the pastor's professional duties. Such feedback will give the pastor support in maintaining appropriate professional ethics.

Even with these structural protections in place, we do have concerns for the woman pastor. As noted in chapter 6, she risks jeopardizing her professional power when she dates a parishioner because of the fragility of women's social power. She also makes herself vulnerable to gossip within the congregation. Because men tend to view women in terms of a dichotomy of "virgin Mary or temptress Eve," few men can relate to a woman pastor without a load of transference issues. One pastor waited until she had left the congregation she was serving before she dated a man from that parish. Even then, she was accused of being the cause of the failure of his marriage, which by then was long since over.

All of these cautions apply to the pastor who seeks to date a parishioner. But some pastors will think that because they intend a committed relationship, some of these cautions do not apply. Even if the dating relationship between pastor and parishioner is public, and even if it leads to committed relationship, there may be a price to pay within the congregation. People who are attracted to the pastor as a potential dating partner for themselves or for their offspring may become jealous and give vent to that jealousy in deceptive and unpredictable ways that make ministry difficult.

If the dating does lead toward a committed relationship, the couple experience tremendous pressure from the congregation to marry. The church, clinging to traditional norms for pastors if not for others, will not allow the couple to live together, or to appear to be too intimate with each other unless they are married.

For example, one of our respondents and the woman he had dated publicly for two years, with full knowledge and general approval from the church, described the intense pressure to marry they have felt from the church. At a wider denominational event attended by several hundred people, this couple shared housing. Members of their congregation were outraged, in spite of the fact that both are middle-aged, divorced people. Some sought the resignation of the pastor for "unprofessional conduct." While the vast majority of the congregation voted to retain the pastor, the whole congregation experienced months of agony. Eventually, this couple decided to marry, even though they had been quite content with their relationship as it was, living in separate homes in the same community.

How, then, do we assess the situation of the single pastor in light of the framework we have developed above? First, we would note that single pastors will have whatever numinosity and power attend the pastoral role. The fact that they are single does not change the situation. While single women pastors may lack some of the cultural power that men have, they do still have the power of the pastoral role. For this reason alone, we would generally not approve sexual relations between pastor and parishioner, and we would put the burden of proof on the pastor to show that the parishioner could give a valid consent. The fact that the pastor has limited opportunities for dating does not, in itself, change the basic dynamics of power and how they operate to provide an ethical framework.

Single pastors need to be aware that the desire to be coupled, and the pressure from society to do so, presents some problems. We would caution single women pastors in particular about this issue. Women have traditionally been viewed as less than whole when they are single, and these cultural images can have significant negative effect on women pastors. The image of women as temptresses or as sexually available to men can also work to the single woman pastor's detriment. While men in general have more power than women in this culture, the single male pastor also has some disadvantages. Being thought of as either a playboy or celibate male can work against his stature in the church.

However, we do not draw an absolute line. The "normal neurotic" pastor who generally seeks an honorable, intimate relationship with a parishioner may be able to act ethically. We do suggest, however, that structural protections are needed for both the pastor and parishioner. And we caution that even under the most honorable of circumstances, there can be unhappy consequences in the church.

9
In the Closet and Out: Gay and Lesbian Pastors

We turn now to looking at the situation for gay and lesbian pastors. Are there any differences that would suggest that a different ethic is needed? Before we can answer this question, however, there are some definitional problems and complexities that need attention.

PROBLEMS OF DEFINITION AND SOCIAL LOCATION

The situation of one of our respondents will illustrate. This pastor gave a poignant response to one of our questions. He said, "I'm sure I'll carry to the grave a sense of unfulfilled desire to act upon the homosexual self I know I am but manage to keep consciously repressed." This pastor has remained in a monogamous, heterosexual marriage. To his community, he appears to be a contented, heterosexual male. Clearly, he has never acted on his homosexual inclinations. Yet he speaks of "knowing" that he is homosexual. Is he then "gay" because of his internal sense of who he is, even though he is perceived as "straight" by the community around him and does not engage in homosexual relationships?

What does it mean to say that someone is gay or

straight? Is it desire for or simple attraction to the same sex that makes someone gay or lesbian? If someone is attracted to men but also relates to women, is she or he then bisexual? What about the person who does not self-identify as gay or lesbian and yet does have attractions to those of the same sex? Some men, for instance, have sexual relations with other men but would not call themselves gay. Are they gay?

There is no single agreed definition for what makes someone gay or lesbian or bisexual. Sometimes when these terms are used, they refer to the self-definition of the person; sometimes they are a designation given by others. The terms *gay* or *lesbian* can refer to patterns of sexual attraction, or they can refer to a more self-conscious political stance of self-identification.

When we speak of gay or lesbian or bisexual pastors here, we are speaking about those who have identified themselves as such. Their experiences do not necessarily represent the experiences of all gay and lesbian and bisexual people, variously defined.

Moreover, although the term *gay* or *homosexual* is sometimes used to refer both to gay men and to lesbian women, there is considerable evidence and argument today that the gay community and the lesbian community are quite different. They may have different norms for sexual behavior. For example, Mary Hunt writes, "while polygamy is practiced openly by men of some religious (and personal) persuasions, the predominant *articulated* sexual more of lesbian women is monogamy."[1] Hunt acknowledges that there are patterns of nonmonogamy in the lesbian community, and Morris Floyd notes that exclusivity may be on the rise in the gay community, [2] but it probably remains true today that the lesbian community is more inclined to monogamous relationships than the gay male community has been. These differences are important, and it will not suffice to label all gay and lesbian people "homosexual" and expect one ethic for both groups. We will need to look at the lesbian community and at the gay community, and not presume that what holds for one holds for the other.

This is doubly true because lesbians automatically encounter the world as women and may experience their primary oppression not as lesbian but as woman. One of our pastors said, "Lesbians are women first and gay men are men first, and we play out all the other things around being a woman or being a man in the culture." This sentiment is reflected in the litera-ture: "For lesbians, their oppression as lesbians often takes a back seat to their primary oppression as women."[3] Thus, not only are there different issues in sexual ethics for gay and lesbian people, but there are also different issues because of being male or female. For all these reasons, it is important to distinguish these two groups.

Complicating the picture even more is the fact that within each group there will be various subgroups. Some gay or lesbian or bisexual pastors are single; others are partnered or in covenanted relationships. Some, like the pastor quoted above, are closeted and not known to be gay or lesbian; others are out of the closet and known as gay or lesbian, or are partially out and known to at least a few in the church. Some serve predominantly straight congregations; others serve mixed congregations; still others serve in predomi-nantly gay and lesbian congregations such as the Metropolitan Community Church. All these differ-ences will affect the questions and issues with which pastors must deal in their intimate relations.

For example, a closeted lesbian minister who is in a covenanted relationship may nonetheless be seen by her congregation as a single and therefore "available" woman. Because she is perceived as single and straight, even though in fact she is covenanted and lesbian, she will nonetheless encounter many of the issues that single, straight women in ministry encounter—propositions from male parishioners, women trying to "fix her up" with a date, and the like. The situation will be complicated for her, and it will be quite different from the situation of a gay male minister serving in a predominantly gay church.

In short, it is deceptive to think that being gay or lesbian is the only important matter of social location that will affect professional and sexual ethics. Being partnered or not, serving a straight or mixed church, being closeted or not—these and many other factors change the situation. There are thus many permutations to what it means to be a gay or lesbian or bisexual pastor. We cannot deal with all of those here.

We will ask whether the complications and permutations of being gay, lesbian, or bisexual present fundamental challenges to the basic framework we have developed here. We will then assess what modifications, if any, need to be made to accommodate the particular issues that face gay and lesbian pastors in and out of the closet.

THE CHALLENGE

There is some evidence that encountering the world as a gay or lesbian or bisexual person is so fundamentally different from encountering the world as a straight person that it might undermine all generalizations about sexual ethics, including the generalizations we have drawn here about sexual ethics in professional practice.

One of our lesbian pastors noted that the gay and lesbian communities are leery of judging anyone's sexual behavior. This hesitation comes, she suggested, from the fact that "we just can't handle being judged around our sexual behavior because it's been beaten over the head to us." The "beating over the head" arises from two aspects of dominant culture.

First, gay and lesbian people are not seen as full people but are defined only in terms of their sexuality. The same pastor puts it bluntly: "Gay and lesbian people for the most part have learned that we are labeled sexual. That's the extent of what many people think of us. That's who we are [to them]: we are sexual." This exclusive focus on the sexuality of a gay or lesbian person means that the full humanity of gay and lesbian people is denied.

Second, not only are gay and lesbian people defined exclusively in terms of their sexuality, but they are automatically judged negatively for their sexual orientation. The official stance of our culture for a long time has been rejection of homosexual orientation and behavior. Although we know that there have always been people who live in homosexual relationship, and that same-sex love has been a reality in practice, in theory we have long condemned it. Thus, the official stance of the culture toward lesbian women and gay men is a judgmental, condemning stance.

In this context of living under constant negative judgment, lesbian women and gay men become hesitant to accept any judgments about acceptable sexual behavior. Because those in the gay and lesbian communities live so constantly with negative judgments about their sexuality, they are leery about contributing to any negative judgments about other gay and lesbian people's sexual choices. They therefore tend to shy away from rules and proscriptions for sexual behavior.

This sentiment is echoed in the literature on gay men and lesbian women in the church. In his discussion of sexual ethics from a gay male perspective, Morris Floyd asserts: "Gay men and lesbians generally lack norms or systems that might be guides for sexual decision making." Noting that the churches have traditionally rejected and excluded gay male experience and lesbian experience, he suggests that few gay men would turn to churches for behavioral guidelines.[4]

Floyd then articulates why those in gay communities might legitimately reject traditional sexual standards:

> A homophobic and heterosexist culture has made most outlets for expression of gay identity both rare and risky. Genital sexual interaction has, therefore, been for many gay men a primary means of expressing our personal identity. Thus, it should be no surprise that few gay men are anxious to subscribe to *any* system of beliefs or norms that might provide a basis for decision making about sexual activity. . . . To do so would seem to be a surrender of self-definition.[5]

An oppressed community that has had to struggle for its own identity will often find that it has to resist anything from the dominant culture that might be associated with loss of self-definition. Since the dominant culture has defined gay and lesbian people in terms of negative judgments about sexuality, gay and lesbian communities will be understandably reluctant to accept such definitions, for they appear to undermine any sense of self-definition.

Part of such resistance is rejection of traditional norms of sexual behavior, such as monogamy. As Peggy Gaylord puts it in an essay on lesbian sexuality, "Pursuing monogamy might just be another attempt for people of other orientations to try to buy acceptance from heterosexuals."[6] Traditional standards for sexual behavior are suspect because they represent the rejection of one's own sexuality.

In sum, gay and lesbian pastors might very well argue that all norms of traditional sexual ethics do not apply to them because of their status as oppressed people. Lesbian women suffer double oppression, as women and as lesbians. But gay men also suffer an oppression that is not typical of men—at least of white men—in this culture. Indeed, because women are allowed more expressions of physical affection generally in this culture, some would say that lesbian women can more easily blend into the general population, and that homophobia affects gay men more than lesbian women. While we see little point in playing "I'm more oppressed than you are," we do take note of the complexities of the experience of oppression within each group.

Gay men and lesbian women experience both homophobia and heterosexism. They live in a culture that not only fears same-sex attraction (homophobia) but has built a social system around that fear that makes heterosexual relations normative and assigns second-class citizenship to any who do not fit the heterosexual norm (heterosexism). Under such circumstances, all traditional norms for behavior become suspect, because those norms reflect homophobic and heterosexist biases. Thus, some might argue that norms for the general population simply are not applicable to gay men or lesbian women, and that a different ethic is needed.

We take this fundamental challenge seriously. There is good reason to be cautious in applying our framework to those from oppressed communities. We recognize that the experiences of our gay, lesbian, and bisexual pastors, both closeted and noncloseted, will be different from the experiences of straight pastors. These differences are to be taken seriously in developing an ethical framework, and we will return to some of them in a moment.

PERSONAL VERSUS PROFESSIONAL ETHICS

Nonetheless, it is important to note that the resistance to traditional standards of sexual ethics appears to apply more in the realm of sexual ethics and personal behavior than in the realm of professional ethics. For example, one gay male pastor in our study indicated that he has always had multiple sexual partners, even during the time that he has been in a covenanted relationship. Thus, on a personal level, he certainly does not fit the monogamous standards of the dominant culture. But when it comes to his professional life, he says: "I have a mind set that I go into when I'm around church which is that this is not a place where I get my sexual needs met." This pastor deliberately avoids dating people in his church, and he noted that twice he has terminated counseling with parishioners who tried to kiss him at the end of the counseling session.

Similarly, a lesbian pastor told a story about what happened early in her training during a time when she was particularly vulnerable. A parishioner and she were attracted to each other, and the parishioner said she didn't need the woman to be her pastor. They became sexually involved. The pastor writes, "We did sleep together and I felt like I sinned." She concludes that even though she felt "sucked in" by the parishioner's overtures, the decision to enter a sexual relationship as well as any problems arising from that decision "is the clergy's responsibility as a professional."

Thus, from our small sample there is at least some evidence that gay and lesbian pastors set the same limits on professional behavior that most of our straight pastors do. They do not see the church as a place to meet their own needs for sexual intimacy, they draw back from sexual involvement with parishioners, and they judge that involvement wrong when it happens. While the gay and lesbian communities may resist traditional norms for personal sexual ethics, there is no evidence that this spills over into professional practice.

Nonetheless, gay and lesbian pastors might have reason to do some "special pleading," as might single pastors. There are some differences between the situation of the gay or lesbian pastor and the situation of the straight pastor. These differences deserve attention to see if they justify a change in the framework for professional ethics.

FINDING A PARTNER

One of the differences that gay and lesbian pastors point to is the lack of available partners. While this is a problem in general for single pastors, it may be a particular problem for gay or lesbian pastors. If we remember that it is estimated that roughly 10 percent of the population is gay or lesbian, this means that the gay or lesbian pastor has a very small population from which to draw potential sexual partners. Just as straight single pastors might plead for some relaxing of guidelines because of lack of availability of partners, so might lesbian or gay pastors.

Moreover, most gay and lesbian people have left the church—or been forced to leave. This means that the gay or lesbian Christian pastor who would like to find a Christian partner has a *very* small pool from which to draw. As one of our pastors puts it, "the juncture between lesbian and Christian is a rarity. . . . It's very attractive then to find someone who is both." If the lack of availability of sexual partners makes us inclined to be sympathetic toward single pastors in general, then it should incline us to be even more sympathetic toward the gay or lesbian pastor.

With regard to this problem, we note that the genuinely bisexual pastor who is attracted to either men or women does not have the same problem as the pastor who identifies only as gay or lesbian. The pool of possible partners for the bisexual pastor will include both men and women. Therefore it will be considerably larger.

In addition to the limited pool of possible partners, lesbian and gay ministers face another problem: within the context of a homophobic and heterosexist culture, they cannot generally advertise their sexual orientation. With a few exceptions (notably the Metropolitan Community Church), pastors who are known to be gay or lesbian find it very difficult to secure placement in churches. Thus, many remain in the closet in order not to jeopardize their particular jobs or their entire calling into ministry. But being closeted makes it difficult for them to look for suitable partners, since the world around them will assume they are looking for partners of the opposite gender. Not only is the pool of possible partners smaller, therefore, but the pastor is in more of a bind in terms of letting it be known that he or she is looking for a partner and, in particular, for a partner of the same gender.

LACK OF POWER

The next set of reasons for special pleading goes more to the heart of the theoretical framework we have developed here. Just as heterosexual women might argue that they do not have the power that men do, so might lesbian and gay pastors. If issues of intimacy in the parish depend on the power of the pastor, then this changes the ethical picture. If lesbian women and gay men are not on pedestals, if there is not a power gap between the pastor and parishioner in the lesbian or gay communities, then a different sexual ethic might be in order. If their communities understand sexual ethics differently, in a way that diminishes the significance of power differences, then we might allow more latitude for sexual contact between pastor and parishioner.

For example, some would argue that the power gap simply does not exist between lesbian or gay pastors and their parishioners. This may be in part because the lesbian or gay pastor is with a person of the same gender, and so male-female power issues are absent. The power gap between two men or between two women is less than the power gap between a man and a woman in this culture.

It may also be that the lesbian or gay pastor is not put on a pedestal in the same way that traditional straight males have been in the church. Since all oppressed people lack power in the culture to a significant degree, it might be argued that the gay or lesbian pastor, similar to the straight woman pastor, does not have cultural power and therefore does not represent authority in the same way or with the same devastating possibilities that a straight male pastor might. If the power gap between pastor and parishioner is therefore lessened, sexual relations might be more acceptable. For instance, one lesbian pastor who had developed relationships with two parishioners at different times implied that there was an equality in their relationship when she said, "Both of these women had trouble seeing me as their pastor."

Finally, within both lesbian and gay communities, friendships are central and are not so rigidly differentiated from lover relationships as they are in the dominant culture. In response to the question whether she had ever been sexually attracted to a member of the congregation, the same lesbian pastor wrote: "Of course, it's a classic line—'we were friends first'—but we really were, in both cases. . . . And when you're friends with people, it's more likely that you'll become lovers."

It is possible that in both instances, the parishioners had trouble seeing this woman as their pastor because she was a woman and did not fit stereotypes of a pastor. But it is also possible that it was her development of a style of friendship rather than professional distance that led to this diminution of the "pedestal effect."

Many women do use friendship as a style of ministry. In Lynn Rhodes' study of women in ministry, one woman pastor declared:

> Within the congregation I am learning to be friends with people. I know that my well-guarded tendency is to say, "You fool, you'll just get burned." But vulnerability is part of friendship. What I do know is that nothing is to be gained in the old model of power. Without friendship ultimately we have nothing, we gain nothing, we lose everything.[7]

This woman, and other pastors as well, chooses friendship as a model for ministry precisely in order to avoid the power dimensions of the traditional models. They see friendship as risky but ultimately the only way to gain the true gifts of ministry.

Where pastors and parishioners are friends, clergy-lay boundaries are crossed and the pastor is no longer on a pedestal. Friendship, in which both partners are seen with all their faults and foibles, tarnishes the "gold" that might otherwise be attributed to the pastor.

The link between friendship and lover relationships is noted in the lesbian community. "While one night stands are not unknown among lesbians, the more common experience is that women friends become lovers."[8] The movement between friendship and sexual involvement may be accepted more readily in the gay community than it is in the straight community. Moreover, the phenomenon of friends becoming lovers is not limited to the lesbian community. One gay male pastor said, "The situation where this would come up is if a parishioner is a friend—I spend a lot of time with him—then something sexual could happen."

The argument then might be that where lover relationships grow out of friendships, there is not the same power gap as there is in the traditional professional-client relationship; therefore, the pastor who is friends with a parishioner might enter a sexual relationship without violating the vulnerability of the parishioner.

This is demonstrated all the more clearly by a line drawn by the gay male pastor quoted here. Although he makes room for the possibility that "something sexual might happen" with a parishioner who is a friend, he draws an absolute line of prohibition around situations where the parishioner is particularly vulnerable: "If I see someone in a counseling session, I would never have sex with them." This distinction is reminiscent of Marie Fortune's qualification that what made Donovan's actions unethical was that "he was her pastor *and* she *a parishioner seeking counsel.*"[9] As we noted in chapter 5, a distinction might be drawn between the situation in which a parishioner seeks counsel or has a special vulnerability and the situation in which the pastor and parishioner simply work with each other in the mission of the church. Gay and lesbian pastors might distinguish situations of *particular* vulnerability for the parishioner, but might think that under normal circumstances a friendship and even a sexual relationship is possible between pastor and parishioner because the power gap is not unduly great.

Thus, we find two possible challenges to our framework: one on a logistical level, pleading for leniency in guidelines because of the lack of partners, and one on a theoretical level, arguing for leniency in guidelines because of structural differences that make the power gap less between gay pastors and their parishioners or between lesbian pastors and their parishioners.

SOME CAUTIONS

In the face of these challenges, we would raise some cautions drawn from the experiences of pastors.

First, it is not clear that gay and lesbian pastors are off the pedestal. Closeted gay and lesbian pastors will not be known as gay or lesbian ("I appear heterosexual") and therefore are subject to the same "pedestal" effects as are straight pastors. Those who are not closeted may also still be on pedestals.

For gay men in particular, the gay pastor may be a particularly potent symbol. "To some I'm a sexual fantasy. I wear robes and look like a minister. It's highly charged. It's a motif in male sexuality—priest, holy, father," said the pastor of one Metropolitan Community Church. This quote from a gay pastor of an openly gay church suggests that numinosity—the dimension of the holy or mysterious or divine—is still an issue for parishioners of gay clergy.

Thus, gay and lesbian clergy may still be on pedestals, or still represent God. Indeed, it is possible that the stakes are even higher here: precisely because the church has traditionally not accepted gay or lesbian people, to be loved by a gay or lesbian pastor can be an extremely powerful experience. As one lesbian pastor put it, "people can confuse feelings, and unconditional love from the minister can have a romantic feeling." A gay pastor noted that he often counsels lovers who are grieving the loss of their partner to AIDS: "I have lovers of men who have died that have transferred their affection and love to me; I'm very cautious of that."

Transference is a phenomenon for all clergy, not just for gay and lesbian clergy. But because of the emotional traumas associated with being rejected by the church for one's sexual orientation, transference is likely to be a particularly keen issue for lesbian and gay clergy. One lesbian pastor explained a common dilemma: "A lot of people come to me who are gay and lesbian who are alienated from the church. . . . One of the boundary issues at that point is, do I tell them I'm lesbian. Do they want a pastor? Or do they want a bridge back to the church? There's a difference." Choosing what to disclose to a parishioner takes on very special meaning because of the rejection of lesbian and gay people by the church.

One pastor said, "I'm more open about myself with a person who is gay, because that is a sub-culture." This pastor shares more because of feeling that sharing within the subculture is more trustworthy and that his identity as gay is less likely to be divulged. But at the same time, sharing that he is gay is likely to be a powerful experience for the counselee or parishioner. "Coming out" to a parishioner or counselee can be a very powerful experience: it can tell that person that someone whom they admire is also gay or lesbian, it can tell that person that gay and lesbian people have a place in the church, it can tell that person that God loves gay and lesbian people. It can also "up the ante" and increase the stakes for any intimate involvement. "When I do counseling with a gay or lesbian person and I end up coming out to them, the emotional stakes go up enormously." Being accepted as a lesbian or gay person is emotionally very charged because this has not been part of the general cultural or church message.

Thus, gay and lesbian pastors do indeed participate

in some of the "pedestal effect." In fact, because of the rejection of gay and lesbian people by society and by the church, acceptance and love by a lesbian or gay pastor can have a powerful valence. We would caution any lesbian or gay pastor, therefore, not simply to assume that belonging to an oppressed group means that the power of the pastoral role is diminished.

Here, there may be differences between gay male clergy and lesbian clergy. Just as women professionals in general are not as much on a pedestal as are men, so we would expect to find that lesbian pastors are not on a pedestal. And yet, it was one of our lesbian respondents who said, "In the pastoral role you represent authority—the church—even God." While there may be some truth that power gaps are diminished for those who are within an oppressed community or who are relating within one gender instead of across gender lines, still there is evidence for a numinous dimension to pastoral presence. There remains a power gap that must be recognized.

In a similar vein, the black and Hispanic communities in general are oppressed in this culture. But the power of the pastor or priest in these communities is considerable. Thus, belonging to an oppressed community does not, per se, diminish the power of the professional person or leader within that community.

Our second caution has to do with special vulnerabilities that gay and lesbian pastors have. Many if not most gay and lesbian pastors are still closeted, or semicloseted, and therefore are perceived as single and straight. The lesbian pastor may therefore have all the problems we noted in the previous chapter for single women in ministry. For instance, one pastor told this story:

> There have been a couple of men in the congregation I've had some trouble with. One man told me he wanted to

take me to dinner. I got in his car and soon discovered
that he was taking me [to another city]. . . . I told him to
take me home, that I was uncomfortable. He just
assumed that he could date me. He tried to hold my
hand and other stuff.

Here, because the woman minister is perceived as
straight and single, the male parishioner *assumes* some
right of sexual access to her.

Having men assume sexual access is a problem for
most women, and for almost all single women, in
ministry as well as elsewhere in this culture. But it is a
particularly delicate problem for closeted lesbian
women, who often hesitate to say "no" lest they be
discovered as lesbian and lose their jobs. "I would be
a lot more outspoken on a lot of issues if I weren't
afraid of being thrown out," said the pastor who told
this story.

Fears of disclosure and of loss of a job put some
lesbian pastors in a situation of hiding their sexuality
in different ways. The pastor just quoted said she
declines to lead the young adult group, since it is seen
as a singles group and has the potential for putting her
in a very awkward situation. Another pastor indicated
that early in her ministry she gained a lot of weight
and "desexualized" herself. One says that "there is a
game I have to play not to avoid men, not to appear
that I hate men."

For those pastors who are gay or lesbian but are
closeted or semicloseted and therefore perceived as
being straight, dealing with sexuality is a bit like
walking through a mine field. No wonder one of our
respondents said, "I do a lot of avoidance of sexual
issues." Such fear of disclosure can lead pastors to
living almost duplicitous lives—or to denying and
avoiding sexuality not only in the public arena but
internally as well.

It can take a heavy toll on ministry as well. One

pastor spoke eloquently about what happened during his ministry while he was closeted and living with internalized homophobia that kept him from recognizing his own limits:

> I've sufficiently internalized my own homophobia that I could kid myself about my limits for a long time. At my previous parish, I fell in love with a man. He was sexually molesting his children, and I shielded him. I finally confronted myself with what was happening inside me. I was having a lot of fantasies. Once I confronted my own feelings, I was able to let him be taken to jail.

Here, the pastor's hidden homosexual feelings and fantasies contributed to his unwillingness to confront a parishioner who was molesting children. Thus, his ministry was directly affected by what he calls his "complicity" in homophobia.

The framework developed here illumines this dilemma and makes clear that the pastor's failure to protect the child is a violation of professional ethics. It also suggests that gay and lesbian pastors must be wary of the dangers of internalizing heterosexism and homophobia: buying into the prejudices of the society may make them hide their true sexual feelings, and this can severely damage their capacity to do ministry.

Another danger for lesbian or gay pastors comes from the mixed messages they are likely to receive from their churches. Churches often offer a double standard, pretending—or genuinely wanting—to be open and accepting of gay and lesbian people, and yet not being willing to allow the conditions under which gay or lesbian pastors could live a truly normal life.

The paradoxes are well expressed by this pastor: "The bishop says we have to be totally open to gay people, but . . . we can't bless holy unions. He is adamantly opposed to promiscuity, and very supportive of committed relationships, but gay people can't be in them. And then, I ask, how do you find a committed relationship without dating, which the bishop thinks is promiscuous?" The double bind is clear: if gay or lesbian pastors are not allowed to date, how will they find partners for the committed relationships that are the only approved form of sexual relating in the church? And if committed relationships are the only approved form, then why are they not approved for gay or lesbian couples?

Even where churches purport to accept homosexual people and unions, they may undermine those people by buying into stereotypes that assume that any gay pastor who dates is being promiscuous, and undermine those unions by refusing to honor them for the lesbian or gay pastor. One pastor noted that he was almost called to one church, "until they found out I was partnered." He concludes, "it's OK to be gay if you don't do anything about it, so most people pretend."

Because few churches are comfortable with homosexuality, the lesbian or gay pastor is always in danger of being perceived through the eyes of a homophobic and heterosexist culture that assumes that all sexual expressions other than heterosexual monogamous marriage are ipso facto wrong. Thus, an attempt to date may be seen as an attempt to seduce or to change someone else's sexual orientation.

For all of these reasons, therefore, we think that lesbian and gay pastors have special reasons to exercise extreme caution in how they handle their sexuality. Whether they are closeted or out of the closet, whether they are partnered or single, whether they perceive themselves as belonging to an oppressed group and lacking cultural power, they are nonetheless walking in a mine field when it comes to sexual behavior. Being afraid of being thrown out is not only a constant fear, it is a realistic fear, given the homo-phobia of this culture.

STRUCTURAL ISSUES

We suggested in the previous chapter that single heterosexual pastors who want to date parishioners are also walking on dangerous territory, but that there are structural steps they can take to protect both the parishioner and themselves. For example, such steps as ensuring that the parishioner has another pastor or telling a pastor-parish relations committee do not completely resolve the ethical issues, but they do provide at least some protections for the vulnerability of the parishioner and the risk to the pastor.

But gay and lesbian pastors may find that such structural protections as well as other protections on which pastors typically depend do not work well in their case.

For instance, we noted in an earlier chapter that many pastors depend on their spouses not only for internal support but for external protection. Some insist on taking their spouse along for any evening pastoral visits. Some make sure that they introduce the spouse and keep the spouse in visible positions in the church. In particular, a number of our male pastors indicated how central their marriages have been in helping them not to cross boundaries.

This protection will be missing for many lesbian or gay pastors, even if they are partnered. Several made clear that they hid their partnerships in order not to be known as lesbian or gay. One woman pastor told a poignant story of not being able to share with the congregation her extreme joy when her partner gave birth. The need to be closeted undermines the ability to depend on covenanted relationships as an external

check and balance, since it means that the congregation often does not know that there is a covenanted
relationship.

Similarly, we argued that the single pastor who
wants to date a parishioner might be able to set up a
protective structure by telling the pastor-parish relations committee. But for closeted gay or lesbian
pastors, this would mean coming out of the closet by
revealing their sexual orientation. One lesbian pastor
told the story of what happened when she decided to
come out of the closet to someone with whom she was
counseling, because of being sure that the woman
was herself lesbian: "I once came out to a woman who
I knew was gay, who said, 'Gee, it must be hard to be
a lesbian pastor.' I was left hanging naked in the
desert." Even coming out to a person who is gay or
lesbian is not necessarily safe for the pastor.

Thus, structural arrangements that might work to
provide some protection for both pastor and parishioner in the heterosexual situation do not always work
for the gay or lesbian pastor. The gay or lesbian pastor
serving a Metropolitan Community Church might be
able to utilize the mechanism of telling a pastor-parish
relations committee or some other relevant board in
the church. So might the rare pastor who is able to be
openly gay in a typical mainline church. But for the
bulk of lesbian, gay, and bisexual pastors, such
structural protections are not likely to be feasible.

While lesbian and gay pastors are correct to understand that sexual ethics differ in oppressed communities, we see no evidence that these differences are
strong enough to change the framework for professional ethics that we have developed here. Friendship
may be a common pattern between gay or lesbian
pastors and their parishioners, but it does not destroy
the numinous dimension of the pastor. Indeed, precisely because the lesbian or gay pastor is dealing with

a particularly vulnerable population, for whom their sexuality has been at the core of being rejected by church and society, the stakes are higher and the potential for damage from an intimate relationship is great. For all these reasons, we do not think that the lesbian or gay pastor can claim exemption from the general prohibition of pastor-parishioner sexuality. We are inclined to agree with the lesbian pastor who had one relationship with a parishioner which she later concluded was wrong. She reflects: "the questions are not hetero or homo, but about how we live out our sexuality."

10
The "Bishop's" Dilemma

The main purpose of this volume has been to establish an ethical framework for understanding pastor-parishioner sexuality. We have attempted to look at both the positive gifts that sexuality brings into the practice of ministry and the boundaries of acceptable sexual contact between pastor and parishioner. We have looked at the power of the pastor and the vulnerability of the parishioner. We have asked whether pastors whose power is diminished or who practice in difficult circumstances should receive dispensation for entering into sexual relations with parishioners.

Throughout this discussion, we have stressed the need for structural protections. We have argued that sexual acting-out is not just a personal problem of the pastor but is a structural issue that demands attention to the practices of ministry and to the cultural expectations of our society. In *Ministry and Sexuality*, Lloyd Rediger argues that the most significant factors that contribute to clergy sexual acting-out are changes in the clergy role in church and society.[1] We agree that issues of role are central.

But this means that clergy sexuality is not just a matter for individual pastors to decide. It is also a matter for denominational adjudicatory bodies. In this chapter, we turn from a focus on the pastor to a focus on denominational structures. We use the term *bishops* in a generic sense to refer to those denominational officials who are responsible for structures, procedures, rules, and regulations within a denomination. Our concern here is for the responsibility of those who represent the denominations.

Bishops are generally responsible for the well-being of pastors and churches. They are often "pastors to the pastor," the ones to whom pastors turn for their own pastoral care. And they are also the watchdog for the institutional church, charged with responsibility to make sure that pastors do their work well and that pastors' behavior is ethical. While not all these functions are carried on by a single individual, and each denomination will structure these important aspects of its polity slightly differently, in this discussion we will use the single term *bishop* to refer to the range of positions or offices that would typically have these responsibilities in various denominations.

Bishops have come under attack lately. In *Is Nothing Sacred?* Marie Fortune offers a scathing critique of the way institutional churches deal with offending pastors. Churches protect their own, she charges. They cover up, sweep the problem under the rug, and move the pastor to a new parish. They blame the victim, shoot the messenger, and misname the problem.[2] Because so many of those in power in churches are men, they tend to side with the male pastor and refuse to believe the women's stories.

Similarly, in *Sex in the Forbidden Zone,* Peter Rutter argues that professional organizations and their responsible officials have been singularly reluctant to deal with sexual violations in the forbidden zone. It is not difficult, he suggests, to understand why sexual violation occurs, but "it was far more difficult to understand why so many of us, bystanders and victims alike, had remained silent in the face of these violations."[3] As noted above, he suggests that male colleagues all too often refuse to bring charges against an offending colleague because they harbor a secret jealousy and envy of the forbidden act.

It is important, then, that we look not only at pastors but also at denominational officials. What should they do when there are hints or accusations of sexual misconduct on the part of a pastor? How should structures be established to deal with these issues? What are the ethical dilemmas faced by the bishop, and how should they be resolved? What happens when a boundary is crossed and a whistle blown?

In order to illustrate the bishop's dilemma, we return to the story of Robert. In fact, Robert's history of sexual involvement with women in several churches he served has never become public knowledge. His past actions have never "blown up" in his face. No one has ever brought charges against him, or accused him publicly of unethical conduct. Robert has been lucky!

Let us assume that someone does bring accusations of unethical conduct. Suppose that this happens during the time that Robert and Adele are making a decision to divorce, and he is seeing Sandy. Let us further suppose that Robert's denomination has had the foresight to put in place a set of procedural guidelines similar to those in Appendix A. Thus, when the whistle is blown on Robert, his bishop is not in the position of having to make up every step along the way, as were the denominational officials described in Fortune's *Is Nothing Sacred?* The guidelines offered in Appendix A are procedural guidelines. They do not attempt to state with precision just what constitutes unethical conduct on the part of the pastor; rather, they assume that such a statement will

come out of the discernment of the community
through the procedures instituted. In our discussion,
we will offer more substantive suggestions that might
help those following the procedural guidelines. In
doing so, we draw on the ethical framework developed in chapter 5.

We will further suppose that the whistle is blown
on Robert not by Sandy, but by someone else in the
church. As the concern is presented, then, it is not a
woman calling to say she has been used or treated
unethically by the pastor, but a third party who is
distressed about what he or she thinks is going on in
the church. Perhaps it is the moderator or chief lay
person in the church who calls the bishop and
declares: "our pastor, Reverend Robert, has left his
wife and is having an affair with a member of the
congregation." What should the bishop do?

We think that the answer to this question will make
clear that the crossing of a professional boundary is
not just a personal or interpersonal act. There are
important questions to be asked about the relationship between Robert and Sandy, and whether she can
give consent to sexual relations between them, and
whether professional trust has been violated by
Robert becoming sexually involved with her. But
these are not the only important questions. There are
consequences not only for Robert and Sandy, but for
Robert's wife, Adele, for the local congregation that
Robert serves, and for the wider church. The bishop
has responsibility for all these parties. By looking at
the dilemma the bishop faces, we can begin to
understand the complexity of the larger covenants
that are involved when pastors are accused of sexual
misconduct.

We cannot answer here all the questions that might
be raised about what the bishop should do, nor can
we explore all the ramifications of Robert's actions.

What we will do is to focus on several of the ethical issues in order to illumine the structural aspects of the situation and suggest some ordering of principles and priorities. The particular dilemmas encountered by the bishop will depend on the circumstances: who brings the charges of unethical behavior, what evidence can be garnered, whether there is any evidence of past behavior of a similar nature, and so on. Our exploration here is, of necessity, limited by the circumstances of the hypothetical case we propose. Even within those limited circumstances, we cannot resolve all the substantive issues. We think, however, that the exploration will illumine the usefulness of having in place both procedural guidelines such as those proposed in Appendix A and substantive ethical reflection such as that offered in the preceding chapters.

DID IT HAPPEN?

The dilemmas faced by the bishop when informed of a possible breach of professional ethics fall roughly into two categories: determining whether something unethical has happened, and determining what to do about it if it has. Each of these is complicated, and can be illustrated by the hypothetical case of the church moderator blowing the whistle on Robert.

Determining that something unethical has happened is no easy task. It is partly for that reason that the procedural guidelines offer several steps: the bishop makes an initial determination as to whether there is sufficient grounds for a more full investigation, and if so, committees and other structures are brought into play.

In the case at hand, for example, the moderator claims that Robert has "left his wife" and is "having an affair." But when the bishop calls Robert, he gets a different story: Robert claims that he has not "left"

Adele, but rather that he and Adele have made a mutual agreement to separate. He also claims that he is not "having an affair" with Sandy, but that he is in love with her and intends to marry her. Further, he claims that they did not become sexually involved until after he and Adele separated. Although Robert acknowledges that he is not technically divorced, he considers himself divorced in the moral sense of the term and therefore considers himself a single person for all intents and purposes. He sees nothing wrong with his relationship with Sandy, whom he considers a competent adult who has willingly entered into a relationship with him. In Robert's eyes, he has done nothing wrong, because he did not have an "affair" while still "married" in a moral sense.

Already, the bishop has a dilemma. Two versions of the story are being told. Whose is to be believed? Is Robert telling the truth about not being sexually involved with Sandy until after he separated from Adele? And was that separation really a mutual decision? Even if those things are true, the sexual relationship with Sandy may still appear to the church to be an "affair," since Robert is still technically married. What understanding of marriage and divorce should guide the bishop's actions?

To complicate matters, the church is beginning to talk. Rumors are flying. Sandy is accused of being a homewrecker. Adele is hurt and angry and is feeding those rumors. Moreover, Adele begins to make public the fact that Sandy is not the first woman with whom Robert has had sexual relations outside their marriage. Sandy is hurt and angered by these revelations and by the way she is being ostracized by church members. She has no one to turn to outside of Robert. Suspicion and distrust are growing on all sides in the church. Ascertaining what happened in the midst of accusations and counteraccusations is no easy matter.

In this case, we will assume the bishop is inclined to believe that Robert and Sandy are indeed sexually involved, but that Robert entered this relationship only after he genuinely saw no hope for his marriage and understood himself to be divorced in the moral sense of the term. The bishop understands that Robert thinks he is genuinely in love with Sandy and that he will marry her after his divorce from Adele is final. In short, the bishop is inclined to believe Robert.

At this point, we would raise a caution for the bishop. The bishop must be wary of assuming that pastors can do no wrong and are always to be believed. The bishop, if male, must be wary of falling into the trap of the "good old boys" network in which males protect males to the detriment of females. In this particular case, the accusation of unethical conduct did not come from the woman with whom the pastor was involved; it came from a third party. But if Sandy herself had accused Robert of unethical conduct, we would think it imperative that her voice be heard and her perspective honored. Female victims of sexual exploitation by clergy have traditionally found local church leaders and denominational officials very reluctant to take seriously their claims. The wall of disbelief and indifference that often answers their appeals for help and for justice has perpetuated a pattern of silence that in turn has prolonged the suffering of an untold number of persons in the church.

Thus, the bishop faces at the outset an epistemological dilemma: whose perspective on truth is to be taken seriously? It is partly because of alternative versions of what happens that it is important to provide structures so that no single person, including the bishop, has the power to discount any voice. We would argue on theological grounds that the perspective of the oppressed or marginalized should count most heavily. If the charge of unethical conduct were brought by a woman who claimed that she was victimized herself, then we think the bishop must take that charge with utmost seriousness. And there must be committee structures or other backup structures such as adequate record keeping to ensure that the bishop does so.

WAS IT UNETHICAL?

But even if the bishop can determine what has actually happened, this will not solve the dilemma of whether it was unethical. We think the answer to this issue involves at least three considerations: Adele's position as Robert's spouse, Robert's position as pastor and his personal relationship with Sandy, and the consequences for the church of Robert's actions.

Nearly all church people would consider it inappropriate for a married pastor to have an affair because of the harm to the spouse and the violation of the covenant of marriage, which is usually understood to include a commitment to sexual fidelity. Even here, however, there is room for disagreement: members of the Professional Ethics Group were once castigated for assuming that "open marriage" is a thing of the past. Not all couples do assume sexual fidelity as central to the marriage commitment. But here, we can assume that Robert and Adele began their marriage with an understanding that sexual exclusivity was part of their covenant. To have an affair, then, would be a violation of covenant. Adele clearly accuses Robert of having had several affairs and thus of violating their marriage covenant.

At the same time, Adele admits that she and Robert have talked of divorce for some time and had agreed to separate on a trial basis. Although they still share the same house, they no longer have sexual relations.

They will move into separate accommodations as quickly as it can be arranged. While still legally married, they have agreed to terminate their marriage covenant and consider themselves separated. While Adele accuses Robert of having had several affairs in the past, she wavers on whether or not Robert's current relationship with Sandy constitutes an "affair" that violates a marriage covenant. Robert clearly thinks it does not.

With regard to the issue of Adele and the marriage covenant, then, the bishop and any committee that investigates the matter must make two decisions: first, whether Robert's current relationship with Sandy does in fact constitute a violation of his marriage covenant, and second, whether such a violation would constitute grounds for disciplinary action on the basis of *professional* ethics. It may be unethical for Robert to have an affair, but it is not necessarily a matter of professional ethics that should come under the purview of the bishop or committee. Our focus in this volume is not on all kinds of unethical conduct, but on questions of ethical conduct *as a professional*.

What makes Robert's conduct a matter of professional ethics is the fact that Robert is relating sexually to a parishioner. This is the question on which we focus. In this context, our discussion of the framework for ethical sexual conduct makes clear that we would find any exploitive or abusive behavior wrong. If Robert had lied to Sandy, or attempted to force sexual relations on her, his actions would be clearly unethical.

Moreover, even without these extremes, there are problems. Any sexual contact with a parishioner (unless that parishioner is already one's spouse) is characterized by an inequality of power between the parties. This inequality of power is ethically problematic and puts the burden of proof on the minister to demonstrate that a valid consent could be given by the parishioner. In no case would we think that a valid consent could be given where the parishioner has been in a special relationship of counseling or where the parishioner is facing particular vulnerabilities such as death or grieving. Thus, if Sandy and Robert became romantically and sexually involved following or during a time of special counseling around issues such as grief or loss, then we would judge Robert's actions unethical.

In this case, then, Robert's claim that he is morally if not technically "single" does not settle the issue of whether his behavior with Sandy is ethical. The bishop would want to know whether Sandy had come to Robert for counseling over some special vulnerability. The bishop would want to know whether Robert has been using Sandy to meet his own needs, and whether he has been exploiting her vulnerability or her admiration for his role as pastor.

When questioned, Robert justified his two previous affairs by pointing to his failing marriage and claiming that his affairs met needs, which enabled him to continue working to improve the marriage while being an effective minister. He used the largely psychological category of "meeting my needs" to justify his actions. When the appropriateness of his relationship with Sandy was questioned, he became angry and argued that such a "special friendship" was necessary to his own emotional health. He further believed that, so far as any lovers were concerned, mutual consent was enough to justify his actions. His partners were mature adults in his view, and they understood what they were doing. He denied that any power differential was at work in his relationship with Sandy, because she was herself a professional family therapist and therefore a professional equal.

We have already argued in chapter 5 that consent under such circumstances is highly questionable, and it is likely that Robert's lovers did not fully understand the risks to them and were not fully free to consent or refuse, in spite of being mature adults. The issue is not whether they were psychologically mature, but whether the structures within which they entered a relationship with Robert undermined their capacity to consent. Where a female parishioner enters a sexual relationship with a male pastor, we have reason to think that there is a large structural power gap, and that this power gap is morally relevant.

Further, Robert's language of "meeting my needs" appears to suggest that he is using the women to meet his own needs. This would be a violation of professional ethics in which the professional is to meet the needs and be focused on the welfare of the client, as so many of our respondents noted. Although Robert undoubtedly thinks of himself as being in love with these women, or at least as loving them, his language suggests that he is using them. Thus, even if we concede to Robert that he is "single" for ethical purposes, we are not ready to concede that he has acted ethically. The bishop and review committees will have to assess whether his relationship with Sandy violates standards for professional ethics in the sexual arena.

Finally, there is the matter of the church. In several of our surveys the question of responsibility to the larger church body or congregation was ignored by many respondents. But among the most serious consequences of any breach of professional ethics are the consequences for the "body of Christ," both in the form of the local congregation and in the form of the larger church.

Whenever a pastor is accused of inappropriate sexual conduct within a church, the bonds of trust between that pastor and the congregation are stretched to the breaking point. The focus of attention within the congregation shifts from the worship of God and the mission that flows out of that worship and begins instead to concentrate on the behavior of the pastor and of church members. In the current case, all eyes are watching Sandy, Robert, and Adele. Some are accusing Sandy of being a tramp; others accuse Adele of not being a good enough wife; a few turn their anger on Robert himself. The energy and spirit of the church is siphoned off into accusations and counteraccusations. Sides are taken, factions formed. The mission of the church suffers.

These changes are costly to the spiritual health of the congregation and very costly to the mission of the church as a whole. Many congregations have been split by such occurrences, although a few do weather the storm. But a storm it is, and the bishop has a significant task in trying to hold together a divided church and work toward setting the church back on track to deal with its primary purpose of worship and mission.

To think of the question of sexual conduct on an interpersonal level only is therefore to ignore one of the dimensions that can make sexual behavior wrong: the good of the whole congregation. Adele is not the only one with whom Robert has a covenant. He also has a covenant with the church, both with the local congregation and with the wider body of Christ. This is part of what it means to be ordained and called. This covenant is at stake in his behavior just as much as his covenant with Adele may be at stake. This covenant should also be part of the equation when pastors are considering their behavior and when that behavior is reviewed by bishops or committees. The breaking of covenant with a church is a serious matter. Churches are not above criticism, and pastors are certainly entitled to stand in prophetic criticism against the church. Nonetheless, even prophetic criticism takes place within a larger framework of covenant.

In assessing whether Robert's behavior is unethical in a manner that raises questions about professional ethics, then, the bishop will want to consider Robert's marriage covenant, Robert's professional position, and Robert's covenant with the church.

WHAT SHOULD HAPPEN?

Whether the bishop and committees decide that Robert's behavior was unethical or merely unfortunate, the bishop faces a serious question as to what should happen now to Robert. No matter whose version of the situation is taken as true and what judgment is made about whether Robert has acted unethically, the situation has serious ramifications for Robert's future in ministry and for the church. The procedural guidelines offered in Appendix A provide for a range of possible consequences to Robert, from disciplinary rebuke to expulsion from ministry. In our judgment, what action should be chosen from this range depends on whether Robert is classified as an "offender," a "wanderer," or a "normal neurotic," as defined in chapter 5.

Robert would no doubt claim that he is a "normal neurotic," a pastor functioning well in general who has happened to fall in love with a parishioner. He would argue that his intentions toward Sandy are entirely honorable, and that he will marry her as soon as his divorce is final. In fact, we know that Robert did marry Sandy, and therefore in retrospect there may be some force in this claim. But at the time the bishop must make a decision, she or he would not yet know what will eventually happen. Whether Robert will in fact marry Sandy, or whether he will go on to "wander" into another relationship and then another, is still an open question.

If Robert is a "normal neurotic," then it is not likely that he will repeat this behavior again. Thus, although the current church is undoubtedly damaged, possibly even severely, by going through this crisis, there would be no reason that Robert could not serve well in another church. Removing a "normal neurotic" from one church setting and placing that pastor into another church may be the best solution all around: it protects the current church and provides some space for healing to happen, but it also allows the pastor to continue in his calling and to utilize his gifts for ministry.

If, on the other hand, Robert is an "offender," then we would judge that Robert should simply be removed from ministry altogether. The offender not only uses other people solely for his own purposes but also uses deception and coercion in the manner of "Rev. Peter Donovan" in *Is Nothing Sacred?* The offender will repeat these actions in other church settings and therefore should never again be allowed to practice as an ordained minister.

In our judgment, Robert is not an offender. Although he has had several affairs with women in the churches he has served, he is not sociopathic. We judge him a "wanderer," who falls into relationships when things are not going well and who has some boundary problems. Thus, in our judgment, his case falls in between that of the normal neurotic and that of the offender. He should neither simply be moved to a new church setting nor simply be removed from ministry altogether. Rather, the bishop and committees will have a difficult decision to make in trying to balance responsibility for the church against responsibility for the well-being of the pastor. Robert should undoubtedly be removed from this particular church. But whether he should be moved to another congregation is more difficult, since his pattern of "wandering" suggests that he may in fact repeat his behavior.

At this point, no doubt some would recommend that Robert enter counseling. This is a common response of denominations to pastors who act out sexually or in other ways. As Robert himself notes, however, much current counseling is not helpful for these kinds of cases. Other pastors have also noted the limitations of traditional counseling and have urged that wandering pastors undergo a twelve-step program based on a model of overcoming addiction. While not all sexual acting-out is necessarily a form of addiction, something along the lines of an addictive model is more appropriate in these cases than is much of traditional counseling.

We note also that Robert indicated he did not have affairs with women while he was in an alternative form of ministry. The bishop should pay attention to the structures within which ministry will be practiced and should consider encouraging placement for Robert in structures that minimize the dangers of intimacy in the parish. For example, Robert could have a supervisor for his counseling with women. He could also change his practice and do only family counseling, in which three or more persons are always present. Such structures might minimize the temptations for inappropriate intimacy in the parish. Or he might be encouraged to seek a non-parish setting.

Whether the bishop will judge that Robert can be placed in another parish depends in part on how each denomination assesses the balance of concerns for the pastor against concerns for the well-being of the church, and what kinds of structural protections for all parties can be brought to bear.

TRUTH TELLING AND HEALING

No matter what decision is made about Robert, all parties need to have an opportunity for a fair hearing and for healing and reconciliation. To that end, we urge the adoption of procedural guidelines such as those proposed in Appendix A. While these may seem cumbersome at first, they are intended to provide structural protections and opportunity for data gathering and fair procedures for all parties. They help the bishop assure protection for persons who may be victimized by clergy, for example, by providing for a separate advocate for women who bring allegations against a pastor, so that the women's concerns are genuinely heard and publicly honored.

Above all, truth telling is a necessary condition for healing for everyone involved. Sexual exploitation of parishioners carries with it many of the same dynamics as those experienced by families in situations of incest. Frequently there is denial on the part of some members of the congregation who cannot believe any wrongdoing on the part of the pastor. These people will justify prevailing patterns of secrecy because they want to protect the congregation from shame. As a consequence of this pattern, many ministers have been moved quietly from parish to parish.

When this happens, healing is thwarted. Typically the pastor not only carries the secret of past behavior but also carries the pattern into present and future behavior. Thus, the pastor receives no healing, because he is not forced to seek help or to confront and acknowledge patterns of behavior.

The victims receive no healing, because their hurt remains unacknowledged and therefore untreated. Unless truth is told, no one will ever say "we are sorry" to the victims. Nor, as Marie Fortune points out, will they be thanked for the risks they take in exposing wrongdoing.[4] Their sense of shame or guilt goes untreated. Their anger gets repressed. They are not offered the grace and love that they are due, and they may carry emotional and spiritual wounds that fester for years. The church is no longer a safe place for them. Sanctuary is now unavailable to persons who desperately need it. Their experience tells them that clergy can no longer be trusted. Typically, no professional person of the same gender as the perpetrator will ever again be trusted. They carry a deep anger toward the church for not being believed and for not having their hurts honored.

Truth also needs to be spoken for the sake of those women who may not see themselves as victims. Sandy was not the one who brought complaints about Robert, and, at least at the outset, would not see herself as being victimized by him. No doubt she feels more victimized by the church's reaction to her. But it is also important that the issues get aired, so she can consider her own situation of relative powerlessness and can ask herself whether she trusts the dynamics that are operating in her relationship with Robert. Sadly, all too often a woman does not protest when a relationship with a pastor begins, but later she feels used (especially when she learns that there have been other affairs, or if the anticipated marriage does not come about). Because she did not protest at the outset, she may feel that she has no right to protest later. While this is not true, it is a dynamic that operates for many women and that blocks their healing.

Among the victims who need truth we might also count the spouse and family of the pastor. In this case, Adele is participating in the innuendo circulating around the church. She needs a forum in which her complaints and allegations about previous affairs can be heard legitimately, but where they can also be

countered and put into proper context. When ministers are simply moved to a new setting without an
honest airing of issues, the minister's family members
are unable to explain why the move has come about or
to get their own pains honored. The spouse carries a
particular burden. If a spouse has been wronged, that
needs to be acknowledged. If a spouse has par-
ticipated in name-calling or in hurting another, the
spouse needs an opportunity for reparation and
reconciliation.

Without truth, the congregation also receives no
healing. Carrying a deep secret fosters the habit of
keeping secrets and of leaving hurts untreated. Hon-
esty is buried, and the church becomes a dysfunctional community. Truth, one of the most cherished
notions of the faith, is abandoned in favor of appear-
ances. The power of grace in repentance and forgiveness is lost to the very community that proclaims this
power as its reason for being. A paralyzing layer of
fear blankets the people and prevents them from
living with the confidence that "love conquers all."
Without truth, distrust will live and fester in the
community. Some will find it hard to trust another
pastor, and a new pastor walking into that congregation may not understand the complicated dynamics
behind problems that arise.

The guidelines that are adopted by denominations
should account for all these consequences. The importance of a process that allows truth to surface—or at
least provides a forum for alternative views to be
heard genuinely—cannot be overstressed.

THE WIDER CHURCH

If the bishop determines that Robert is a wanderer
or a normal neurotic, not an offender, and that it is
therefore possible for Robert to continue in ministry in

some capacity, this does not end the ethical dilemmas. What should a bishop say to a search committee or to a bishop from another region when a church is interested in Robert as a potential minister?

Under the best scenario, Robert himself should be encouraged to share with his potential new church what has happened to him and how he is setting up structures to make sure that it does not happen again. Doing so may mean that a church or bishop gets nervous and decides not to call or place Robert with that church. There is a risk. But if Robert can begin a new ministry setting with a clean slate, and with structures in place to help him avoid any future difficulties, this is the best beginning. A covenant of disclosure and consultation might be established with the church board or with a "pastor-parish relations committee" in the church. This covenant should be a three-way covenant, involving the pastor, the church, and the bishop. It should specify clearly what is expected of whom, and what steps will be taken should anyone suspect that untoward behavior is occurring.

In Robert's case, the bishop who assisted him in finding placement in this church had heard rumors that he had previously engaged in extramarital relations. However, not until Adele began to make some of that information public did the bishop know whether to credit those rumors. The grapevine is not a particularly reliable source of information. How is the bishop to discern truth from vicious rumor? Should the bishop have shared rumors with the church prior to placing Robert? To do so would almost certainly have cost Robert that placement, and might very well have done so based on unfounded rumor. No charges had ever been brought against Robert by any of the women with whom he was involved, nor had Adele at any previous time sought to expose Robert's history.

The handling of rumor and the obligation to be truthful in the search process is one of the most difficult ethical dilemmas the bishop will face. After hearing about Robert's previous affairs, the chairperson of the search committee that called him complained to the bishop. "We should have been told," she said. "Now we feel betrayed by our denomination, and we will never again trust the denominational placement system to give us the whole truth about candidates." Congregations expect to be told if their prospective pastor has a history of destructive behavior. Yet, the bishop will hesitate to pass on information that was received through rumor and cannot be substantiated.

Such dilemmas would be minimized if all denominations in all regions adopted a policy of truthfulness and procedural guidelines designed to ensure that voices could be adequately heard. Current legislation in some states, and legal suits brought against denominational officials in others, are clarifying the obligation of bishops to warn congregations if a pastor has previously been charged with inappropriate conduct. For example, Minnesota has recently passed a statute providing that an employer of a psychotherapist (including clergy) may be liable for failing to ascertain whether there is a history of inappropriate sexual contact with clients and also for failing to take action where such a history is known or should be known.[5] We recommend as policy that the bishop respond and follow through on all rumors of sexual misconduct on the part of pastors. Such response will help to protect both the possible victims and also the good name of a pastor who has not engaged in misconduct.

The bishop will also have to counsel the congregation with some care regarding the selection of a successor for Robert. Where possible, we recommend that a woman be considered as his successor, in order to allow for healing within the church and to allay suspicions about the behavior of the next pastor.

Nowhere is the power of the pastoral office more clearly illustrated than when that power is abused through inappropriate sexual conduct. The whole church is affected: the pastor, the pastor's family, the parishioner(s), the local congregation, and the wider church. The whole church, including denominational offices and institutions of theological education, must work together to prepare for ministry people who understand the dimensions of this power and who are prepared to be good stewards of it. Confronting the fact that it is an issue of power is the first step. Having adequate structures and procedures is the second step.

Conclusion

"My theology of sexuality is in little pieces, like pieces of a puzzle that I haven't put together." This is the pastor's lament with which we started this volume. Our search has been for an ethics of sexuality in the parish. That search does not put all the pieces of the puzzle together, nor does it provide a full theology of sexuality. But it does begin to suggest the shape of a picture for sex in the parish.

It is a picture of joy and danger, of power and vulnerability, of covenant and struggle, of role and responsibility. It is a picture in which sexuality can be used in the service of God, and the power of the pastoral role can be understood and brought into covenant with the congregation. It is a picture in which the church can be a "safe place" and people can trust pastors and open their lives. It is a picture of denominational officials taking seriously their role as pastor to the pastor but also as watchdog for the church.

In building that picture, we have tried to hold together insights from psychology, sociology, and theology. Ethical dimensions are elaborated by integrating these sources and reasoning our way through dilemmas.

THE PARADOX

Sexuality is powerful, and precisely because it is powerful, it becomes an arena for particular concern in ministry, where we deal with people's spirits. Sexuality misused has the capacity to destroy all that is trustworthy, holy, and true. There can be no worse event in human life than to feel that one has lost God. And this is precisely the feeling that so many women have when they are sexually abused by a pastor. Because of the representative role of the pastor, to be betrayed or used by the pastor is to be betrayed or used by the church and even by God. Thus, on the one hand, it is absolutely essential that churches and ministers develop an ethical framework to prevent and control sexual abuse. This must be a number-one priority.

On the other hand, we are not content with approaches to the problem that simply assume that sexual acting-out is a sign of inadequate ministerial character. Our analysis in the preceding chapters demonstrates that character is not all that is at issue. Until such time as women are genuinely equal with men in our culture, there will be power differentials between men and women that raise ethical questions. These power differentials exist because of sexism, and they are not overcome by the efforts of any one person or pastor. Until such time as patterns of child rearing in our culture are changed, it is likely that men will tend to genitalize their deep feelings. These patterns are cultural patterns, not weaknesses of character of a few misfit pastors. In order to develop healthy patterns of sexual relating in the church, the cultural patterns have to be changed.

To say this is not to exonerate the male pastor who acts out sexually. The offender who preys on women must be stopped. The wanderer who goes from relationship to relationship must also be stopped. Both will do irreparable damage. Even the normal neurotic whose intentions are honorable must bear the burden of proof that there is no power differential that invalidates the parishioner's consent. Structures are needed to ensure that pastors' behavior is ethical. So we do not excuse the pastor. But we do recognize that behavior is not separable from culture, and that there are patterns in the culture that need to be changed.

At one and the same time, we must understand both the devastation wreaked by inappropriate sexual conduct on the part of clergy and the very human elements that engender that inappropriate conduct. When sexual misconduct happens, it is difficult to talk about having empathy for the women who are abused without appearing to condemn and blame men. It is difficult to talk about having sympathy for the male pastor without appearing to belittle and deny the pain of the women. Yet this is precisely the paradox with which we must work, for we are convinced that only by trying to understand all the dynamics at work can we arrive at an adequate ethical framework. An adequate ethical framework must hear the pain of women who are victimized without jumping to simplistic conclusions about men who act out.

THE FRAMEWORK

Throughout this discussion, two issues have loomed large. The first is the pastoral role and the power that attaches to it. The framework we offer here is largely based on understanding that being a pastor means carrying the power that attends that office: both the power one has as a professional person and the more specific power of the pastor in the spiritual arena. It is because of the significance of this power that pastor and parishioner are never simply equals who can consent to sexual involvement. Popular images of pastors today tend to emphasize the humanity of the pastor. This emphasis may make us ignore the very real power that goes with the role of pastor.

The other issue that has loomed large for us is the question of institutional structures. Under this term we include not only specific institutions such as churches and how they are constituted and governed, but also larger cultural issues. The images that we hold of what it is to be adequately male or female, the specific ways that we come to understand our sexuality—these are socially constructed and culturally conditioned. No framework for ethical analysis of sex in the parish would be adequate if it did not attend to these questions. To point blaming fingers at a pastor is not the appropriate response to the problem of sex in the parish. While we would put responsibility on the pastor, we do so precisely because of the pastor's role. However, we also understand that the role of pastor and the pastor's own experience of her or his sexuality are conditioned by a culture that develops addictive, sexist, and other unhealthy patterns of sexual relating. These are to be deplored, to be sure. But they are at root structural problems, and it would not be realistic to assume that the answer to a structural problem lies in admonitions about the character of the minister.

THE CONTRIBUTION

We are at root in agreement with Rutter that professional-client relations are a "forbidden zone" for sexuality. Like Rutter, we locate the grounds for that forbidden zone in the power of the professional and the vulnerability of the client. Yet our argument departs from his. Rutter takes as his model the one-on-one situation typical for counseling and therapy. Although he extends his argument to include teachers, lawyers, and ministers as well as doctors and therapists, he clearly has in mind the situation of the professional who works very closely with an individual client in situations where the deepest sorts of intimacy and self-revelation are expected on the part of the client.

The practice of ministry sometimes has this character. But much of a pastor's work has more the character of being a co-worker in a cause. Pastor and parishioner work together in the mission of the church, just as co-workers might work together for the good of a company. Pastor and parishioner are colleagues who work side by side, not just professional and client who work in hierarchical relationship. To be sure, we have argued that the power of the pastor should never be ignored. But we also make room for the possibility that pastor and parishioner might meet as co-workers for whom sexual involvement is risky but not impossible. The burden of proof of this equality of power is always on the pastor, and we suggest structural protections for both parishioner and pastor. Within these limits, nonetheless, we would find some exceptions to the forbidden zone. Here, we are closer to some of the nuances found in Marie Fortune's arguments.

At the same time, the pastor has a covenant not just with the individual parishioner (nor just with a spouse) but also with the congregation and wider church. Decision making about one's sexuality is not only a question of protecting the trust and vulnerability of the individual parishioner. It is also a matter of honoring covenant and furthering the mission of the church. One of the saddest results of sexual acting-out on the part of the pastor is deflecting the energy of the church away from its mission in the world.

With Fortune, we agree on the importance of consent to sexual relations, and on the way in which professional power undermines the equality and mutuality necessary for valid consent. Indeed, a more thorough examination of the elements of consent than is offered by Fortune begins to suggest precisely why some consents are inadequate, even when the people involved appear to be "consenting adults." Moreover, attention to the specific vulnerability of the sexual arena shows why consent to sexual involvement might not be acceptable in the parish even when people are able to consent to other shared activities.

Fortune's model appears to be drawn from the extreme case of the sexual offender and his victims. This model is not adequate for dealing with all possible instances of sexual relating between pastor and parishioner. In this volume, we have taken as our prototype the wanderer. This choice is significant, for it allows us to explore a range of factors that do not enter into the discussion of the sexual offender. Whereas the offender is a sociopath, the wanderer displays more characteristics of typical male behavior in this society, and therefore allows us to extend a sympathetic glance toward the male who is affected by social conditioning and sexual socialization. Without exonerating the pastor, who carries responsibility for setting and keeping boundaries, we nonetheless can put the pastor's behavior into a broader context of social and psychological factors.

In addition to the offender and the wanderer identified by Fortune, we also identify the category of the normal neurotic pastor. A sexual ethic must be broad enough to account for the full range of behavior, including both the wanderer and the normal neurotic, and not be confined to egregious instances of sexual abuse. Whether sexual involvement with a parishioner is wrong, and how it should be handled by denominational officials and others in the church, depends largely on whether the pastor involved is an offender, a wanderer, or a normal neurotic.

With both Fortune and Rutter, we stress the power of the professional person in the role or office. Indeed, the power of the professional person is the key to the ethical analysis offered here. Our analysis of professional power is nuanced, however, by understanding the effects of sexism. In sexist culture, men and women are not equal. Rather, men have power in general. Since unequal power renders consent problematic, women often cannot give valid consent to their sexual involvements.[1] Certainly, when a woman faces a man who has professional and pastoral power in addition to male power, it is highly questionable whether she can give a valid consent to sexual involvement. Thus, there are strong grounds for urging that sex between a male pastor and a female parishioner constitutes a forbidden zone.

On the other hand, the situation is quite different if the pastor is a woman. The professional woman's power is undermined by the fact that she lacks power in general. These factors change the ethical picture: "men and women in ministry are as different as night and day." We would still urge caution for the woman pastor who develops a sexual interest in a male parishioner, but here our concern focuses on protecting her as well as him.

What we offer here is an attempt to fit together the pieces of a very difficult puzzle, the puzzle of sexual ethics in the parish. We offer no aphorisms such as "celibacy in singleness, fidelity in marriage." Rather, we offer a framework based on understanding the power and role of the pastor and the special vulnerabilities associated with sexuality in human life. It is these central factors with which we work throughout. Yet we also recognize that power, role, and even our experiences of sexuality are socially constructed. No ethical framework is adequate, therefore, unless it attends to the cultural forms and social structures within which sexual behavior gets its meaning.

Having said all of this, and having attempted to provide an initial ethical framework for examining sex in the parish, we are finally brought up against human limits. Ethical frameworks and human structures are necessary, but they are not sufficient. One pastor declared: "It is difficult in ministry to achieve a balance in the area of sexuality: no repression on the one hand and care about inappropriate expression on the other. I believe the only real hope for balance lies in the integration by the Spirit with its fruits of freedom and self-control."

The church needs ethical frameworks and appropriate structures to deal with sex in the parish. Such frameworks and structures will allow the joy of sex to be honored and yet the dangers and limits of sexual encounter to be recognized. Such frameworks and structures will help us to avoid repression of sexuality on the one hand, while also guarding against inappropriate expression of sexuality on the other. But even with frameworks and structures in place, above all we need the Spirit of God.

Appendix

PROCEDURAL GUIDELINES FOR LOCAL CHURCHES, ASSOCIATIONS, AND CONFERENCES REGARDING ALLEGATIONS OF INAPPROPRIATE SEXUAL CONTACT BY PASTORS AND PASTORAL COUNSELORS IN PROFESSIONAL RELATIONSHIPS*

I. Introduction: The Nature of the Problem

In this document, we address the very serious issue of unethical sexual behavior on the part of local church pastors with members of their congregations, or pastoral counselors with people they are counseling. Our purpose is fourfold: 1) to name the issue; quite simply, we want to break the conspiracy of silence surrounding sexual abuse in pastoral relationships; 2) to propose guidelines for making and responding to allegations of sexual misconduct, including policies and procedures for the local church, the minister and the Conference staff; 3) to identify areas in which healing and reconciliation can be supported within the church community; and 4) to suggest strategies for education and prevention of sexual abuse and misconduct.

The church, in both the local and the wider church arena, only recently has openly recognized the extent and seriousness of this problem. For too long, our church leaders, both clergy and lay, have refused to acknowledge such unethical practices and have failed to respond to them. There has been a longstanding tradition of concealing the facts of such events, as well as a reticence to discuss

---

*Used by permission of the Northern California Conference of the United Church of Christ and the United Church of Christ Office for Church Life and Leadership.

the problem with local church congregations. Often this is done in the interest of confidentiality for the victims, or to protect the professional image of the church or of the accused pastor. However, because of this conspiracy of silence, the victims have rarely been protected or helped, the accused have been quietly and inadequately dealt with, and the congregations have been misled and kept in the dark.

The effect of this silence has been devastating. The personal lives of those involved are shattered. The ongoing mission of the local church is severely curtailed. The silence prevents any movement toward forgiveness, reconciliation, and healing. It is our hope that these proposed policies and suggested strategies for prevention and education will help to break this silence, promote open and fair assessment of accusation, and encourage needed healing and reconciliation.

We must assume that most pastors and pastoral counselors are competent and ethical and do not have unethical sexual contact with parishioners or clients. But when such coercive and/or exploitive contact does occur, the church, local and wider, must address the problem immediately.

II. Preventive Strategies for Church Members and Leaders

Church members and leaders, as well as pastors/pastoral counselors, should be informed that inappropriate sexual contact does sometimes happen between a pastor or pastoral counselor and his/her parishioner or client, and that this situation constitutes a violation of ministerial ethics.

It is essential that the religious community understand the inadvisability and sin of a pastor or pastoral counselor (or any other person in a position of similar trust) becoming inappropriately involved with a parishioner who comes for counseling. Pastors or pastoral counselors who violate this proscription increase the likelihood that the parishioner will be harmed and not helped by the counseling.

It is recommended that:

A. Conferences educate church leaders and members through seminars, workshops, classes, women's and men's support retreats, written materials, pastoral comments in newsletters or in worship.

B. Conferences designate one or more persons (in addition to Conference officials) who are well known and respected, as a person with whom those persons who understand themselves to be victims of inappropriate sexual conduct can consult. These resource persons should be familiar with the judicatory processes and should be willing to listen in an atmosphere of trust, confidentiality, concern and compassion. They should have the authority to call upon the Committee on Ministry to convene a Pastoral Concerns Committee.

C. Conferences, at the time of the calling or appointment of a new pastor/pastoral counselor, should encourage the appropriate body or person within the Conference to have information available to review with both the new pastor and the congregation the Conference policy on sexual harassment and the Working Document on Guidelines Regarding Inappropriate Sexual Contact Between Pastor/Pastoral Counselor and Parishioner/Client. Informing a new pastor/pastoral counselor about the denomination's method for handling situations in which a pastor/pastoral counselor has inappropriate sexual contact with a parishioner/client may be one effective preventive strategy.

D. Conferences encourage, in cooperation with seminar sponsors and extension theological education resources, theological work by lay people as well as pastors and pastoral counselors in understanding human sexuality, sexual violence and abuse, inclusive language, masculine and feminine images of God, positive images of the human body, the role of women and men in society. Negative images of men and women, sexuality and the human body, contribute to exploitive sexuality and sexual abuse.

III. GUIDELINES FOR LOCAL CHURCHES

In the United Church of Christ, the local church is seen as the primary community of faith and the locus of accountability. Local churches covenant with each other through Associations and Conferences for the purpose of mutual cooperation and support in the accomplishment of the mission of the whole church.

Ministers in the United Church of Christ are in covenantal relationships with the local churches through which they serve. They are also in covenantal relationship with the whole church by means of the covenant of Ministerial Standing.

When questions are raised concerning the conduct of a Minister, these questions will ordinarily be raised in and through the local church in which that Minister serves. When the questions are of a serious nature, it is appropriate for the local church to work in cooperation with the Association/Conference in which Ministerial Standing is held.

In order that it may fulfill its responsibility to protect the well-being of its members and the integrity of the pastorate, we recommend that the local church include the following in its bylaws, policies and procedures:

A. Bylaws

1. Pastors/pastoral counselors serving this congregation may continue their professional practice only as long as they maintain Ministerial Standing within this Association/Conference.

2. Provision for a standing Pastoral Relations Committee.

B. Policies
Local churches are responsible to develop and establish standing policies relating to alleged violations of professional ethics, including sexual contact between pastors/pastoral counselors and parishioners/clients. Such policies should contain at least the following:

1. Statement that any coercive or exploitive sexual contact by clergy persons with parishioners/clients in a professional relationship is totally inappropriate;

2. Provision that allegation of any such violation of professional ethics that may have any validity, or that may be multiple in nature, will be immediately ad-

dressed. The local church moderator will contact the Conference to seek its support and assistance in investigating and adjudicating this matter; the Conference will immediately initiate an investigation as stipulated by the Policy on Sexual Harassment as adopted in September, 1987;

3. Provision that appropriate specific officials or governing bodies of the local church (following consultations with the Conference) can call for and enforce immediate leave of absence of the pastor/pastoral counselor without prejudice (and with continued pay) pending resolution of such charges. This can be done in conjunction with, or independent of, related Conference action;

4. Statement that one of the church's first concerns is for the support, welfare, and protection of the complainants and immediate prevention of further possible abuses to others. Equally important is the need for the accused pastor/pastoral counselor to have an opportunity for a fair hearing. The accused, if found guilty, needs opportunity for acknowledgment of the violation, repentance, treatment, rehabilitation and support;

5. Statement that these policies and procedures will be communicated with maximum candor and caring to the whole congregation.

C. Procedures for Initiating a Complaint

1. Origin of Complaint: The initial report to local church officials of alleged inappropriate pastoral sexual contact or abuse can come from the victim(s), a member of the victim's family, a friend of the victim(s), from a witness to such an event, or from other sources.

2. Conference Contact: Upon receipt of such report, the local church Moderator shall make immediate (within 36 hours) contact with the Conference. Con-

ference representatives shall take immediate steps to investigate the allegations and notify the accused.

3. Log: The local church and conference shall each begin at this point to keep a log of all events, meetings, contacts, etc., which are related in any way to the charges.

4. Local Church Coordination Committee: The existing local church Pastoral Relations Committee or similar group shall serve as the local church coordinating body. Such a committee of at least five persons, including a balance of female and male church members, shall be instructed by the governing body to take the following actions:

a. Cooperate with the Conference in its conduct of its investigation, since Ministerial Standing is held in the Conference.

b. If allegations appear to have sufficient basis for investigation, cooperate with the Conference in making every effort to identify other possible victims.

Realizing that it is often very difficult for a victim of sexual abuse to come forward and make a complaint, anonymity and confidentiality must be assured to anyone who offers information at this point; however, confidential statements must be submitted in writing to the Conference Pastoral Concerns Committee by the complainant as basis for the Conference investigation.

c. Cooperate with the Conference and local authorities (police, judicial) in providing immediate (within 12 hours) support, counsel, and assurance of physical protection to all parties.

Since a primary concern is for the welfare of the complainants, they should be offered support and counseling as needed to deal with the experiences which precipitated their complaint.

Complainants should be informed of all options available to them for dealing with their complaints, including making formal charges through established denominational procedures, initiating civil litigation to recover damages, filing criminal charges, etc.

A referral list of trained, competent counselors sensitive to the issues of sexual abuse should be readily available to all parties.

Where there are multiple complainants of one accused, an opportunity for voluntary sharing among them should be made available. These persons may gain healing insight and provide occasions for mutual support in a group facilitated by an experienced, caring counselor.

In addition, they should be given fullest assurance that steps are being taken to prevent other possible abuses.

Since an equally primary concern is for the welfare of the accused, support and counseling should be offered to the accused.

d. Assure that all parties are kept regularly informed as to process, progress, and conclusions of the investigations and procedures being taken to resolve the issue.

5. Local Church Governing Body

Upon charges being brought to the Conference Pastoral Concerns Committee by the local church, the Conference Minister or the complainant(s), there shall be immediate notification (within seven days of the charges being brought) of every member of the local church congregation. This notification shall be in writing and delivered by U.S. Postal Service. Notification should include that charges have been brought (the complainant shall not be named), and that the pastor/pastoral counselor is being given a leave of absence without prejudice, pending resolution of the charges. There should be a telephone number of a responsible church official whom members can call with their concerns.

The local church governing body may also need to take action on several matters which may include:

a. Allocating resources, including staff time, to assist in the conduct of the investigation;

b. Allocating necessary resources to give support to complainants;

c. Allocating resources necessary to cover replacement of pastor/pastoral counselor during leave of absence;

d. Reassigning staff duties as necessary during the leave of absence, especially counseling responsibilities; and

e. Monitoring the ongoing cooperation between the local church committee involved and the Conference, assuring that

(1) proper thorough records are being kept,

(2) complainant(s) are given support and protection,

(3) the congregation is being kept informed as to progress, and that

(4) the accused is given support and pastoral care.

IV. Pastor/Pastoral Counselor Responsibilities

A. Ministerial Standing

Ministerial Standing is that status by which ordained ministers are authorized to perform ministerial functions in the United Church of Christ.

In the Northern California Conference, UCC, Ministerial

Standing is held in the Conference by adhering to the following criteria:

1. Ongoing participation in a community of faith and worship;

2. Continuance in the performance of the tasks of ministry;

3. Engagement in processes for continued theological, spiritual and professional growth in order that the tasks of ministry may be more adequately performed;

4. Ongoing participation in peer group fellowship and also activities related to the cooperative life of the UCC churches. An ordained minister of the United Church of Christ will remain in communication not only with those he or she is called to serve but also with the ministers and representative laity of his or her Association and Conference, that the work he or she may do shall bear the stamp not only of his or her own individuality but also the mark of the Fellowship. Discipline for the ordained shall mean a ready and voluntary sharing of the life of faith and the life of service, that the Church may both support and be supported by the ministers of the Church.

5. Periodic self-evaluation and interpretation of one's work in terms of a Christian theological framework; and

6. Acknowledgment of and adherence to the Ethical Guidelines of the Northern California Conference and of the United Church of Christ as presented in the Manual on Ministry of the UCC.

B. Counsel

In matters where ministerial character is called into question by charges of inappropriate sexual conduct, professional incompetence, financial irresponsibility, moral turpitude, criminal behavior, or other breach of ministerial ethics, the minister in question is urged to seek the help and counsel of the Conference Minister.

Such charges may be brought in writing, to the attention of the Committee on Ministry by the minister in question, by the Conference Minister, by the local church in which the minister holds membership, or by an Association Moderator.

C. Compliance

The pastor/pastoral counselor's responsibility, once allegations have been brought, regardless of the source, is to comply with the investigative responsibilities of the Conference. There is no option not to appear.

V. GUIDELINES FOR CONFERENCES

The Conference with the Associations bears responsibility for establishing and maintaining standards for ordained ministry within its boundaries. It can best fulfill that responsibility by: educating clergy and churches concerning ethical standards and procedures; carrying the burden of investigating alleged breaches of those standards; providing for and holding hearings to insure justice for all parties; helping all parties to move toward reconciliation and new health following a situation in which a pastor/pastoral counselor has been accused of inappropriate sexual contact with a parishioner/client.

A. Educational Responsibilities:

The Conference shall:

1. Provide to local churches copies of Conference and UCC procedures and policies which have been established to handle any complaint of inappropriate sexual contact that may be received by any local church or the Conference;

2. Provide guidelines to local churches for development of local church policies and procedures for these issues.

3. Provide a procedure whereby the Conference, independent of the local church, may require a leave of absence pending resolution of charges;

4. Encourage, in cooperation with seminar sponsors and theological education resources, programs in local churches which help people become aware of, understand, talk about, and seek help for the problems of sexual and domestic violence which are so widespread in society.

B. Investigative Responsibilities

Allegations may be brought to the attention of the Committee on Ministry by the pastor/pastoral counselor in question, by the Conference Minister, by members of the local church in which the pastor/pastoral counselor holds membership, or by an Association Moderator. The direct channel to the Conference for local church members is absolutely necessary to protect members of churches whose church officers are unresponsive to members' allegations.

1. Conference Minister's Responsibilities:

Generally, it is the responsibility of the Conference Minister to assure, overall, that the process works.

Upon initial notification from any source of an alleged inappropriate sexual contact by a pastor or pastoral counselor within the Conference the Conference Minister or his/her designee shall:

a. Take immediate steps, within 48 hours of notification, to meet with the accused and to further investigate the charges. This shall be done confidentially in conjunction with local church officials if possible. Informal resolution of the complaint with satisfaction to all parties shall be attempted. However, anonymity of the complainant(s) must be maintained at this point if desired by complainant(s).

b. Begin keeping a detailed log of every event, meeting, testimony, contact, etc., related to the investigation, documenting every action and agreement with any party.

c. Meet with the complainant(s) and other affected parties, listen to their concerns, and share how the case will be processed. It is important that the complainants trust and understand the process.

d. Work with the Pastoral Concerns Committee to select for the complainant(s) an advocate who does not have other official duties as staff or Conference committee member but who has expertise on the issue and who also has an understanding of the denominational structure and process. This advocate shall be compensated by the Conference for his/her work.

e. Make a decision as to whether the allegations are substantiated or not substantiated.

(1) Allegations Not Substantiated: If the Conference Minister deems the allegations not to be substantiated after meeting with the complainant(s) and the accused, the Conference Minister shall take appropriate steps to assure that the accused is not harmed by the allegations, and steps to assure that the complainant receives appropriate support, counseling, etc. to reinstate a positive working relationship with the local church or calling body.

(2) Allegations Are Substantiated: If the Conference Minister deems that the allegations may be substantiated or at least deserve further investigation, he/she shall convene the Conference Committee on Ministry within 72 hours after meeting with the complainant(s) and the accused.

Even when an individual complainant chooses not to follow through with a formal complaint, if the Conference has reason to believe that there has been some breach of ministerial ethics, then he/she should counsel the pastor/pastoral counselor in question and give clear warning as to the consequence of future misconduct.

The Conference Minister shall then inform the Committee on Ministry of the Allegations, and whether they have been deemed substantiated.

2. Committee on Ministry Responsibilities:

The Committee on Ministry shall appoint a Pastoral Concerns Committee. This Committee shall consist of two representatives appointed from the Conference Committee on Ministry Section A and two representatives appointed from Conference Committee on Ministry Section B, and the designee of the Conference Minister, who will serve as chairperson. The Pastoral Concerns Committee should embody a balance of lay and clergy, female and male members.

The complainant(s) shall not be identified at this point to anyone except the Pastoral Concerns Committee and Conference staff.

3. Pastoral Concerns Committee:

This committee shall operate as a neutral investigating body. Their process will be designed to protect innocent and injured parties.

   a. First Investigations

   1. After careful consideration of allegations, if there is no cause to believe that the complaint is valid, the committee should be instructed to cease its process and respond with care and concern to the person placing the allegations. Such care might include recommendations for pastoral counseling, and structured opportunities for reconciliation. In addition, a record of the proceedings and the disposition of the allegation should be retained for the Conference file of the person against whom the complaint was made. Access to this file is allowed only under secure circumstances, to Conference staff and to the individual pastor/pastoral counselor.

   2. If it is determined that the pastor/pastoral counselor has been wronged by such com-

plaints, the Committee on Ministry shall endeavor to make public its adjudication in every area where such charges have been raised—the congregation, the Conference, the community and the wider church.

3. The Pastoral Concerns Committee shall, by its counsel and advice, endeavor to bring a solution that will effectively clear the reputation of the pastor/pastoral counselor, and seek the welfare of the community which the pastor/pastoral counselor serves.

b. Further Investigation, Supervision, Reporting:

If the Pastoral Concerns Committee deems further investigation and/or action is appropriate, the Committee shall:

1. Arrange Meetings with the Congregation and Its Governing Body: Instruct Conference staff to meet with the local church governing body, then with the congregation, listening to their concerns and sharing the procedures which are outlined in these guidelines. Subsequently, frequent reports will be made to the governing body and the congregation.

2. Provide a Resource Person for the Congregation: Instruct the Conference staff to make available a trained resource person who can assist the congregation in any additional steps needed in the healing process so that the congregation can work through the pain of this trauma and return to its regular mission. This person must help the local church understand these procedures as a part of the healing process.

3. Document Testimony: Fully hear and document the experience(s) and allegations of the complainant(s).

4. Support Complainants: Take immediate (within 12 hours of the end of their first meeting)

steps to assist the local church in providing support, counsel, and physical protection for the complainant(s) if desired.

5. Formulate in Writing All Official Charges.

6. Meet with the Accused and Deliver Formal Charges: Meet, as a full committee, with the accused minister, present the charges, and carefully document the meeting.

7. If a solution which will satisfy all parties can be reached, no hearing is scheduled. Efforts will be made to restore the welfare of the community.

If no solution which will satisfy all parties can be reached, the Committee will:

8. Schedule a Hearing: If a solution cannot be reached which is satisfactory to all parties (within two weeks of the meeting with the accused), the Pastoral Concerns Committee will schedule the mandatory ecclesiastical hearing before the whole Committee on Ministry. The hearing should be held as soon as possible. Once formal charges are brought and no solution can be reached a hearing is mandatory.

9. Suspension of Ministerial Standing: The Conference, on recommendation of the Pastoral Concerns Committee and the Committee on Ministry, by action of the Board of Directors, may at this time enforce immediate suspension (not negotiable) of Ministerial Standing, pending resolution of all charges. Such action will be taken in cooperation with the local church, if possible.

10. Report to the Local Church: Report back to the local church governing body within one week regarding their findings. The report should contain at least:

a. Preliminary summary of charges to date;

b. Summary of initial response of the accused;

c. Any other findings;

d. Actions taken; e.g., recommendation for leave of absence of the accused, recommendation for suspension of Ministerial Standing, Conference notification of other judicatory bodies, etc;

e. Explanation of further action;

f. Report the date set for ecclesiastical hearing before the Committee on Ministry.

11. Notify the Accused: Notify the accused of the date and location of the hearing and outline the accused's rights and privileges for due process.

12. Notify Complainants: Notify complainants of the date and location of the hearing and of the procedures to be followed.

C. Hearing Responsibilities

1. Responsibilities Prior to the Disciplinary Hearing:

Following completion of the investigation of initial charges and notification of all parties of the date set for the hearing, the Committee on Ministry shall:

a. Complete Investigation: Complete any further investigation it deems necessary to prepare for the hearing.

b. Assure Due Process: Abide by denominational policies and procedures in conducting the hearing.

2. Procedures for the Disciplinary Hearing:

a. The charges made against the minister shall be in writing and shall be mailed to the minister by registered mail, return receipt requested, marked "personal and confidential."

b. The committee shall not consider any charges other than those embraced by the written charges mailed to the minister. If after mailing of the charges, additional charges are made or information pointing to the conclusion that additional charges should be made against the minister, those new charges shall be reduced to writing and either given or mailed to the minister and the minister shall be given a reasonable opportunity to respond to said additional charges.

c. In no event can the committee, over the minister's objection, consider any charges not first mailed to the minister.

d. The minimum time between the mailing of the charges and the commencement of the hearing shall be two weeks. Requests for extensions of time by either the minister or those bringing the charges shall be submitted to the chair of the committee or in his or her absence, the vice chair who may then either grant or deny the request for continuance after taking into consideration all of the facts, including but not limited to, the nature and extent of the charges.

e. The chair shall appoint a hearing panel which shall consist of no less than five and no more than nine members. A quorum shall consist of a majority of the appointed members and all action of the hearing panel shall require a majority of the members present and attending.

f. Upon serving the written charges upon the minister, the hearing panel may elect to proceed in his or her absence in the event that the minister does not appear before the panel.

g. No person shall be a member of the hearing panel who has any interest, bias or relationship to or against either the minister or anyone bringing the charges.

h. The minister will have the right, at his or her option, to be represented by counsel of his or her choosing at the minister's sole expense. Neither the hearing panel, the Committee on the Ministry or the Northern California Conference shall have an obligation to provide counsel for the minister.

i. Prior to the commencement of the hearing, the hearing panel shall determine whether or not it wishes the services of a court reporter. The charges of the court reporter will be borne by the Committee on the Ministry unless those services are requested by the minister and in that event, those charges shall be assessed against the minister or divided between the minister and the Conference in any equitable manner that the hearing panel determines.

j. No witness appearing before the hearing panel shall testify to any facts not embraced by the written charges previously provided the minister.

k. The hearing panel may, in its discretion, request the services of an attorney to advise it on any legal or procedural matters. Such an attorney may meet with the hearing panel in private session, but shall not participate in its final decision and shall have no vote.

l. Both the individuals making the charges and the minister shall be given a reasonable and adequate time to be heard by the hearing panel. A good faith effort shall be made by the chair of the hearing panel to give an equal amount of time to those making the charges and to the minister in presenting their respective positions.

m. If new information or charges are obtained through the hearing process, the panel must continue the hearing for sufficient time in order to allow the minister to prepare his or her defense against those allegations.

n. No rules of evidence need to be followed by the hearing panel whose purpose is to conduct a full and complete hearing allowing each side a full opportunity to be heard and to present their respective position. However, the minister shall be given the opportunity to confront any of those individuals making charges against him or her.

o. The hearing may consist of more than one session and any subsequent sessions will be set so as to give the minister and those making the charges a reasonable opportunity to be present.

p. At the end of the presentations before the hearing panel, the chair shall declare the hearing closed. The panel shall issue its decision, in writing, and mail it to the minister, the Conference Minister and the persons bringing the charges within thirty days of the close of the hearing.

q. Report in writing to the Conference Board of Directors

Report of Findings: The Committee on Ministry shall file with the Conference Board of Directors a report of the work of the Pastoral Concerns Committee, Conference Staff, and the Committee on Ministry concerning the events leading to the action being recommended. This report shall include the process followed by the Committee on Ministry and the evidence upon which its recommendation is based.

3. Process of the hearing: (quoted from the United Church of Christ *Manual on Ministry* pp. 199f. with permission)

   a. Sequence of the Hearing Process

      1. Statement of the role of the Association Committee on the Ministry in disciplinary matters in

contrast to that of a civil court. The church seeks to address issues of behaviors which are unbefitting for ordained, commissioned, or licensed ministers of the United Church of Christ.

2. Introduction of all persons present for the hearing and their role in the hearing.

3. Statement about how the hearing will be conducted.

4. Prayer for guidance.

5. Reading of the allegation being made against the person.

6. Presentation of evidence supporting the allegation against the person. This normally would be done through information provided by persons who have pertinent information about the allegation. A specific amount of time should be allocated for this step. The number of persons providing information may be limited to a manageable number.

7. Presentation of information or testimony refuting the allegation against the person. This normally would be done through the testimony of the person in question and any witnesses which she or he has secured to offer evidence. A specific amount of time should be allocated for this step comparable to the time allowed for the presentation of the allegation against the person. The number of persons providing information may be limited to a manageable number.

8. Opportunity for those making the allegation to respond to the presentation of the defense.

9. Opportunity for the person in question or those representing her or him to respond to the presentation of those representing the allegation.

10. Questions from the Committee on the Ministry to any of those offering testimony.

11. Closing statement by those representing the allegation.

12. Closing statement by the person in question or those representing her or him.

13. Prayer for continued guidance and comfort for those involved in the situation and for those who must make a decision about the allegations.

14. Dismissal of all except the Committee on the Ministry.

b. Decision by the Committee on the Ministry

The Committee on the Ministry considers all of the evidence and makes its decision. The Committee decides from among the following options:

1. to exonerate the person,

2. to prescribe a program of growth and development,

3. to censure the person,

4. to suspend the person's ministerial authorization, or

5. to terminate the person's ministerial authorization.

D. Board of Directors' Actions

The function of the Conference Board of Directors is to determine whether there was substantial evidence to support the findings and to take action on the recommendations of the hearing body. The Board shall rely exclusively upon the written record of the hearing before the Committee on Ministry in making its decision. No party shall be entitled to a trial de novo (new trial) before the Conference Board of Directors.

E. Pastoral Follow-Up

Disciplinary hearings happen infrequently in the life of the Church and are difficult, painful and stress-producing experiences for all involved. Once the hearing is complete, decisions made, and actions taken, there needs to be intentional effort made at reconciliation and healing.

The Church needs to offer ongoing support and concern to those who made the allegation or who were wronged and find ways to express forgiveness and grace to those who have been disciplined.

God's grace and compassion need to be extended to all parties involved.

Notes

INTRODUCTION: THE SEXUAL PUZZLE

1. Charles L. Rassieur, *The Problem Clergymen Don't Talk About* (Philadelphia: Westminster Press, 1976).
2. G. Lloyd Rediger, *Ministry and Sexuality: Cases, Counseling and Care* (Minneapolis: Augsburg, 1990).
3. Marie M. Fortune, *Is Nothing Sacred? When Sex Invades the Pastoral Relationship* (San Francisco: Harper & Row, 1989).
4. Peter Rutter, M. D., *Sex in the Forbidden Zone* (Los Angeles: Jeremy P. Tarcher, 1989).
5. Rassieur, *The Problem*, p. 27.
6. Ibid., p. 45.
7. Titled "Sexual Ethics in Ministry," the videotape is produced by the Department of Health and Human Issues, the University of Wisconsin-Madison.

1. THE JOY OF SEX

1. E.g., the May 25, 1987, issue of *Time* magazine carried a cover story titled "Whatever Happened to Ethics?"
2. Lisa A. Mainiero, *Office Romance: Love, Power, and Sex in the Workplace* (New York: Rawson Associates, 1989), p. 42.
3. G. Lloyd Rediger, *Ministry and Sexuality: Cases, Counseling and Care* (Minneapolis: Augsburg, 1990), ch. 4.
4. *Open Hands*, vol. 3, no. 3 (Winter 1988), pp. 9–12.

5. James B. Nelson, *Between Two Gardens: Reflections on Sexuality and Religious Experience* (New York: Pilgrim Press, 1983), p. 4.

6. Ibid., p. 5.

7. Ibid., p. 4.

8. United Church of Christ, *Human Sexuality: A Preliminary Study* (New York: United Church Press/Pilgrim Press, 1977), p. 87.

9. Ibid., p. 12; they draw here on Eleanor S. Morrison and Vera Borosage, eds., *Human Sexuality: Contemporary Perspectives* (Palo Alto, Calif.: Mayfield, 1973).

10. Anthony Kosnik et al. (The Catholic Theological Society of America), *Human Sexuality: New Directions in American Catholic Thought* (New York: Paulist Press, 1977), p. 85.

11. Ibid., p. 85.

12. Ibid., p. 86.

13. United Church of Christ, *Human Sexuality*, p. 94.

14. Nelson, *Between Two Gardens*, p. 22.

15. See ibid., p. 29.

16. For a selection of sources, see Appendix B.

17. It is not only Methodists who use these four sources, however. In *Between the Sexes* (Philadelphia: Fortress Press, 1985), p. 5, Roman Catholic moral theologian Lisa Sowle Cahill recommends four analogous sources for ethical reflection on sexuality.

2. DYNAMICS OF DESIRE

1. Robert J. Carlson, "Battling Sexual Indiscretion," *Ministry* (January 1987), p. 4.

2. Peter Rutter, M. D., *Sex in the Forbidden Zone* (Los Angeles: Jeremy P. Tarcher, 1989), p. 7.

3. Ibid., p. 55.

4. Carlson, "Battling Sexual Indiscretion," p. 5.

5. Rutter, *Sex in the Forbidden Zone*, p. 11.

6. Ibid., p. 2.

7. These statistics are reported by Richard Exley in "A Support System: Your Way of Escape," *Ministries Today* (May/June 1988), p. 36.

8. Carlson, "Battling Sexual Indiscretion," p. 5.

9. Ibid.

10. See Sissela Bok, *Lying: Moral Choice in Public and Private Life* (New York: Pantheon Books, 1978), p. 93.

11. Roy M. Oswald and Otto Kroeger, *Personality Type and Religious Leadership* (Washington, D. C.: Alban Institute, 1988).

12. Nancy Chodorow, *The Reproduction of Mothering: Psychoanalysis and the Sociology of Gender* (Berkeley, Calif.: University of California Press, 1978).

13. James B. Nelson, *The Intimate Connection: Male Sexuality, Masculine Spirituality* (Philadelphia: Westminster Press, 1988), p. 42.

14. Nelson, *Intimate Connection*, pp. 59–63.

15. See ibid., p. 37.

16. Rutter, *Sex in the Forbidden Zone*, p. 56.

17. Ibid., p. 41.

18. Ibid., p. 139.

19. Ibid., p. 166.

20. Ibid., p. 92.

21. Carlson, "Battling Sexual Indiscretion," p. 4.

22. Ibid., p. 6.

23. Rutter, *Sex in the Forbidden Zone*, p. 151.

3. THE FAILURE OF LIMITS

1. Anne Wilson Schaef, *Co-Dependence: Misunderstood-Mistreated* (San Francisco: Harper & Row, 1986).

2. Ibid., p. 46 and passim.

3. Ibid., p. 44.

4. Schaef, *Escape from Intimacy* (San Francisco: Harper & Row, 1989), p. 79.

5. Anne Wilson Schaef and Diane Fassel, *The Addictive Organization* (San Francisco: Harper & Row, 1988), p. 51.

6. Ibid., p. 61.

7. Ibid., p. 74.

8. Ibid., p. 74. Indeed, some professionals in the treatment field "contend that the helping professions themselves become the practice of the disease of co-dependence," p. 75.

9. Ibid., p. 135.

10. Ibid., p. 74.

11. Ibid.

12. Robert J. Carlson, "Battling Sexual Indiscretion," *Ministry* (January 1987), p. 5.

13. Schaef and Fassel, *Addictive Organization*, p. 66.

14. Ibid., p. 108.

15. Schaef, *Escape*, p. 1.

16. Schaef and Fassel, *Addictive Organization*, p. 92.

17. Schaef, *Escape*, p. 96; we will return to this theme in ch. 7.

18. Ibid., p. 111.

19. Peter Rutter, M. D., *Sex in the Forbidden Zone* (Los Angeles: Jeremy P. Tarcher, 1989), p. 10.

20. Carlson, "Battling Sexual Indiscretion," p. 5.

21. Ibid.

22. Gaylord Noyce, *Pastoral Ethics: Professional Responsibilities of the Clergy* (Nashville: Abingdon Press, 1988), p. 99.

23. Karen Lebacqz, *Professional Ethics: Power and Paradox* (Nashville: Abingdon Press, 1985), pp. 137–139.

24. Marie M. Fortune, *Is Nothing Sacred? When Sex Invades the Pastoral Relationship* (San Francisco: Harper & Row, 1989), pp. 47, 156.

25. Schaef, *Escape*, p. 137.

26. See also Rutter, *Sex in the Forbidden Zone*, p. 21.

4. Pastoral Power

1. David S. Schuller, Merton P. Strommen, and Milo L. Brekke, eds., *Ministry in America* (San Francisco: Harper & Row, 1980), p. 30.

2. Marie M. Fortune, *Is Nothing Sacred? When Sex Invades the Pastoral Relationship* (San Francisco: Harper & Row, 1989), p. 42.

3. This definition of closeness in the marriage context is offered in G. Lloyd Rediger, *Ministry and Sexuality: Cases, Counseling and Care* (Minneapolis: Augsburg, 1990), p. 138.

4. Peter Rutter, M. D., *Sex in the Forbidden Zone*, (Los Angeles: Jeremy P. Tarcher, 1989), p. 5.

5. Ibid., p. 25.

6. Fortune, *Is Nothing Sacred?* p. 103 and passim.

7. Rutter, *Sex in the Forbidden Zone,* p. 21.

8. James L. Lowery of Enablement, Inc. (Boston, Mass.), letter to the editor of *The Christian Century,* December 14, 1988, p. 1163.

9. Rutter, *Sex in the Forbidden Zone,* p. 28.

5. AN ETHICAL FRAMEWORK

1. Peter Rutter, M. D., *Sex in the Forbidden Zone* (Los Angeles: Jeremy P. Tarcher, 1989).

2. The United Church of Christ, *Human Sexuality: A Preliminary Study* (New York: United Church Press/Pilgrim Press, 1977), p. 104.

3. Anthony Kosnik, et. al. (The Catholic Theological Society of America), *Human Sexuality: New Directions in American Catholic Thought* (New York: Paulist Press, 1977), p. 95.

4. Marie M. Fortune, *Sexual Violence: The Unmentionable Sin* (New York: Pilgrim Press, 1983), p. 82.

5. Marie M. Fortune, *Is Nothing Sacred? When Sex Invades the Pastoral Relationship* (San Francisco: Harper & Row, 1989), p. 16.

6. Ibid., p. 27.

7. Ibid., p. 30.

8. Ibid., p. 25.

9. Fortune, *Sexual Violence,* p. 82.

10. Fortune, *Is Nothing Sacred?* p. 46.

11. Lebacqz, "Appropriate Vulnerability: A Sexual Ethic for Singles," *The Christian Century,* May 6, 1987.

12. Rutter, *Sex in the Forbidden Zone,* p. 73.

13. Ibid., p. 51.

14. Ibid., p. 207.

15. Ibid., p. 124.

16. Ibid., p. 91.

17. Ibid., p. 60.

18. Lisa A. Mainiero, *Office Romance: Love, Power, and Sex in the Workplace* (New York: Rawson Associates, 1989), p. 130.

19. Ibid., p. 136; emphasis deleted.

20. Fortune, *Is Nothing Sacred?* p. 46; emphasis added.
21. Ibid., p. 101.
22. Rutter, *Sex in the Forbidden Zone,* p. 124.
23. Fortune, *Is Nothing Sacred?* p. 47.

6. WOMEN IN MINISTRY: SEX AND SEXISM

1. Peter Rutter, M. D., *Sex in the Forbidden Zone,* Los Angeles: Jeremy P. Tarcher, 1989), p. 21.

2. See, for example, Rosemarie Tong, "Sexual Harassment," in *Women and Values: Readings in Recent Feminist Philosophy,* ed. Marilyn Pearsall (Belmont, Calif.: Wadsworth, 1986).

3. Ibid., p. 150.

4. Ibid.

5. Ibid., p. 157.

6. Lisa A. Mainiero, *Office Romance: Love, Power, and Sex in the Workplace* (New York: Rawson Associates, 1989), p. 123.

7. Ann Douglas, *The Feminization of American Culture* (New York: Avon Books, 1977), p. 90.

8. Mariana Valverde, *Sex, Power and Pleasure* (Philadelphia: New Society Publishers, 1987), p. 40.

9. Margaret Adams, "The Compassion Trap," in *Woman in Sexist Society: Studies in Power and Powerlessness,* eds. Vivian Gornick and Barbara K. Moran (New York: New American Library, 1972).

10. Laurel Fingler, "Teenagers in Survey Condone Forced Sex," *Ms.* February 1981, reported in Marie M. Fortune, *Sexual Violence: The Unmentionable Sin* (New York: Pilgrim Press, 1983), p. 2.

11. Carol Turkington, "Sexual Aggression Widespread," *APA Monitor* 19/13:15 (1987), quoted in Polly Young-Eisendrath and Demaris Wehr, "The Fallacy of Individualism and Reasonable Violence Against Women," in *Christianity, Patriarchy and Abuse,* eds. Joanne Carlson Brown and Carole R. Bohn, p. 136.

12. See Andrea Dworkin, *Pornography: Men Possessing Women* (London: Women's Press, 1981); also Valverde, *Sex, Power and Pleasure,* pp. 129–131.

13. Nancy C. M. Hartsock, *Money, Sex, and Power:*

Toward a Feminist Historical Materialism (Boston: Northeastern University Press, 1983).

14. Valverde, *Sex, Power, and Pleasure*, p. 40.

15. See Nancy Friday, *My Secret Garden: Women's Sexual Fantasies* (New York: Pocket Books, 1973), p. 110.

16. Judith Weidman, ed., *Women Ministers* (New York: Harper & Row, 1981).

17. In 1981, only 3 percent of ordained clergy were women. Ibid., p. 3.

18. Janice Riggle Huie, "Preaching Through Metaphor," in ibid., p. 50.

19. Patricia Park, "Women and Liturgy," in ibid., p. 78.

20. Brita Gill, "A Ministry of Presence," in ibid., p. 99.

21. Huie, in ibid., p. 49.

7. GOD AND EROS

1. Haunani-Kay Trask, *Eros and Power: The Promise of Feminist Theory* (Philadelphia: University of Pennsylvania Press, 1986), p. 116.

2. Rita Nakashima Brock, *Journeys by Heart: A Christology of Erotic Power* (New York: Crossroad, 1988), p. 40.

3. See also Trask, *Eros and Power*, pp. 147–154.

4. Mary Field Belenky, Blythe McVicker Clinchy, Nancy Rule Goldberger, and Jill Mattck Tarule, *Women's Ways of Knowing: The Development of Self, Voice, and Mind* (New York: Basic Books, 1986), p. 54.

5. Ibid., pp. 68–69.

6. Ibid., pp. 93 and passim.

7. Ibid., pp. 57–58.

8. C.f. ibid., p. 94: "Truth lies hidden beneath the surface and you must ferret it out" is one of the claims of women who have moved beyond pure subjectivism into procedural and rational knowing.

9. Ibid., pp. 54–55 and 112–114.

8. SINGLE AND SEXUAL

1. John R. Landgraf, *Singling: A New Way to Live the Single Life* (Louisville, Ky.: Westminster/John Knox Press, 1990), p. 71.

2. John Shelby Spong, *Living in Sin? A Bishop Rethinks Human Sexuality* (San Francisco: Harper & Row, 1988), p. 209.

3. Landgraf, *Singling*, p. 69.

4. Ibid., p. 100.

5. United Church of Christ, *Human Sexuality: A Preliminary Study* (New York: United Church Press/Pilgrim Press, 1977), p. 103.

6. Charles L. Rassieur, *The Problem Clergymen Don't Talk About* (Philadelphia: Westminster Press, 1976), p. 63.

7. Spong, *Living in Sin?* p. 47.

8. Ibid., p. 48.

9. Ibid., p. 210.

9. IN THE CLOSET AND OUT:
GAY AND LESBIAN PASTORS

1. Mary E. Hunt, "Sexual Ethics: A Lesbian Perspective," *Open Hands*, vol. 4, no. 3 (Winter 1989), p. 10.

2. Morris L. Floyd, "Sexual Ethics: A Gay Male Perspective," *Open Hands* vol. 4, no. 3 (Winter 1989), pp. 11, 13.

3. Ibid., vol. 5, no. 3 (Winter 1990), p. 11.

4. Floyd, "Sexual Ethics: Gay Male," p. 11.

5. Ibid.

6. Peggy R. Gaylord, "Striving Toward Wholeness," *Open Hands*, vol. 4, no. 3 (Winter 1989), p. 15.

7. Lynn Nell Rhodes, *Co-Creating: A Feminist Vision of Ministry* (Philadelphia: Westminster Press, 1987), p. 123.

8. Hunt, "Sexual Ethics: Lesbian," p. 12.

9. Marie M. Fortune, *Is Nothing Sacred? When Sex Invades the Pastoral Relationship* (San Francisco: Harper & Row, 1989), p. 38, emphasis added.

10. THE "BISHOP'S" DILEMMA

1. G. Lloyd Rediger, *Ministry and Sexuality: Cases, Counseling and Care* (Minneapolis: Augsburg, 1990), p. 113.

2. Marie M. Fortune, *Is Nothing Sacred? When Sex Invades the Pastoral Relationship* (San Francisco: Harper & Row, 1989), pp. 120–122.

3. Peter Rutter, M. D., *Sex in the Forbidden Zone* (Los Angeles: Jeremy P. Tarcher, 1989), p. 10.

4. Fortune, *Is Nothing Sacred?* p. 127.

5. Minnesota S. F. #1619 Chapter 372, passed on August 1, 1986, amending Minnesota statutes (1984) sections 609.135 and Chapter 148A.

CONCLUSION

1. See Karen Lebacqz, " 'Love Your Enemy': Sex, Power, and Christian Ethics," *Annual of the Society of Christian Ethics* (Washington, D. C.: Georgetown University Press, 1990).

Selected Bibliography

PROFESSIONAL ETHICS: GENERAL

Battin, Margaret P., *Ethics in the Sanctuary: Examining the Practice of Organized Religion*. New Haven, Conn.: Yale University Press, 1990. A philosophical examination of selected issues, such as conversion practices, confidentiality, professional responsibility in pastoral counseling.

Callahan, Joan C., ed., *Ethical Issues in Professional Life*. New York: Oxford University Press, 1988. An excellent collection of essays on a range of topics in professional ethics.

Campbell, Dennis M., *Doctors, Lawyers, Ministers: Christian Ethics in Professional Practice*. Nashville: Abingdon Press, 1982. Argues for the professions as forms of ministry and for the "quadrilateral" approach to ethics (utilizing scripture, tradition, reason, and experience).

Guggenbuhl-Craig, Adolph, *Power in the Helping Professions*. Irving, Tex.: University of Dallas, 1979. From a Jungian perspective, author cautions professionals to attend to their "shadow" side and to power issues.

Kraybill, Donald B., and Phyllis Pellman Good, eds., *Perils of Professionalism: Essays on Christian Faith and Professionalism*. Scottdale, Pa.: Herald Press, 1982. Essays from an Anabaptist perspective challenging the values that underlie professionalism.

Lebacqz, Karen, *Professional Ethics: Power and Paradox*. Nashville: Abingdon Press, 1985. Offers a framework for professional ethics based on an understanding of role morality and attending to the power of the professional person.

Noyce, Gaylord, *Pastoral Ethics: Professional Responsibilities of the Clergy*. Nashville: Abingdon Press, 1988. An overview of ethical issues in various aspects of pastoral ministry.

Reeck, Darrell, *Ethics for the Professions: A Christian Perspective*. Minneapolis: Augsburg Publishing House, 1982. A general approach to professional ethics, including definition of *professional* and attention to specific issues.

Shaffer, Thomas L., *Faith and the Professions*. Provo, Utah: Brigham Young University, 1987. Drawing on stories of professional life, the author argues for a "character" approach to ethics and for the significance of the "outsider."

SEXUAL ETHICS

Barbach, Lonnie, and Linda Levine, *Shared Intimacies: Women's Sexual Experiences*. New York: Bantam Books, 1980. Dated but helpful study of how women experience sexuality in this culture.

Boswell, John, *Christianity, Social Tolerance, and Homosexuality: Gay People in Western Europe from the Beginning of the Christian Era to the Fourteenth Century*. Chicago: University of Chicago Press, 1980. Reexamines scriptural tradition and Christian history to show the place of homosexuality.

Brock, Rita N., *Journeys by Heart: A Christology of Erotic Power*. New York: Crossroad, 1988. Argues for a recovery of the "erotic" in the broadest sense as integral to spirituality.

Brown, Joanne Carlson, and Carole R. Bohn, eds., *Christianity, Patriarchy and Abuse: A Feminist Critique*. New York: Pilgrim Press, 1989. A collection of essays relating Christian belief and practice to phenomena such as domestic violence, rape, and misogyny.

Carnes, Patrick, *Out of the Shadows: Understanding Sexual Addiction*. Minneapolis: Compcare, 1983. The classic text on sexual addiction; deals primarily with male sexual addiction. (For the parallel for women, see Kasl, below.)

Countryman, L. William, *Dirt, Greed, and Sex: Sexual Ethics in the New Testament and Their Implications for Today.* Philadelphia: Fortress Press, 1988. A thorough review of sexual ethics in the Hebrew scriptures and New Testament with profound implications for contemporary interpretations of sexual conduct.

D'Emilio, John, and Estelle B. Freedman, *Intimate Matters: A History of Sexuality in America.* San Francisco: Harper & Row, 1988. A review of the changing cultural shape of sexuality in the United States.

Ehrenreich, Barbara, Elizabeth Hess, and Gloria Jacobs, *Re-Making Love: The Feminization of Sex.* New York: Anchor Books, Doubleday, 1987. The authors argue that women went through a significant "sexual revolution" in the late 1960s, with profound implications.

Fortune, Marie, *Is Nothing Sacred? When Sex Invades the Pastoral Relationship.* San Francisco: Harper & Row, 1989. An in-depth study of a case of clergy sexual violence; particularly valuable for delineating elements of justice in the abuse situation.

―――, *Sexual Violence: The Unmentionable Sin.* New York: Pilgrim Press, 1983. A classic, offering definitions of sexual violence, exploding myths, and providing an ethical framework based on consent and mutuality.

Freeman, Jo, ed., *Women: A Feminist Perspective.* Palo Alto, Calif.: Mayfield Publishing, 1979. Contains some classic studies of rape, discrimination, and sexual socialization practices.

Friday, Nancy, *My Secret Garden: Women's Sexual Fantasies.* New York: Pocket Books, 1973. A bit dated, but still the classic on the subject.

Glaser, Chris, *Uncommon Calling: A Gay Man's Struggle to Serve the Church.* San Francisco: Harper & Row, 1988. Autobiography of his "coming out" and discussion of issues of sexuality and spirituality.

Greer, Germaine, *Sex and Destiny: The Politics of Human Fertility.* San Francisco: Harper & Row, 1984. A provocative look at child-rearing and sexual patterns, challenging some contemporary beliefs.

Hartsock, Nancy, *Money, Sex, and Power: Toward a Feminist Historical Materialism*. Boston: Northeastern University Press, 1985. Argues that sexual experience is culturally conditioned and that in our culture, sex and violence are inextricably linked.

Hill, Ivan, ed., *The Bisexual Spouse: Different Dimensions in Human Sexuality*. New York: Harper & Row, 1987. Interviews with couples experiencing bisexuality in their marriages.

Hite, Shere, *The Hite Report: A Nationwide Study of Female Sexuality*. New York: Dell Publishing, 1976. Like the studies by Barbach and Levine and by Friday, this one depends on women's own experiences and statements. Dated but helpful for setting some context.

Kasl, Charlotte Davis, *Women, Sex, and Addiction: A Search for Love and Power*. New York: Ticknor & Fields, 1989. The first complete study of sexual addiction in women.

Kosnick, Anthony, et al., *Human Sexuality: New Directions in American Catholic Thought*. New York: Paulist Press, 1977. Argues for new understandings of the classic "purposes" of sexuality.

Landgraf, John R., *Singling: A New Way to Live the Single Life*. Louisville, Ky.: Westminster/John Knox Press, 1990. One of the few serious treatments of the growing phenomenon of singleness before and after marriage.

Mainiero, Lisa A., *Office Romance: Love, Power, and Sex in the Workplace*. New York: Rawson Associates, 1989. Uses case studies to argue for the positive contribution that romance makes in the work place, but cautions against romantic involvement between people in hierarchical relation.

Nelson, James B., *Between Two Gardens: Reflections on Sexuality and Religious Experience*. New York: Pilgrim Press, 1983. A look at sexuality in religious tradition, exploring links between sexuality and spirituality.

————, *The Intimate Connection: Male Sexuality, Masculine Spirituality*. Philadelphia: Westminster Press, 1988. Exposes the psychosocial dynamics of male sexuality and the way it is incorporated into power issues in society. An excellent treatment of male spirituality and sexuality.

Oswald, Roy, and Otto Kroeger, *Personality Type and Religious Leadership*. Washington, D.C.: The Alban Institute, 1988. An application of the Myers-Briggs Type Indicator to pastors, with discussion of the strengths and weaknesses of different personality types for different functions of ministry.

Pearsall, Marilyn, ed., *Women and Values: Readings in Recent Feminist Philosophy*. Belmont, Calif.: Wadsworth, 1986. A collection of essays and excerpts from important feminist texts, both philosophical and theological, of the past several decades. Important analyses of sexual harassment, pornography, etc.

Rassieur, Charles L., *The Problem Clergymen Don't Talk About*. Philadelphia: Westminster Press, 1976. A bit dated, this classic first effort to talk about sexual problems in the church still contains some helpful advice.

Rediger, G. Lloyd, *Ministry and Sexuality: Cases, Counseling, and Care*. Minneapolis: Augsburg, 1990. Focuses on clergy sexual problems, drawing on the author's long years of experience counseling clergy.

Rutter, Peter, *Sex in the Forbidden Zone*. Los Angeles: Jeremy P. Tarcher, 1989. An exploration of the psychological dynamics of sexual contact between men in power— therapists, doctors, lawyers, teachers, and clergy—and the women for whom they have professional responsibility.

Schaef, Anne W., *Co-Dependence: Misunderstood-Mistreated*. New York: Harper & Row, 1986. One in a series of books about addiction and co-dependence, delineating the personality characteristics of people from addictive and dysfunctional families and arguing that society perpetuates these characteristics.

———, *Escape from Intimacy: Untangling the "Love" Addictions*. San Francisco: Harper & Row, 1989. In this book, Schaef modifies her definition of co-dependence and argues that sex, romance, and relationship can also become addictions.

Spong, John Shelby, *Living in Sin*. San Francisco: Harper &

Row, 1988. Bishop Spong proposes controversial stands on divorce, gays and lesbians in the church, etc.

Tyrrell, Thomas J., *Urgent Longings: Reflections on the Experience of Infatuation, Human Intimacy, and Contemplative Love.* Hopedale, Mass.: Affirmation Books, 1980. An attempt to understand infatuation and intimacy as parts of a spiritual journey. Very helpful for delineating the components of infatuation and how to deal with it.

United Church of Christ, *Human Sexuality: A Preliminary Study.* New York: United Church Press/Pilgrim Press, 1977. A general discussion and review of scriptural and theological foundations, in the form of a study document for churches.

Valverde, Mariana, *Sex, Power, and Pleasure.* Philadelphia: New Society Publishers, 1987. An honest look at sexuality for women in Western culture, exposing myths and dealing forthrightly with questions of pleasure and power as they relate to sex. The closet parallel for women to Nelson's *Intimate Connection.*